STEPHEN LEACOCK

Humorist and Humanist

Ralph L. Curry

DOUBLEDAY & COMPANY, INC.
GARDEN CITY, NEW YORK
1959

For permission to quote personal letters the author and the publishers are grateful to: Faith Baldwin, for one of her own letters. Mrs. R. F. Curry, for letter Mr. Curry wrote to Leacock. Mr. N. R. Crump (Canadian Pacific Railway), for letter from Sir Edward Beatty. Estate of E. V. Lucas, for two letters from Mr. Lucas. Mrs. D. P. Morgan, for letter from Frank Crowninshield. Mr. D. L. Thomson (McGill University), for letters from and to A. P. S. Glassco, A. E. Morgan, Gerhard Lomer, Dean Martin, Dean Woodhead. Mrs. Gertrude Benchley, for telegram from Robert Benchley. Thomas Costain, for letter to Leacock. Lord Beaverbrook, for letter from R. B. Bennett.

Selection from *My Discovery of England*, copyright 1922 by Dodd, Mead & Company. Reprinted by permission of Dodd, Mead & Company and John Lane, The Bodley Head. Selection from *Hellements of Hickonomics*, copyright 1936 by Dodd, Mead & Company. Reprinted by permission of Dodd, Mead, and Company and John Lane, The Bodley Head. Letter to Jefferson Jones reprinted by permission of Dodd, Mead & Company. Telegram to Frank Dodd reprinted by permission of Dodd, Mead & Company. Excerpt from "General Currie: An Appreciation," as published originally in the Montreal *Herald*, reprinted by permission of the Montreal Star Company, Ltd. Letter from Kenneth Roberts, copyright by Anna M. Roberts and the Canal National Bank of Portland, Portland, Maine, Executors of the Estate of Kenneth Roberts. Reprinted by permission. Letter from F. Scott Fitzgerald reprinted by permission of Harold Ober Associates.

To Sis, Jane, and Cindy

Introduction

Stephen Leacock represented in a way the paradox which is Canada. Born in England, he moved to Canada and wrote American humor. But this was the simplest of the inconsistencies that his life and personality presented. He was the untidy man with the orderly mind, the man who could not drive a car but who could explain the theory of relativity. These are true paradoxes, however, because they only seem to represent incongruities. At the source, Leacock was a humanist in the broadest sense: his study and his interest was humanity, not facts and figures. The man was at the same time lecturer, teacher, economist, scholar, political scientist, humorist, historian, and *bon vivant*. Everything he wrote and everything he did was based upon a recognition of human dignity.

Leacock's total work, varied as it was, was unified by its continual insistence that man, and only man, was important. Leacock, the economist, wittily declared that Malthus was "the apostle of the empty cradle." Leacock, the historian, said of one of his books, "Read the pages on Toronto in the Confederation period. It's real history, being my own recollection of 1876–78." Leacock, the

7

teacher, head of his department, said to his staff, "Bite off a small piece of your subject and chew it well." Leacock, the political scientist, explained, "Socialism won't work except in Heaven where they don't need it and in Hell where they already have it." Leacock, the humorist, believed quite seriously that "the very essence of good humour is that it must be without harm and malice." These statements suggest what Leacock proves to be, one who believed with Pope that "the proper study of mankind is man."

This work had its genesis as a small paper, "Mark Twain and Stephen Leacock," written under the tutelage of Professor Clarence Ghodes, then visiting professor at the University of Pennsylvania. The study grew toward its present form under the able and patient direction of Professor Sculley Bradley, University of Pennsylvania, to whom the author owes much gratitude.

It takes many people to write a biography; the present study is no exception. Fortunately Stephen Leacock was so loved by his friends that they were more than willing to help record his life and establish his memory. To the following the author is grateful for interviews, aid in research, and introductions to additional source material: Harold Hale, Paul Copeland, James McGarvey, Mrs. Harry T. Shaw, Miss Maude Ardagh, Miss Marjorie Tudhope, William Arthur Deacon, Henry Janes, T. E. Harris, Dr. Stewart Ramsey, John Hackett, Kaye Lamb, and especially Gladstone Murray and J. E. McDougall. Special notice should be given Raymond Bond, for

the Dodd, Mead and Company correspondence; Thomas B. Costain, for the Doubleday and Company correspondence; and Mrs. Robert C. Benchley, for Leacock's letters to her husband.

Dr. Leacock's family was also very helpful. Members to whom particular thanks are due are Stephen L. Leacock, his son; George and Mary Leacock, his brother and sister-in-law; and Mrs. Donald Nimmo, his niece and literary executrix.

Canadian scholars remember Stephen Leacock as one of themselves. Much gratitude is due the following faculty members or students of Canadian universities: Professor C. T. Bissell, Professor A. S. P. Woodhouse, Professor H. A. Needler, Professor A. L. Phelps, and Miss Selma Skoll.

Libraries, the foundations of any research project, and library staffs which proved very helpful to the author are: Redpath Library, McGill University; University of Toronto Library; Margaret I. King Library, University of Kentucky; University of Pennsylvania Library; New York Public Library; Louisville Public Library; Cincinnati Public Library; Stephen Leacock Memorial Home; and the Library of Congress. Particular gratitude is due Dr. Gerhard Lomer, retired librarian of the Redpath Library; Miss Virginia Covington and the staff of Georgetown College Library, Georgetown, Kentucky; and Miss Mary Sheridan, sometime librarian of Orillia Public Library.

For financial assistance and encouragement, the author acknowledges his debt to the Humanities Research

Council of Canada, the Penrose Fund of the American Philosophical Society, and most of all the author's own institution, Georgetown College, and its president, H. Leo Eddleman, whose personal influence and encouragement helped bring this book to a successful culmination.

For the final drudgery of manuscript work, the author deeply thanks Professor Robert W. Canzoneri, who argued valiantly and successfully over most of the problems of knotty syntax; Peggy Bradley, who typed far beyond the call of duty; Thomas E. Boone, Mrs. D. P. Curry, and Professor Dorothy G. Melzer, who graciously took the thankless task of reading proof; and most of all his wife, who wrestled with the manuscript and two children at the same time.

RALPH L. CURRY

Georgetown College
December 24, 1958

Contents

STEPHEN LEACOCK

Humorist and Humanist

I

1869–1881

THE little boy stood on the deck of the *Sarmatian* as she pulled into the Montreal harbor. Wide-eyed he watched as a new city and new country unfolded before him. Young Stephen Butler Leacock did not know it, but he was coming "home" for the first time. He was to become Canada's minister at large to the rest of the world, and he was to write "the most Canadian book ever written." But that was still in the future; for the time being Stephen looked at this new land with excitement, comparing it with the only place he had known, England.

For a little while Stephen Leacock enjoyed "with Homer," he said, a "disputed birthplace." He knew that he was born in Swanmore, but he did not know which Swanmore. Stephen's great-grandfather, John Leacock, after making his fortune in Madeira plantations and the wine trade, had retired to Oak Hill, near Ryde, on the Isle of Wight. It was at Oak Hill that Stephen's father, Walter Peter Leacock, known as Peter, was born. This

15

being the family situation, it seemed reasonable, as
Stephen Leacock assumed for years, that he was born
in the village named Swanmore near Ryde. A search of
church records, however, proved he was born December
30, 1869, at Swanmore, county of Hampshire, where his
father had unsuccessfully tried farming for a while.[1]

Peter's life had been an irresponsible one. About the
middle of the century, Peter's mother, Stephen's grand-
mother, joined the Roman Catholic church. In spite
of the shock to the Anglican Leacocks, Peter and the rest
of the children joined the new faith with her.[2] Born to
wealth and good family, Peter led a casual life, sailing
his own boat and attending school irregularly. In this
period of England's rapid increase in population, many
younger sons were being forced to leave home; Peter
was already destined for the colonies. At the age of
eighteen he courted and then secretly married Agnes
Emma Butler, Stephen's mother.

The Butlers were, perhaps, a more notable family, but
socially the marriage should have been a good one. On
her mother's side, three of Agnes's uncles were university
educators: Granville Bradley, headmaster at Marlbor-
ough; Herbert Bradley, dean of Merton College, Oxford; and Andrew Bradley, classical master at Liverpool College. On her father's side, she was descended
from Sir Henry Lushington. Other members of the
paternal line had distinguished themselves in military
and clerical endeavors. Agnes's father, Stephen Butler,
was a hard-working Anglican minister, whose living was
so large that he required two curates. The death of his

wife, when Agnes was five, was evidently a blow, for he shortly began to exhibit signs of epilepsy, having to be carried from the pulpit on one occasion. He soon died, leaving young Agnes to the care of his brother Charles, vicar of Carlington, Hampshire.[3]

The Leacocks and the Butlers had been friendly for years, though the friendship had been a little uneasy, it must be admitted, with the "Romish" members of the family. In 1866, Agnes visited the Isle of Wight with her Uncle Charles. At Seaview, near Oak Hill, she met Peter for the first time since they were both grown. Peter sailed to Seaview every day, and Agnes would frequently slip out of the house in the evening, after her uncle thought her in bed, to join Peter in his boat. They were soon engaged, though the arrangement was a secret from both families. After the Christmas holidays, Uncle Charles having bought her a round-trip ticket to Waterloo Bridge, Agnes went to London. The return portion of her ticket was never used, for Agnes and Peter were married at All Saints' Church, Norfolk Square. Evidently Peter did not take very seriously the responsibilities of his religious belief: All Saints' is an Anglican church. Peter and Agnes took rooms in Burand Street while awaiting their passage to the colonies. Thus began a marriage which was destined to be a prolific though not a very happy one.[4]

In March of 1867 Peter and Agnes sailed for Natal, the closest port to Maritzburgh, South Africa. Stephen Leacock told something of this part of his parents' life in the fragmentary *The Boy I Left Behind Me*, but his

version, although interesting, was hardly reliable. It was not the journey of tremendous hardship that Stephen made it appear. Agnes took with her an Irish maid who "was very pretty but not much good" and a pet dog. And in her diary she complained, though not pettishly, that there was no way to get to the town except by walking while the Kaffirs carried the luggage (with Tom, the retriever, snapping at their heels because they frightened him).[5] At Maritzburgh, Peter tried to farm a plantation bought for him by his father, but the locusts ate up the crops and the climate proved too much for the seemingly delicate Agnes, who had suffered a brain concussion as a child. The next year they returned to England, bringing with them Thomas James, the first of eleven children to be born to this union.

Back in England the Leacocks lived at various times in Swanmore, Shoreham in Sussex, and Portchester, while Peter, awaiting another farm of his own, tried to learn farming by "drinking beer under the tutelage of Hampshire farmers—who, of course, could drink more than he could."[6] Agnes was extremely glad to be back where she could visit her family at the Butler family seat of Bury Lodge, Hambledon, Hampshire; but Peter, because of the secret marriage and his Roman religion, was never invited to her home.[7] Bury Lodge, which his father never saw, formed a rather important part of the English heritage of Stephen Leacock. It was here that the local hunts began every year, and it was here on Broadhalfpenny Downs that some of the very first real cricket matches were played, several of the earliest

scores still being preserved on a fire screen in the lodge.[8]

While his parents were temporarily at Swanmore, Stephen was born, he significantly remarked, in "exactly the middle year of Queen Victoria's reign." His method of dating his birth is indicative of his lifelong political loyalties. For though to many people he seemed the spirit of Canada itself—at his death the Native Sons of Canada urged that his birthplace, which they supposed to be in Canada, be made a national shrine[9]—Leacock always thought of himself as a citizen of the British Empire, and he loved Canada because it was a part of that Empire.

The Leacocks were not to remain at Swanmore for very long, and indeed the only part of England which made any lasting impression on young Stephen at all was Portchester, where he lived from the time he was four years old until the family moved to Canada when he was seven. Here he became familiar with English commons, the celebration of holidays, the veneration of all military heroes. Here he learned of the English complacency: Uncle Charles, the rector, considered himself "singularly fortunate" to be in Portchester, "where there was no outbreak of 'religion'. . . . No people got sudden 'salvation'; they got it gradually over eighty years of drowsy Sundays."[10] It was in Portchester too that he began his long academic career, when he and his two older brothers attended a "dame's school." What he remembered of this school is important in relation to the inquiring mind and the antidogmatic wit he was to display later:

. . . the dame held up a map and we children recited in chorus, "The top of the map is always the north, the bottom south, the right hand east, the left hand west." I wanted to speak out and say, "But it's only because you're holding it that way," but I was afraid to. Cracks were as easy to get in a dame's school as scratches down on the Rio Grande.[11]

The only other occurrence which seems to have stayed with the boy had almost nothing to do with England but was rather itself a reference to America. While visiting on the Isle of Wight, he received from his grandfather Leacock a small block of wood about six inches long, labeled "A Piece of the American Frigate 'Chesapeake'—Captured 1813." This small scrap of wood he very carefully preserved the rest of his life. It was still occupying a prominent place on the mantel of his study at his death. Stephen Leacock liked history he could touch. Although it would be difficult to say that here began his interest in history, the gift meant enough to him that years later he traced precisely what happened to the captured vessel, and he was boyishly pleased when he discovered that its timbers were still in use in the mill constructed of them at Wickham.[12] Still later he was to write movingly of the battle in which the *Chesapeake* was captured.

Perhaps the only reason that the family settled down in Portchester long enough for Stephen to remember it is that his father was out of the country. Peter's father had bought the family another farm, this time in Kansas, "sight unseen." Agnes, as she was often to do in the next

years, had to serve as both parents. Life was not, of course, easy. As Stephen wrote one time:

My dear Dadda

I thank you for the letter. Mama has burnt her hand so I write for her I am 5. We each had a crackker [sic] at tea I send you an almanac.

Mamas hand is straped [sic] on a board and it is no use there is to be a Xtmas [sic] tree at the school on the 8th We shall go

> Your affec
> Stephen[13]

But school and holidays followed each other, and the time passed. The Christmas tree custom was catching on in England and Stephen wrote his father once:

> Portchester
> Ja

My dear Dadda

I thank you for the book. Jim has a young Xtmas [sic] tree We have got a new Baby he was born on the 6th We very often go in to Fareham

> Your affec son
> Stephen[14]

While such homely details in the letters from home may have been cheering to Peter, his local prospect in Kansas was not. This venture in farming was no more successful than the last. In South Africa it had been locusts, in Kansas it was grasshoppers that ate up the place.[15] It would be difficult to prove that Peter was responsible for

the locusts or the grasshoppers, but misfortune persistently dogged his agricultural efforts. He did not like farming and had no real training or background for it. Even when he really worked hard at it, farming was not very profitable for him, and he soon turned his attention to other things. At any rate he soon returned to England to prepare for another major move, this time with the whole family.

Peter's father showed more persistence than his son; for the third time he established his son on a farm, this one a large tract in Upper Canada, as Ontario was called then. Peter went on ahead to prepare the place for the rest of them, and in the spring of 1876, the family sailed, from Liverpool, on the *Sarmatian* for Montreal. For the boy Stephen, the *Sarmatian* was a very impressive experience, combining the enchantment of an old ship with the thrill of a new. The masts of a sailing vessel towered above the decks, but below was the newer, more efficient steam engine. This ship later served as a troopship in the Ashanti war and still later brought Queen Victoria's daughter, Louise, to Canada as the wife of the Governor-General, the Marquess of Lorne.[16] Stephen followed the *Sarmatian's* career with interest until she was broken up after the turn of the century. The ship was exactly the sort of thing that could always arouse Stephen's interest: it blended the best of the old and the new; it experienced the adventure of military exploit; it performed dutiful service to the Crown.

From Montreal they took a river steamer to Toronto, then a leisurely trip, which gave the immigrants an op-

portunity to observe their new country. During a stop
at Kingston on May 24, the children had their first introduction to one of the colonial customs, the celebration
of the Queen's Birthday. This holiday was never observed
in England, but Mrs. Leacock had lived in South Africa
and was able to explain it to the astonished boys. That
such a voyage, even though uneventful, was exciting
to young Stephen is self-evident; at the age of six he was
old enough to realize something of the importance of
such a permanent move. He was also old enough to
notice how different things were from those he had
known in England.

The big, friendly, noncompartmented cars in use on
the Toronto-Newmarket Railroad seemed very public
to the boy familiar with the snug, closed cars of the
British lines. From Toronto the train carried them north
to Newmarket, where Peter met them with a buckboard
and a lumber wagon, the only possible vehicles for the
remaining thirty miles to the farm.[17]

The farm which Stephen's grandfather had bought
his errant son this time was a one-hundred-acre tract near
the village of Sutton. As Leacock described it, the country
was real frontier, but it is in this phase of his life that
one must most discredit his own account. Stephen Leacock hated the animals, hated the isolation, and hated
the chores with a passion which he never forgot. He spoke
of the farmhouse, built of cedar logs covered with clap-
boards, with other rooms stuck on; of the stable, a log
structure, chinked and plastered; of the barn built of
loose logs with the wind whistling through them.[18] What

he failed to make clear was that there could be no tighter
stable than the one he pictured and that a barn needs to
be weatherproof, not cozy. And in this account, one of
the few places he ever displayed bitterness, he neglected
to tell that the other rooms stuck on were an eight-room
house connected to the older house by a breezeway. The
original "log house" had, among other conveniences, a
large drawing room furnished with good English furni-
ture. He revealed more of his true situation than he perhaps realized when he wearily said that there were nine
stoves in the house and the job of cutting wood was
endless; it takes a good house to support nine stoves.

Whatever the Leacocks' financial situation, life in
Upper Canada was not easy. Rugged living conditions
were made more difficult by the inexperience of the
Leacock family. The best available light was from coal-
oil lamps, but Agnes Leacock, unused to them, preferred
homemade candles at first. The farms were as widely
scattered as on the frontier in the United States, the
nearest neighbor being a half mile away, and a trip to the
village meant an overnight visit. Roads, some of the
sturdy but bone-rattling corduroy construction, were not
good, and one had to walk the mare up the hill. Farm
work, never easy, was lightened for the Leacocks by the
addition of a hired man and three other servants: "a 'hired
girl' and a 'little girl' and generally an 'old woman.'"
Sutton, the nearest town, had little to offer—two mills,
two churches, and three taverns—a proportion that an
older Stephen Leacock considered about right.[19]

The Leacock farm was situated on pleasantly rolling

land which had been the scene of the Iroquois massacre in 1649. An arrow-straight stretch of road led to the house, which stood on the highest hill in immediate view. From the front of the house, Stephen could see the long gentle slope into the valley and the miles of undulating land beyond; from the crest of the hill behind the house, he could see Lake Simcoe with its ever-changing surface. Peter Leacock, like everyone else of his area, chose wheat as his principal crop because it was suited to the land; but it did not pay even in good years. Fields were of a regular seven-acre pattern with snaky rail fences around them.[20] These picturesque fences not only afforded protection to an occasional rebellious tree which had resisted the clearing of the forests, but also provided work for the farm boy who had to grub out the fence corners. Undoubtedly the boy Stephen had jobs to do, as any resident of a farm had, but it is unlikely that he shared in any heavy labor since his education began almost with his arrival in Ontario.

The next formal education young Stephen experienced after the dame's school in Portchester was in School Section No. 3, Township of Georgina. It was a regular little red schoolhouse "that has helped make America." Here the usual academic life of early rural North America prevailed. The boys and girls were together in their classes, but never outside; they did their ciphers on slates which they cleaned with the sides of their hands; they all gathered around the pump in the yard and drank out of the same tin cup. The boys came to school barefooted in the summer, though Leacock re-

calls that he did not—"a question of caste and thistles." There were the Friday afternoon "school entertainments" so common to the United States and Canada, when the trustees made speeches "or shook their heads and didn't" before the children said their pieces and the fiddler played. Stephen and his schoolmates studied reading, spelling, writing, arithmetic, geography, and no nonsense.[21] But when her children began to lose their Hampshire accents, Agnes Leacock, gentle Englishwoman that she was, decided that she must teach them herself.

During this period of instruction at home Leacock read T. W. Higginson's *Young People's History of the United States,* which he received as a gift from a cousin in the States. This was his first introduction to the other side of the American Revolution, and he felt, he said, a "new sense of the burning injustice of tyranny." From then on, he claimed, he had no use for an hereditary title which always seemed to him merely an hereditary evil, "saving out the British monarch."[22] Leacock's statement may easily be the result of his habit of seizing on one particular to dramatize a whole concept. If so it is a particular, well selected, and the sentiments expressed here seem to have been those of the humorist through his life.

When their mother started to teach the Leacock children, she dug out of her trunks her own schoolbooks carried all the way from England. Although somewhat dated by this time, perhaps, they were sound volumes. The children studied Colenso's *Arithmetic,* Slater's

Chronology, Olendorf's *New Method of French,* and *Peter Parley's History of Greece and Rome.* This latter was constructed on the basis of questions, the answers to which were simple affirmative or negative ones; generally a simple "yes" would suffice. This educational substitute worked well enough for a while, but at the rule of three the good mother's instruction broke down; besides, said Leacock, "it was no good . . . we knew it was only Mother." To this minor crisis, Grandfather Leacock once more responded, this time by paying for a tutor for the children.[23]

The tutor, Mr. Harry Park, was reduced to teaching on this elementary level so that he might continue his work toward his degree. Park did his job admirably, however. In a room given him for that purpose, he set up a school with regular classes, dividing it into forms like the English system. Stephen, in spite of the fact that two brothers were older than he, was the highest ranked of the scholars, evidencing even at this age his talent for the studious life. By the time he was eleven, Stephen had become a good speller—an accomplishment much admired in those days—and knew all Park could teach him about simple grammar. He knew British history and the history of English literature and was through vulgar fractions in arithmetic.[24]

It was during this time that Leacock began to do some reading on his own; his mother had brought some good books from England, which must have been added to from time to time since Leacock spoke of reading *Tom Sawyer,* published the same year he came to Canada. At

this time he read *Pickwick Papers,* an auspicious beginning which culminated in his biography of Dickens. He read all of the Jules Verne stories, remembering *The Mysterious Island* with particular affection because the men did something and there were no women to clutter up the story. He joined almost the total juvenile population of his day in reading all the "half-dime" novels he could get; Leacock never tired of adventure. With an appreciation almost equal to that which he gave Dickens, he read all of Mark Twain's works which had been published. Although he greatly admired the others, he recalled in one place, "*Tom Sawyer* I never cared for."[25] This was written in 1920; in 1944 he recalled Injun Joe's being sealed up in the cave as one of the incidents he remembered most vividly from his childhood reading. It seems logical that in the earlier criticism he was speaking about literary merit while in the latter he was referring to what the boy really liked at the time. Like other boys of his age, he read and thoroughly enjoyed the Waverley novels as well as such children's classics as *Robinson Crusoe.* The only remarkable thing about Stephen's reading was that he perhaps read slightly more than the average boy. However, he had begun to show signs of the constant and quick reader who makes a good scholar.

After 1880, the Leacocks spent a good part of each summer at Sibbald's Point on Lake Simcoe very near the church they had attended, weather permitting, ever since their arrival in Canada. Their first house at the lake, as a matter of fact, had been the residence of the

rector and was still called the Parsonage. In his autobiography, Leacock more than modestly declared that the "old log building" was unfit for habitation by even the most unassuming of clergymen.[26] But the fact remains that his mother rented a summer cottage and drove to it in her own phaeton behind her own harness mare. It is true that rents were not high—a larger house they took later demanded only eight dollars a month rental—but although the Leacocks were not rich, they did not live in the genteel poverty which the author presented.

Before they were able to move to the lake for the summer, each Sunday during the warmer months, the children had enjoyed an outing when they came to church. The church building was in the process of construction when the Leacock family first attended it, and the children had eagerly watched its growth from Sunday to Sunday. On June 10, 1877, they attended the first service held in it.[27] Sunday was the only day the children really met other children, and the lake offered many opportunities for new and interesting play.[28]

The Lake Simcoe of Stephen Leacock was not the Mississippi River of Mark Twain, but its influence was obviously important. During these Sunday interludes Leacock first explored the lake that never lost its fascination for him. He swam in it when boys "looked on girls in the water as a damn nuisance." He early learned the possible treachery of an offshore wind when the first raft he built was carried out and he had to be rescued. He and his brothers built flat-bottomed boats and found by the hard lesson of experience that such boats are not

suitable for sails. Stephen must have at this time started fishing, a sport that he was to enjoy all his life. The four small steamers of Lake Simcoe, in the romantic eye of Stephen, became fine big ships.[29] Making regular runs, they were a commercial necessity, but Leacock ultimately saw them replaced by the railroad and then the automobile; he lived to regret the passing even of the excursion steamer. The lake traffic also supplied several broad-beamed sailing vessels which tacked awkwardly across the lake, carrying heavy freight to Newmarket, the nearest rail point below.[30]

The railroad was finally extended northward to Sutton and Jackson's Point. Stephen was present at the celebration on the arrival at Sutton of the first train from the south; amid the clanging of bells and the shrills of whistles the train pulled to a chuffing stop beside the grist mill. Toronto, to which he now had access, was a wonderful city to Stephen. It was already a city with character, though it was still growing. The parliament buildings with their flags flying, the wharves even more crowded than those of Lake Simcoe, the dignified University of Toronto, even the rush of business so different from his own rural life must have impressed the boy who had long forgotten what he had known of London.[31]

However much fun Sibbald's Point and Toronto might afford, Stephen spent most of his time on the farm which his father was erratically trying to make pay. Peter Leacock, raised a child of leisure, never really adapted himself to a life which required productive labor. He worked hard when he worked, but between such periods he

spent his time in thorough and evidently dissolute idle-
ness. He drank and gambled and loafed. Through these
times Agnes Leacock held the family together. She was
a woman of high humor, hearty laughter, and joyous
nature. A religious woman, she served as a spiritual and
even temporal matriarch for her children the rest of
her life. They drew strength from her and paid her the
ungrudging admiration she was due. She had much of
the casualness noted later in her son, encouraging her
brood to bring home any number of guests whenever and
as often as they wished, disregarding the difficulties
which such a welcome presented. She covered up as well
as she could the behavior of her husband, no doubt understanding something of his character and temperament
that was unsuited to the life they were leading. To Peter's
credit it might be said that times were genuinely hard
in the late 1870's; Ontario, having what was largely an
agrarian economy, needed real money, and the little
currency in circulation was beginning to flow westward
to boost the paper profits of the exciting new Winnipeg.

Into this unstable domestic and economic situation of
1878 came Peter's younger brother. E. P. Leacock, like
Mark Twain's Beriah Sellers, was a man of vision. As
immortalized by his nephew in "My Remarkable Uncle,"
E.P. was probably the most fantastic and fabulous person Stephen Leacock ever knew. He immediately rushed
into local politics and emerged on the winning side;
he moved on to Toronto for a short while and then hit
Winnipeg at the real rise of the boom. Here he bought
and sold real estate, won a seat in the new Manitoba

legislature, obtained a government grant for his own railroad that was never more than a letterhead, and drew after him his own brother, Peter, in 1881 and still later Stephen's oldest brother, Jim.[32] This was the life Peter had been searching for, a life in which a man got ahead not on work but on ideas. E.P. and Peter, with Jim following more solidly behind, plunged into the

> . . . magic appeal in the rush and movement of a "boom" town—a Winnipeg of the '8o's, a Carson City of the '6o's. . . . Life comes to a focus; it is all here and now, all *present*, no past and no outside—just a clatter of hammers and saws, rounds of drinks and rolls of money.[33]

To finance the move, Peter held a sale at the farm of equipment and stock. This was just successful enough, recalled Stephen, to pay for the whiskey consumed at the sale. With this unsuccessful gesture Peter left the farm to his wife and children; but Stephen was not to remain on the farm long either. It was time for him to go off to school.[34]

II

1882–1891

RIGHT after Christmas, in January, 1882, Stephen helped his mother pack his clothes and his favorite books. With much excitement and some apprehension, Stephen went to join Dick and Jim at Upper Canada College. They had come to Toronto the year before and were thoroughly established in the smart school that Stephen wanted very much to attend but which he was a little afraid of. Although he recalled that he enrolled in February of 1882, the school records indicate that his official entry was made in January of that year. In either case, the classes were already started.

When Arthur Murdock (Dick) and Thomas James (Jim) had registered, they had listed their father as "W. P. Leacock, Farmer, Sutton, Georgina, Ont.," but Stephen found it necessary to identify his father as "Land Agt., Winnipeg, Man."[1] The boy, twelve years old now, found his new situation very difficult; in spite of the presence of his brothers, with whom he shared a room, he was unbearably homesick. Undoubtedly, like all other

boys who attend boarding school, he would eventually have made the adjustment, but less than a week after he arrived at the school he became ill with scarlatina. Attended by a kind matron, he was removed to a make-shift isolation ward in a converted tool shed behind the school. Before his recovery was complete, his mother came, and it was thought best for him to return to the farm with her. This decision was probably a very wise one, since part of Stephen's trouble stemmed from classes having begun some time before he enrolled. (If his introduction to algebra was an example, the decision was certainly wise. As Leacock told it, the teacher turned to one of the students and said, "McKeown, take this boy to the back of the room and explain to him what algebra is.") Quite happy about the turn things had taken, the homesick boy returned to the farm with his mother and, during his convalescence, attended the "little red school-house" again to learn Latin.[2] Leacock believed he went back to Upper Canada College after Easter, but again the school roll contradicts him, showing his second entry into the school to have been September, 1882.[3]

Stephen Leacock's return to boarding school was a much happier experience for him. This time he fitted into the routine without any difficulty and soon was as proud of being an "Upper Canada Boy" as any of his classmates. U.C.C. had been patterned after the English public schools, with some notable differences. There were no real social class distinctions and there was no fagging. Upper Canada College was connected by its endowment and its administration to the University of

Toronto, a school founded to be a secular institution because there could be no agreement as to what sect or denomination should control education in publicly supported schools. This secular origin meant that U.C.C. did not have the church ties that its English counterparts had. There was church, said Stephen, but not too much. Another difference from the English school, called for by the climate, was the arrangement of study hours. School was over at three, and the boarders played the rest of the afternoon while the day students went home.[4]

Upper Canada College then occupied a spacious campus on King Street between Simcoe and John. The buildings were large, square, red brick edifices with a solid look about them. The academic building was an imposing three stories; on either side were the masters' houses. The Boardinghouse or residence hall was a two-story T-shaped building, housing all boarding students except a few who lived with the masters. The junior form lived in the Old Wing under the watchful eye of a resident master on each floor; the senior form, in the New Wing, were under the care of the senior resident master, who held a position which in the eyes of the students afforded sheer luxury. This position, held during Leacock's time by "Gentle" John Marland, carried with it a suite of rooms and a waiter of its own. The campus supplied almost the total environment for its students; they were allowed off it for only a few minutes a day—to go to the candy store, called the "Taffy"—except on weekends. But on those weekends Leacock might amuse himself in Toronto. He found that Toronto, like the school, was based

on an English pattern, but "the barbershops spoke American."[5] At the end of his first full year at U.C.C., Stephen returned to the farm for the summer with a good record, though he had not really applied himself.

The summer vacation was an eventful one for Leacock. The family went to Sibbald's Point as had been their custom for many years, but, in addition to this, Agnes Leacock decided to rent the farm for enough to make the payment on the mortgage and move to Toronto on the basis of a "casual legacy" from England.[6] Though Stephen made no mention of it, his father evidently returned either to help with the move or to try to get the legacy, and Agnes bore their tenth child, Rosamond Mary Butler Leacock, the following May 28.[7] Because this is also the year that Jim left school to join his uncle and father in Winnipeg,[8] it is reasonable to assume that his father took him back. Although again at this point in his autobiography Leacock made much of the poverty of the family, in September his mother moved to Toronto with a large family, took a very good house on John Street, employed two maids, and kept a team and a carriage. The answer cannot be that Stephen was used to a luxury greater than this, for he was not. Part of the answer may lie in the peculiarity of their financial situation. The casual legacy which he mentioned was one of many, so that while there was generally enough money, no one ever knew when the next solvent relative would die or who it would be. Perhaps, too, there was some economy in the move, since it allowed Stephen and his brother Dick to re-enter Upper Canada as day students in the fall of 1883.

In contrast to the summer which preceded it, the school year of 1883–84 saw little change in the fortunes of Stephen. He was still a better than average student, but not very outstanding. He rather bragged once of being "licked" by Major Charles Gordon, a resident master, later to become famous as the writer "Ralph Connor."[9] But while Leacock probably took his lickings along with the rest, none of them were administered by "Ralph Connor." Although his brother, Gilbert, was a master at U.C.C., Charles Gordon never was.[10] At the end of this year, Dick, renouncing education, returned to the farm to work, and Stephen again reported home with good marks, easily won.

The summer holidays were always great fun for Stephen, because he loved the lake and because the rest of the family had already preceded him there. He wrote his father one time about seeing the family off for Sutton:

My dear father,

The little ones all started for the lake this afternoon; they went this morning but they missed the train. The party were 8 in all, carrying about 10 trunks and some ½ dozen dogs and cats. In order not to be late they went to the station about an hour early, and, true to their orders not to go on to the platform, they sat patiently in the car for the best part of an hour before the train started. Of course they forgot some of their luggage. Miss Wilson headed the young Israelites and Miss Bertha made an able second. There will be probably be [sic] a notice about in tomorrow's mail headed

"Departure for happy hunting grounds." or something of that sort. Do you remember the fuchia which you got mother at a butcher's shop on Queen st.? There are 76 buds on it now & the Italian primroses & violets are doing well. I got some checkers down town and Mother & I played three games, I beat her in all of them, but she says it was only because she got stupid at the last, or the baby cried in the middle, or she thought that king was a common, or something of that sort.

Mother wants me to tell you that it was not the children's fault that they missed the morning train, as they were all up at half past four, in fact they hardly slept at all, and their trunks had been packed about a week before.

Mother was out in the yard for the first time yesterday and had the pleasure of beating me in a game of croquet; she put in [sic] down in her diary (at least its very likely) in red letter capitals.

Yr. affec son

Stephen B. Leacock[11]

The family always had fun together, and Stephen always particularly enjoyed them at Sutton, but this was the last vacation which was more important to him than his schoolwork. Before, he had studied easily and looked forward to the summer.

With his return to school in the fall of 1884, having been inspired by the competitive rankings of the system, young Stephen started to study. He said that his younger

brother, Charles, took his departed brother Dick's place,[12] but Upper Canada shows no record of his having attended at any time. At the end of the third form, Stephen, the rededicated scholar, was first in everything except mathematics, and was given as a "prize for book-keeping" a copy of Hawthorne's *Mosses from an Old Manse.*[13] Buckling down to his studies even more, Stephen did still better the next year by memorizing everything in mathematics. In 1886, having completed the fourth form, he was declared first in every subject. When he left school for the year, his father was home from Winnipeg.

The boom was over. Peter Leacock returned broke and bitter, and the family moved back to the farm. The interlude which followed was a "shadowed, tragic family life."[14] The father who had been something of a hero to his children turned into a tyrant. Stephen and the others were further driven from their father by his treatment of their mother, who had proved herself strong and dependable. In spite of his behavior, Agnes Leacock implied in her diary that the affection which caused her to marry Peter never completely died. Perhaps the way the children saw him was different from the way Agnes saw him; maybe she saw the man who had watched three farms financially rot out from under him; maybe she saw the dreamer betrayed by reality; or maybe, more probably, she still saw the dark-haired boy who sailed his boat up to Seaview and romantically called for her to slip out to sea with him. For whatever reason, she returned to the farm even though her small legacy which was supporting

them in Toronto seems to have been the only money they had.

In the fall of 1886 Stephen again became a boarding student at Upper Canada College. Preferring as always to enter wholly into whatever he was doing, he liked being a boarding student much better than being a day student. Leacock's increased activity is evidenced by his being selected as editor for the *College Times*, the weekly paper of the school.[15] In January he debated the question, "The execution of Mary, Queen of Scots, was justifiable," Stephen taking the negative against Pelham Edgar, later famous for his scholarship, for the affirmative. One would like to prove that it was Leacock who wrote of himself in an unsigned report:

> The speech of one learned member (who shall be nameless) would have been more appreciated if he had known which side he was arguing for. The order of the meeting was, on the whole, excellent with the exception of a few factious remarks from some of the "funny" members. . . .
>
> N. B.—After the close of the debate the President might have been seen at the "Taffy," in company with the champions of the negative.[16]

Certainly the style does not keep it from being Stephen's, since it is no more adolescent than his first identifiable publication which appeared the same year, "The Vision of Mirza (New Edition)."[17] This piece, a take-off on the school and its faculty, is done in typical sophomoric style, filled with outrageous puns and references which

are extremely local. Even with his added duties, Stephen graduated in the spring of 1887 as head boy. No distinction granted Stephen Leacock in his honor-filled life ever pleased him more than that of being head boy at U.C.C. The title gave one a notability which followed him through life. Years later, in his biography of Dickens, he mentioned a little too casually that Dickens was not head boy of his school.

Following his successful year at school, Stephen, now seventeen, added other responsibilities to his life. In the summer of 1887 the family difficulties came to a head. At this time Peter left his family for the last time and never came back. Leacock said simply, "I never saw him again,"[18] but a member of the family says it was Stephen who, pushed beyond endurance by the treatment of his mother, took his father to the Sutton station in the cutter. He picked up the buggy whip and flatly stated, "If you come back I'll kill you." It is true, then, that he never saw his father again, but it was by choice. Peter Leacock, probably relieved to be rid of his responsibility, moved to Nova Scotia where he lived more than a half a century longer under the name of Captain Lewis, having survived his wife by six years at his death August 4, 1940.[19] Leacock, who did not ordinarily hold grudges, never forgave his father and refused to go see him even in his old age when some of the other children did visit him briefly on business. His father's departure left Stephen the oldest child at home, Jim not having returned with his father from Winnipeg and Dick having joined the Northwest Mounted Police in 1885. Stephen felt the responsibility

of being head of the family, though his mother had managed on her own for a number of years. Of this part of his life, Leacock again spoke heavily of abiding poverty, but his duties as head of the family were not so onerous that he could not continue his education the next year. Neither was their financial condition actually desperate, though his mother had to remain on the farm when he returned to Toronto.

In June, 1887, Stephen took the matriculation examinations for entrance into the University of Toronto. The results of the examinations not only verified his scholastic honors at U.C.C. but indicated a bright academic future. Except for mathematics, he ranked in the first class in all his subjects, second in the first class in French, history and geography, third in classics and English, and sixth in German. In mathematics he was sixteenth in the second class.[20] In November of 1887, Stephen entered University College, whose residence halls must have been filled, since he took quarters at Wycliff College where he remained until the following spring.[21] Leacock recalled in his autobiography that he did two years of academic work in one year, giving him full third-year status after 1888. This memory, proud as it was, must be judged faulty; the records of the university show that he took the normal complement of six courses. It is true that he attended the university only three years, but many people who had had the good preparatory school training he got at Upper Canada College were granted junior status after one successful year at the university.

The same matriculation exam which qualified him for

second-year status showed results sufficient to grant him a scholarship of one hundred dollars for that year. Leacock's first year at University College seems to have been patterned after his early days at Upper Canada. He was a good student, as the results testify, but he made little impression on the social life of the campus. Undoubtedly he entered into the usual freshman activities, but the freshman of his day was supposed to be humble and reticent, an easy task for the shy young Leacock. At the end of the year he was tied for the General Proficiency Scholarship and had taken honors in all his subjects, being first in French, German and Italian, second in history and classics, and eighth in English.[22] Having taken his work in modern languages, Leacock found that his education had prepared him for "nothing except to pass it on to other people." His mother, living on the farm and caring for eight children on eighty dollars a month, could ill afford more financial help at the time. Besides, he did not want to ask for more help; he saw himself as a young man responsible certainly for his own expense, wanting to contribute to the welfare of the family. He found that three months as a teacher in training would qualify him to teach in a high school, because he had the equivalent of two years at the university. Since teaching seemed the only solution, he sent in his application for teacher training and went home for the summer.

In September, 1888, Stephen was assigned with half a dozen others to the Strathroy Collegiate Institute, Strathroy, Ontario. He took the train to Strathroy, carrying his effects in a wooden trunk tied with an old piece

of clothesline and a valise "of imitation straw or of imitation something else."[23] This indiscriminate luggage was typical of the bags Leacock carried the rest of his life. He never seemed to care what his clothes were in as long as he could carry it, or better yet have it carried. Leaving his trunk at the station and tugging his valise with him, he walked down the first street he came to until he found a sign ROOMS WITH BOARD. This was his first boardinghouse, a kind of living quarters he was to know well before he finished his education. His stay in this house was short indeed. Unused to the accommodations of a boardinghouse, so different from his home or his rooms at school, he wrote his mother, as soon as he had unpacked, of his safe arrival in Strathroy, adding "but the boarding-house I am in looks a pretty rotten place, so I don't expect to stay long"; then he went down to dinner leaving the letter on his desk. Going back upstairs from dinner, he met the landlady coming down from his room. She glared at him and announced huffily, "If you find this boardinghouse such a rotten place I guess you better not stay in it," and charging him a quarter for the meal she put him out.[24] Perhaps it was she who was responsible for the idea he proposed later in "Boarding House Geometry," that

The landlady of a boarding-house is a parallelogram—that is, an oblong, angular figure, which cannot be described, but which is equal to anything.[25]

But he soon found another place, where he exercised more caution.

When he reported to the Institute, he found the same system in effect that young teachers all over North America were finding; the prospective teacher listened to classes being conducted by regular teachers, and after a time of observation he took over the classes. Because he was a modern language student, Leacock was assigned to James Wetherell, principal of Strathroy and teacher of modern languages. Wetherell, known to the students as "Jimmy," was to become one of the great figures in Canadian education. Like all good teachers, Wetherell was distinctive in his teaching, even to mannerisms of voice and gesture. One day after Leacock had been observing for some time, Wetherell turned to him rather abruptly and said, "Now will you take the lesson over at that point and continue it?" Leacock, bored by the professional education requirement which he considered mostly humbug until his death, did precisely what the man asked; he took over. He copied every gesture and intonation of speech. He did it so well and carried it on so long that even the teacher, who of course expected no such thing, caught on. He flushed when Leacock finished and said with some sharpness, "I am afraid I admire your brains more than your manners." Stephen Leacock, the man who in less than ten years would be publishing humor, was crushed. He had made people laugh, but someone else had gotten hurt. This injury he had neither intended nor expected. It was at this time, said Leacock, that he learned first that human kindness was a necessary element of good humor.[26] No one remained angry with Leacock very long and, since Stephen

was contrite, the teacher and the pupil became rather close friends as Stephen continued to conduct the class. In this class Leacock taught Arthur Currie, later Sir Arthur, and James T. Shotwell, later professor at Columbia and member of the American Commission to negotiate peace in 1918.

When he had successfully finished his teacher training, Leacock went back to the farm and applied for every teaching job he heard of. But, in the usual fashion of the academic world, positions were hard to find at midyear, and the inexperienced teacher could offer little competition for the few which could be found. But in January of 1889 his luck changed. Harry Park, the "Mr. Park" who was his tutor on the farm in earlier days, had gone on to get his degree and had become headmaster at Uxbridge High School. He wrote Stephen that Uxbridge needed a modern language teacher and that his recommendation should be enough if Leacock wanted the job. In February he entered Uxbridge's new brick building to take his first paying job. Uxbridge was a small central Ontario town of about fifteen hundred, only eighteen miles from his mother's farm. It was larger than Sutton and, though not the familiar metropolis of Toronto, seemed a good place to live at the time.[27]

It is well that Uxbridge was a quiet town; his monthly salary of $59.33 would hardly have gone far in riotous living. As it was, Leacock found that the salary was sufficient. Board was twelve dollars a month, clothes— he could buy all he needed for about a hundred dollars a year—eight dollars a month, laundry around two dol-

lars. His two beers a day at five cents a glass came to "about two dollars and a half a month, the bars being closed on Sunday." With his first pay check he felt so rich that he hired a cutter and drove the day's journey to the farm to visit his mother. Once there he made his first contribution to the support of his mother—ten dollars from this first check. Thus Leacock entered a role he continued throughout the life of his mother. The other children were able to help as they grew up, so that finally, in her advanced years, Agnes Leacock lived in comparative comfort.[28]

The life at Uxbridge was not a very hard one for Stephen. He was a successful teacher from the start; he did not think much of the system of teaching modern languages, but his students were learning as much as anyone else's. Although teaching was not difficult, it appeared a kind of treadmill existence to him, because Stephen wanted to go back to the university. His salary was not sufficient to allow enough savings to take him back, and he was certainly not satisfied to stop where he was in his education. For a while he tried reading texts from the university; it was a poor substitute.

The Uxbridge period made only one contribution to his accomplishments; while here Leacock decided that shorthand would be valuable. He got Pitman's *Phonographic Dictionary* and learned passable though not perfect shorthand in about three weeks, a skill of which he was inordinately proud the rest of his life. This seems a small thing, but Stephen Leacock liked men who did things themselves. The man who had learned to fly a

plane, or use a hammer, or explore a river, or take short-hand occupied a higher place in his estimation. At the time this craft seemed a new toy to play with until he could return to the university, but it was small consolation.

Finding nothing better to do, Stephen signed a contract with Uxbridge for the next year and left for the summer. Agnes Leacock had taken the Parsonage at Sibbald's Point again, and he went back to the lake and the boats he loved. A few years earlier he had bought an awkward vessel known as a double lugger, and now with his new wealth, for five dollars he had transformed it into a sailing sloop.[29] This was his first boat, but it was the first in a long line. It must have been in this sloop that he began to gain real skill at sailing. Stephen whiled away the summer restlessly, not wanting to return to Uxbridge, but having little choice. He swam and fished and sailed, exploring the shore line of Lake Simcoe until he boasted he knew it as well as a river pilot knew his river. He played tennis and organized cricket games. Next to sailing and fishing, Stephen loved cricket, but Upper Canada was not very active in the preservation of this grand old game. Good cricket required too good a pitch and too many players for casual play. But Stephen would get up a game and, as his brother George said, "He would carry a bucket of beer out to second base and then shout them around the field."

Leacock had just gone discontentedly back to school when Napanee High School offered him two hundred dollars a year more than his Uxbridge salary to teach

modern languages for them. The trustees of his school refused to release him from his contract, and he settled down more obstinately than ever to do a job he hated. With a precedent already established, he received another offer three weeks after the term had started, and this one was even more tempting. Upper Canada College needed a junior master at a salary of seven hundred, exactly equal to his Uxbridge pay. A position at a school in Toronto would allow him to re-enter University College and continue work toward his degree while teaching. He again applied for a release; the trustees again refused, and Stephen, even now only nineteen years old, stubbornly demanded an audience with the board. They granted his unusual request and stonily heard out his arguments. Then, as the chairman was explaining in tones of finality why they could not let him go, one of the men—"his name was Britton, and I am glad to honour it," said Leacock—interrupted and insisted that a young man who was trying to get ahead should not be denied. Stephen quickly pressed his advantage by asking for a week to find them a replacement, and he was free. It was at this point that the "remarkable uncle," E. P. Leacock, again entered Stephen's life. Modern language teachers were very hard to find, but E.P. with his political connections and his flair for managing other people's affairs finally found one who was "far from modern and short on language." But he served the purpose, and Leacock moved back to the university.[30]

Leacock's position of assistant master at Upper Canada College did not require residence, so he moved into

another of an estimated seventeen boardinghouses[31] he occupied during his university days. Even Leacock could not remember where this one was, but it was in the vicinity of McCaul, D'Arcy, and St. Patrick streets, a small area right across College Street from the campus. He lived in this neighborhood until he became a resident master at Upper Canada. Since the *Varsity*, the college publication, was not published in 1889–90, Leacock's campus activities were lost along with those of everyone else. Leacock resumed his modern language program with five languages and history. He evidently had a great interest in the classics, for people who knew him well make the mistake of saying he did honors work in classics. Throughout his life it is obvious that he never lost the facility in Greek and Latin which he gained in his earlier education. At any rate, at the end of the year, Stephen had won the Julius Rossin Scholarship in third-year German and had taken honors in all his courses.[32] He was first in English, Italian, and Spanish and second in French, German, and history.[33]

Leacock's splendid record upon his return to college may indicate his relief in getting back, or it may suggest a limited social life. Certainly his activities on the University College campus were widespread enough the next year, when his marks were not quite so good. It was this year that he joined Zeta Psi, the oldest fraternity at the university. He was elected poet of the class of '91 at the same time his roommate, G. Howard Ferguson— later Premier of Ontario—was selected as president. While in school, Leacock began to get some reputation as

a speaker. When the Medical College had their annual dinner, they requested that he be the representative from University College. The *Varsity* reported that S. B. Leacock and T. E. Bennett spoke.

> These gentlemen covered themselves with glory, Mr. Leacock especially distinguishing himself, making what many considered the speech of the evening. It was certainly the wittiest, very cleverly constructed, and delivered in a most pleasing manner.[34]

Also, Leacock was chosen by his own fraternity to reply to the toast, "The Queen," at their spring banquet.[35] Evidently the young Leacock showed some of the charm for women that the older man was to abound in. The *Varsity*, just before his twenty-first birthday, carried this sly comment:

> The Ladies '91 have suggested that the male portion of the Senior Modern Language Class furnish himself with a chaperone.[36]

However much his classmates were attracted to him, Stephen Leacock, who had refused even to think of quitting short of the completion of his education, was still a man's man with little time for women.

Certainly the most important of Leacock's extracurricular connections was that with the *Varsity*. The Zeta Psi fraternity had gotten control of the weekly magazine in 1880, but by 1889 had run into financial difficulty in its publication. In 1890 publication was started again, this time in the hands of the whole student body. Per-

haps it was his membership in the fraternity or perhaps
it was his demonstrated skill, but the masthead of the
revitalized *Varsity* listed S. B. Leacock as an associate
editor. One of Leacock's duties was the reading of un-
solicited material. Two of his classmates had had so
many offerings rejected by him that they spitefully submitted a sonnet by Keats. This was returned as speedily
as the other submissions. Gleeful at first, the boys were
afraid to reveal that Stephen had apparently fallen into
their trap. Knowing Leacock's almost phenomenal memory, they could never be sure he had not simply recognized the poem and returned it without giving them the
satisfaction of an argument.

Besides editing, Stephen contributed a column which
appeared irregularly under the nom de plume of "The
Sanctum Philosopher." Some half dozen short articles
seldom more than half a column long bore this heading,
and three or four longer pieces rated the byline S. B.
Leacock. Like the one short bit done at Upper Canada,
these were humor, but they were done with far greater
skill. The Leacock style was beginning to mature. There
were still many local references, as in "A Lost Work,"
a long parody of *Hiawatha*, but they were handled more
universally so that they still have some meaning for the
present-day reader. He had become a critic sufficient to
the task of parody. He did not simply follow the odd
metrics of Longfellow, the cumulative repetitions came
at the same speed, the narrative progressed at the same
rate. He still had an addiction to a bad pun, as when the
braves

> Gathered in their neighboring temple,
> Gathered round the shrine of Mouph-tai
> Gathered round his bier, and drank it.[37]

The other longer pieces were parodies also, one of German philosophical fiction, another of the medieval romance.

The duties of editorship proved too much for the young man carrying a full academic course at University College and teaching a full load at Upper Canada College. On December 20 the *Varsity* regretted to announce "that Mr. S. B. Leacock has been compelled to resign his position as editor on the *Varsity* staff, owing to lack of time in which to fulfill his duties to his own satisfaction."[38] But the damage was done; when examination time came Stephen found himself less adequately prepared than he liked. Like Harry Park earlier and many other people later, a friend came to his aid. His Italian teacher, young Professor Needler, had just joined the University College staff a year before. When he volunteered to take Leacock's classes at Upper Canada while he prepared for his exams, Leacock was saved. In his last examinations at the University of Toronto, Leacock gained the honors class in French, German, Spanish, and Italian, but only the third class in English and ethnology.[39]

One of his contemporaries explained that Leacock thought he was taking an examination in English philology and that he was quite surprised when three weeks later he was given credit for ethnology, albeit in the

third class.[40] This is patently false; no one of the intelligence of Stephen Leacock could have confused a test in ethnology with philology. It remained for Howard Ferguson to reveal the truth. Leacock and Ferguson were due to take an examination on algebra, but since both of them were language majors they were quite worried about it. Leacock, still trying to bring the mountain to Mohammed, searched through the fine print of the catalogue and found an option. One could choose an examination in ethnology instead. Ferguson, recognizing Leacock as the superior student, was willing to do whatever he said. Leacock hurried to the library and discovered that Sir Daniel Wilson, principal of the university, had written two books on the subject. He carried the books back to their room and, sitting up all night, they took turns reading the books aloud. The next day Leacock and Ferguson took the exam and were happy to get even third class.[41]

III

1891–1901

WITH his B.A. from the University of Toronto secure, Leacock found himself a university graduate with a degree he was dissatisfied with. Needler had appreciated him as a bright and quick student but thought him little interested in his course. Leacock's discomfort stemmed from a very real belief that languages could not be taught in school by the only method he had been trained in. He was a very good language student himself, but no one was required to speak the languages he was learning. So, certain that it was wrong but vague as to what should be done about it, he applied himself to his teaching at Upper Canada College.

Leacock had come to Upper Canada College as an assistant master in modern languages in 1889. After the granting of his bachelor's degree in 1891 he was elevated to second modern language master and assistant house master with residence in the Old Wing with the junior boys. Advancement almost always came fast to Leacock; the next year he became the first modern language master

in an impressive staff.[1] Few schools of any size, and fewer still of the size of U.C.C., could boast such a collection of young men who were to become important. W. Allan Neilson, later one of America's greatest Renaissance scholars, professor of English at Harvard, and still later president of Smith College, taught with Leacock. The young mathematics master, Edward Peacock, later Sir Edward, became one of the most important financiers of the British Empire. Stephen's closest friend was Pelham Edgar, who became professor of English language and literature at the University of Toronto, a noted Henry James scholar, chief literary historian of Canada, and an influential Fellow of the Royal Society of Canada. These men were naturally exceptions, but Upper Canada had a good faculty; they were pleasant companions for Leacock and it was a good place to work.

Stephen, a young man now, wore a light, sandy mustache, and his hair always seemed to need both combing and cutting. There was less of carelessness about his toilet than of casualness; his tousled but not unkempt hair lent a boyish quality that even his dress could not dispel. His clothes gave an effect of academic negligence which ordinarily comes with age to the absent-minded professor. Leacock had a kind of sleepy look about him except in his eyes which were, to the lower-form boys, almost frighteningly alive. In spite of his lack of attention to fashion and appearance, he had something of the look of the sport about him; he was early dubbed "Stevie" in private by his students. They liked him in spite of his quick sarcasm and his equally quick and knowledgeable

use of the light cane he carried under one arm. Leacock had occupied the "Old Wing" and the "New Wing" and he knew the practices of the boys who lived there. Whenever he found it necessary to punish a boy, he delivered his blows sharply on the fingertips, for schoolboy folklore taught that there were many ways the palm might be toughened in anticipation of falling from grace.[2] The methods the boys tried were, of course, generally ineffective, but Stephen Leacock liked to stay a step or two ahead of his students, and he liked for them to know it. He said once:

> It is the beginning which counts. Face the class. Begin talking to them at once. Get to business, not with one of them but all of them. Talk: don't mumble. Face them: don't turn your back. Start work: don't get fumbling about with a class list of names and a roll call, which you may pronounce correctly or may not. Leave all that till later. Start work, and, once started, they are lost as far as disorder goes. In fact they won't expect any. Above all, don't try to be funny; feeble teachers attempt a footing of fun as a means of getting together. The real teacher descends to fun only when he has established a sufficient height to descend from.[3]

Leacock was far from a martinet, but when he entered the dusty, stuffy classrooms on the upper floors, lighted by bare, faintly hissing gas jets in the darkness of winter months, both he and the students knew who was in charge.

If he took his teaching seriously, Leacock was less strict about his other duties. Some of the masters were assigned the duty of escorting the boarders to the churches they chose on Sunday morning. Leacock admitted that he wrote down some of his best ideas while his attention was distracted from the service to which he had taken the Church of England boys. One day at the beginning of a term a young master named Collinson burst excitedly into Stephen's room. "My word, Leacock, do you know what they've done to me?" he said in a shocked tone. "They have asked me to take the Methodist boys to church!" "That's terrible, isn't it," said Leacock sympathetically. "I'll tell you what I'll do; I haven't any religious prejudices, as you know. We'll simply swap boys. You take mine to St. George's, where you want to go, and I will take care of the Methodists." This arrangement suited Collinson splendidly, but he was horrified to return from church the next Sunday and find Stephen at work in his room, dressed so that it was obvious that he had not been out of the house. Leacock calmly explained that since there were only two or three Methodists in school it had been no trouble to turn them over to a Methodist master who was going anyway.[4] It was by such measures that he was able the rest of his life to do a tremendous amount of work, yet seem to be a man of great leisure.

Because he was so cunning at finding time to get his work done, he had time to pursue almost anything that struck his fancy. For instance, it was during this time that he became interested enough in economics to take

up the study on his own. Edgar introduced him to Professor Mavor at the University of Toronto as a man who might guide his reading, but from the first Leacock and Mavor could not get along. There seemed to be no reason that they irritated each other, but Leacock pursued his studies on his own. This extra studying along with preparation for classes, grading papers, administrative duties, and other reading took a great deal of time, but Stephen still found time to visit his mother on the weekends and holidays.

Stephen, increasingly dissatisfied with teaching on the secondary level, looked forward to his summers, spent wherever his mother was. She had left the farm in 1891 and lived variously at Sutton and Beaverton, and about 1895 settled at Orillia, where Lake Simcoe and Lake Couchiching meet. Stephen liked this little town: two lakes were better than one. And it was eventually here that he established his own summer home. Before the move, while his mother was still living at Sibbald's Point near Sutton, Leacock visited Pelham Edgar at Roach's Point a few miles down the lake. From here, with Gordon Laing, schoolmate of Stephen's at University College and later dean at the University of Chicago, Leacock and Edgar made a two-week voyage around Georgian Bay. Edgar declared that Stephen was neither a skilled sailor nor a fisherman of note at the time of this early cruise.[5] Perhaps he was not familiar with the schooner-rigged boat they were using, perhaps the others were willing to do most of the work. Whatever the reason, there is abundant evidence that Stephen

was far better than the usual amateur sailor. One day while sailing his own sloop, the *Pilot*, in a heavy wind he boasted that he could bring his boat in close enough to Snake Island to throw a biscuit ashore. This was a tricky maneuver at best, but Leacock did it perfectly. Stephen frequently went sailing with his brothers, but he found that he had to do most of the work; they liked the ride but they were not as keen on the sport as he. He demonstrated both his skill and his confidence on the water when a yachting party he had gotten up was forced to spend the night on a sand island because of a storm. He put the party ashore safely and then sailed through the booming wind and the running sea to get and deliver blankets and food for the women and children in the group.[6]

Not all of Stephen's fun came from the lake, of course; there were many things going on ashore which he joined in. As in his earlier days, he played cricket whenever he could. Stephen played rather good cricket for a nonserious player, but Edgar, who had made the first eleven at Upper Canada, called him a "hit or miss player." He played at Sutton and on the Sibbald lawn at Sibbald's Point.[7] Later he played on what was probably his best team at Orillia. Harold Hale, who was Leacock's teammate, remembers that "Leacock was a good batsman but he was no bowler." Although in "Cricket for Americans" Leacock claimed that he once played in an All-Canada match before the Governor-General at Ottawa, he failed to explain that the All-Canadian Cricket Team was one he had made up himself to travel around for the

lark. Certainly Leacock's ability was not All-Canada caliber. But, champion or not, he played cricket as he did everything else, with great enthusiasm; and he was an avid cricket spectator the rest of his life.

Perhaps it was his intense vitality that made the young man popular with his own social set. He was too much alive to need affectation. He did not feel the need to pretend disinterest when he failed to beat Miss Maud Osborne at tennis. She was to become the women's champion of Ontario, but Leacock could play only hard enough and well enough to give her practice when she was just a good girl tennis player. Without conceit Leacock was too satisfied being himself to pretend to be something else. One of his companions of this time recalls seeing Stephen sitting on the rail of the excursion steamer, *Enterprise*, dressed in the old shirt, rumpled flannel trousers, and worn tennis shoes which were his sailing costume. At the next moment he was gaily dancing with the young people, none of whom wore an outfit quite so casual as his. When they sang songs he sang with them in a voice slightly better than average. He was a good mimic and could copy to perfection the voices and mannerisms of the farmers, the local merchants, and the vacationers from the city, but, his friend remembers, his imitations were very carefully without malice.[8] He had learned his lesson at Strathroy well. As he sat among his friends, abstractedly twisting his forelock, he was still shy; he never learned to be completely at ease with others. But Stephen Leacock fitted into society because he was at ease with himself.

While a master at Upper Canada, Leacock made his debut as a professional humorist. On October 6, 1894, *Grip,* a noted humorous magazine of the time, carried his first commercial offering, a one-page sketch called "That Ridiculous War in the East," for which he received the magnanimous sum of two dollars. Others of his writings have been claimed as first, but a careful study of the extant bibliographical sources allows only the *Grip* piece. Leacock's rise as a writer was not fast; it was hardly a rise at all. He was a dilettante writer, having no thought of becoming a professional. Leacock still thought of himself as a teacher, though he was not pleased with what he was teaching. From 1894, a year in which he had only one published article, through 1897, he saw twenty-one of his essays and sketches appear in print. After that first year, he published five the next year, eight the following year, and seven in 1897. The level of this early production was high—seventeen of the twenty-one were to appear in his first book—some of his best and best-known pieces were published in these years. His most famous single sketch, "My Financial Career," was among these, as were "Boarding House Geometry," "An Experiment with Policeman Hogan," and "The Awful Fate of Melpomenous Jones." This last bears the mark of Upper Canada College, since the name though not the character must have come from Septimus Jones, the rector of St. George's where Leacock took his group of boys on Sunday.

The genesis of Leacock as a writer is interesting. He had done some undergraduate publishing but had tried

nothing for payment. In the summer of 1894 he doggedly followed to Colorado a young lady with whom he was smitten. The romantically pale girl, suffering from tuberculosis, was taking a series of treatments on top of a mountain. Queenlike, from her heights, she directed that Leacock must remain at the foot of the mountain. Here he languished most of the summer in the most approved fashion, feeling very sorry for himself and working up a very sentimental mood. Late in the summer the lady fair relented, feeling that she was better, and allowed her courtier to visit her. Leacock arrived only to be treated to an evening of hymns, the girl and her mother and Leacock gathered around the piano. When he reached his quarters at the foot of the mountain, he didn't even stop; he packed up and headed back to Toronto. But the mood he had manufactured for himself was not disspelled so easily. He tried about a half dozen highly sentimental stories, submitting them to *Harper's.* Charles Dudley Warner rejected them as enthusiastically as Leacock had sent them.[9] Leacock, never bothered much by criticism, having gotten the habit of writing, turned his creative talent to the field of humor. From the beginning, Leacock refused to handle his writing carelessly, though he did not think of it as his career. He carried a small book into which he scribbled story ideas and parts of the stories themselves; across some of them he very carefully wrote SOLD.[10] This literary bookkeeping was a practice he continued until his death, but it is indicative of the man that, even when writing was only a pastime, he was going to do it in style.

In 1895 the entire faculty of Upper Canada College received notice of dismissal. Every member from Principal George Dickson to the lowest assistant master was fired. The board of governors had become dissatisfied with Dickson and deemed this the best way to solve the problem; the principal had split the faculty into factions, and the board had difficulty in determining which were his supporters. Though Leacock had been unhappy about his teaching, he had not taken sides, nor was he prepared for the action of the administration. Seeing that he was so upset about it, Pelham Edgar forged a note and placed it in his mailbox on April 1. Leacock came into the room, waving the letter and shouting, "Look! I've been asked to stay." When the date was pointed out, Stephen was, of course, chagrined, but he rebounded with his usual good humor. In time, as a matter of fact, he was rehired by the new principal.[11] During the uncertain period, Pelham Edgar had decided to go to Johns Hopkins to work on a Ph.D. rather than wait for reappointment at U.C.C.

When Leacock was retained as the first modern language master, he was also raised to the position of senior house master, the highest ranking faculty member. Stephen got along well with Principal Parkin, the new man, and Parkin, like other of Leacock's superiors, later came to depend on the young man. He confided one day, "Leacock, I wish I could break this pernicious habit of smoking and swearing in school." Leacock, who had enjoyed his pipe since the days on the lake and whose language had a restrained masculinity about it, soberly

replied, "I know it's a difficult habit to break oneself of, Dr. Parkin, but if you will put all your energy into breaking yourself of it, I am sure that grace will be given you."[12] Stephen liked this easy camaraderie, and he appreciated the accolade of having been chosen senior house master at the age of twenty-five, but he realized too that this was as high as he could go. Principals were chosen from men with higher degrees than his, and he was not certain that he wanted to be even a principal in a secondary system.

In 1899 one of the most important books in Leacock's life was published; Thorstein Veblen produced his *Theory of the Leisure Class*. Stephen had continued his serious but perhaps dilatory reading of economics and political science. Veblen was exciting; here was a man who could and did write of economics with a biting wit, and he was accessible, at the University of Chicago. Stephen evaluated his own situation. He had reached the top where he was. The instability of his position had been shown four years earlier when the whole staff was fired; he might not be so lucky next time. Others of his friends, such as Neilson and Edgar, had already departed to earn higher degrees. At Orillia, he had met the girl he intended to marry, Beatrix Hamilton. Not having written anything for two years, he had, at least for the moment, given up any pretensions to authorship. Teaching French and German was becoming just busy work for him. He had become seriously interested in political economy. The University of Chicago offered a good degree, and it had Thorstein Veblen. Putting ten

and a half years of schoolteaching behind him, he resigned his position at Upper Canada College to enter Chicago in the fall.

His first year at the University of Chicago was a success. He had entered the university September 25, 1899, and in the three quarters that followed he scheduled a heavy program, completing ten courses by the end of the spring quarter. He did so well that he was granted a fellowship in political economy for the next year. On the strength of his proved academic aptitude for his course and the financial help he would be getting, Leacock married Beatrix Hamilton on August 7, 1900.[13]

Leacock had met Beatrix at a tennis game at Orillia. Henry Pellatt, her grandfather, had a large summer place near Orillia called Southwood, where Beatrix and her mother, Mrs. R. B. Hamilton, frequently spent the summers. Southwood held open house on Friday nights, but the Leacocks were closer friends and their visits were not confined to these affairs. Henry Pellatt had retired as a broker while quite successful, and had turned his business interests over to his son, who later became Sir Henry Pellatt. It was Sir Henry who squandered the family fortune—partly on the elaborate Italian castle, Casa Loma, which he built in Toronto at a cost of three million dollars—so that neither Leacock's wife nor her heirs received much from the estate. Beatrix's father was Colonel R. B. Hamilton, member of the Toronto City Council and commander of one of the most famous military units in Canada, the Queen's Own Rifles.

Trix, as all of her friends called her, was an accom-

plished person. Having had quite a bit of voice and dramatic training as part of the education of a proper young lady, she surprised her circle by going to Boston for further study; she added amazement to surprise by going on the stage. Physically she was admirably suited for a theatrical career. Above average in height, she was slight, dark, striking, and even beautiful, with lively dark eyes. Beatrix had a rather extensive amateur stage experience, playing at one time a role which all young actresses dream of playing, Juliet. Her professional dramatic career was necessarily short; she was young and whatever fame she might have gained she gave up in favor of marriage. She was, however, a good enough actress to have appeared at one time with Maude Adams. Because of her theatrical commitments in New York City, Trixie and Stephen were married there. Probably at her suggestion, the ceremony took place in the actors' church, "The Little Church Around the Corner."[14]

The Leacocks returned to Chicago in the autumn and took a small apartment while Stephen continued his graduate studies. They entertained frequently, but not elaborately; both Stephen and Trix had the faculty of enjoying themselves as they were. In the middle of the year 1900–1, Leacock got a minor appointment at McGill University so that their time was divided between Montreal and Chicago. He spent only the spring quarter at Chicago in the school year 1901–2, and evidently the same in 1902–3. During this time he had been preparing his dissertation, "The Doctrine of Laissez Faire." On May 16, 1903, Stephen appeared for his oral examination.

The usual method at the university at this time was for one member of the examining board to give the student a topic on which he was to talk for ten minutes. To Leacock, the chairman of his committee proposed, "Mr. Leacock, discuss for us the tax system of the State of Illinois." Stephen either brashly or desperately replied, "Gentlemen, let me say that I know nothing of the tax system of the State of Illinois, but, if you will allow me, I will speak on the theory of values." When he had spoken brilliantly on his own subject for fifteen minutes, the committee, evidently charmed by him, declared the oral over. On June 16, 1903, he was granted his Ph.D. in political economy and political science, *magna cum laude*.[15]

IV

1901–1911

O N A gray January afternoon in 1901, Stephen Leacock began his long and distinguished alliance with
McGill University in Montreal. Although he grew to love
both the school and the city—both had an air of the
cosmopolitan which he liked—neither had been his first
choice. He had applied for a position at his own alma
mater, the University of Toronto, hoping to continue
what had been for him a most happy association. But
Professor Mavor, with whom he could not agree years
before when he had started his study of economics, would
have none of him.[1] Somewhat regretful and a little
piqued, he turned to McGill. Not yet having his degree,
Leacock could demand no more than they offered, and
he accepted a position of sessional lecturer in economics
and political science bearing a salary of five hundred
dollars a year.[2]

Stephen gave his first lecture at McGill the day before
Queen Victoria died. Even with his flair for the dramatic,
he could not have planned it better himself. His whole

life—politics, economics, manners—was to have a Victorian touch, and he was proud that his career in political economy had started in the reign of "the Queen." That this might legitimately be called a beginning is indicated by the fact that he entered, on that January 21, the room which was to be his for the next thirty-five years, Room 5 in Arts Hall.[3]

Stephen Leacock was not yet the popular teacher he was to become; no young man influences either institution much when he is teaching part-time at one school and taking courses at another. Stephen still had to commute to Chicago occasionally to keep up with his work there, and, shortly after his arrival at McGill, he set a precedent he was to follow for the next two years by spending the spring quarter in Chicago to meet residence requirements. Teaching at McGill and commuting for two quarters, then moving to Chicago meant a rather unsettled life for Stephen and Trix, but he recalled to his friends that cheese and crackers and a quarter's worth of beer made a party for their circle. Their stimulating life as academic nomads went on until 1903, when Stephen was granted his degree and was appointed to the full position of lecturer at McGill.[4]

Celebrating the new Doctor of Philosophy degree, Leacock and his wife took a delayed wedding trip to Europe, one of the periodic casual legacies having come through at just the right time. Acutely aware of his new position, he said, he placed his name on the passenger list as "Dr. Stephen B. Leacock." The boat had hardly cleared the harbor when there came a knock on the door.

When Leacock opened it, he found the steward standing there, cap in hand. "Excuse me, sir," he said, "but the stewardess has injured her leg and the captain wonders if you would mind having a look at it." Stephen said that, mindful of his responsibilities, he hurried off behind the steward; but he was too late. A Doctor of Divinity had outrun him. Leacock returned from Europe to take up his duties at McGill at a salary of little more than two thousand, even including extra pay for night classes.[5]

Stephen had been living on savings for some time; the five hundred dollars McGill had been paying him had not been enough to support his wife or his education. He found the two thousand of the lectureship still inadequate. In hunting for a solution, he made the decision that any young teacher might. He determined to earn a reputation as a scholar so that he might command a higher salary. It is typical of the ability and confidence of Leacock that his first scholarly publication was not an article but a book. When his *Elements of Political Science* appeared in 1906, it was a much-needed work. In a short time after the book had been published, it had been chosen as the standard text by thirty-five universities in the United States. It was the first such textbook used in China after the establishment of the Republic, and it was translated into Urdu for its use in the Mohammedan college of Hyderabad. Before the text was replaced by newer ones, it was translated into nineteen languages. It showed at an astoundingly early date, said one critic, "a surprising grasp . . . of the signifi-

cance and influence of the South African Campaign then just concluded."[6] In spite of the phenomenally quick success of some of his later books of humor, *Elements of Political Science* was its author's biggest money-maker. In striking boldly, Leacock had cut the Gordian knot of his difficulties. He had made money and had made a good start toward his establishment as a scholar. In a further step toward scholarship the same year, he addressed the Canadian Club of Toronto on "The Imperial Crisis."[7]

The publication of Leacock's book and its ready acceptance drew the attention of the university, as did the increasing impression he was making as a splendid teacher. One of his students, Dacres Cameron, upon becoming secretary to the Canadian Manufacturers' Association, proposed to the executive committee that Leacock address their Montreal meeting. There were many objections to the idea of having to listen to a college professor, but Cameron prevailed, insisting that Leacock was amusing as well as learned. Leacock made his first speech before a nonacademic group at their hesitant invitation. His speech, as witty, charming, and thoughtful as the man, was so well accepted that he was asked to address the larger annual meeting in Toronto. This part of his career he had not counted on, but Leacock found himself in demand as a public speaker. The success of his *Elements of Political Science,* his outstanding success as a speaker, and his ability and popularity as a teacher encouraged the university to raise him directly to the rank of associate professor in 1906.[8]

The four articles and the book Leacock published the next year were early indications of his variety of interest and accomplishment. "Education and Empire Unity" and "Greater Canada" were discussions of political science on a near popular level; Leacock took his responsibility as a teacher seriously. "The Psychology of American Humor" was literary criticism in a field which he was so successfully to enter later. And "Responsible Government in the British Colonial System" was a scholarly political science article appearing in a learned journal, *American Political Science Review*. The book *Baldwin, Lafontaine, Hincks: Responsible Government* was a mixture of political science and history. The fourteenth volume of the Makers of Canada series, it was concerned with Canada's early struggle toward effective autonomous government. Leacock proved himself to be not, as the titles might indicate, a hack-writing jack-of-all-trades, but a thinker of genuine ability and range.

His stature as a scholar, his popularity as a speaker, and his success as a teacher made him the choice of the Cecil Rhodes Trust as their lecturer. Under the auspices of this organization, Leacock toured the British Empire in 1907–8, speaking on "Imperial Organization."⁹ Although Leacock, at thirty-seven, could not be considered too young for this honor, the selection was genuinely surprising. A man only three years a Ph.D. and only one year a professor, he was chosen over a great many of his contemporaries who felt themselves equally well qualified and who knew themselves to be of longer service. In spite of his ostensible inexperience, Leacock proved the

choice to have been a wise one and was received everywhere with acclaim. The ability with which he took part
in a discussion at the Royal Colonial Institute in London,
on May 14, so pleased the group that they elected him a
nonresident member at the next meeting.[10] After an almost triumphal tour, Leacock returned to McGill to a
series of successes which made for him a banner year.

In 1908 Stephen Leacock was appointed William Dow
Professor of Political Economy and at the same time became chairman of the Department of Economics and
Political Science. This position carried with it a salary of
thirty-five hundred, which he supplemented to the extent
of five hundred dollars by special lectures. It was in 1908
that he helped found the University Club of Montreal.
The same year he bought his summer home in Orillia,
Ontario. The Old Brewery Bay, the University Club, and
his department at McGill were the three things that Leacock cared the most for during the remainder of his life.

The University Club, in which Stephen Leacock was a
guiding force throughout his active years, furnished the
relaxation and the congenial companionship which he
required. Stephen liked a place where he could sit in a
deep leather chair and smoke his pipe. He liked the restricted maleness of the "club." Situated near the McGill
campus, the University Club offered a convenience and
a quiet luxury that suited the character of Leacock. He
did not like ostentatious living, but in contrast to the
modest means of his youth he wanted to live as a man of
more comfortable resources now. The club served as a
place to invite the visiting professor for a drink, as a

place where he could find a partner for a spirited, if casual, game of billiards. As the years passed and circumstances changed, the University Club became a kind of second home for him, and gradually the big, easy, leather chair, second from the window in the reading room, became known as "Stephen Leacock's chair."

When Leacock was appointed chairman of his department, he was as far up the administrative ladder as he ever cared to go. He did not want to be a dean, or even principal, though with his friends' help he could probably have accomplished either. Although he dearly loved to take a piece of Bristol board and neatly work out the schedule of his department, and he performed the other duties of the department with equal ease, he liked teaching too much to ever have more than the nominal duties of the chairmanship. Stephen Leacock was a master teacher with the rare ability to guide the young graduate student toward important thinking of his own. As chairman he felt a high responsibility for the teaching done by the rest of his staff, and to that end he instituted a practice afterward adopted by other departments at McGill. At the beginning of the term, any lecturer or professor, regardless of rank or tenure, had to prepare a one-page précis of a new course or an old course he had not taught recently. This was not an instance of a new department head's coming in with sweeping, new, untried ideas. Leacock had been doing this in his own teaching for years, and he knew that having to reduce the major aim and content of the course to a concise state-

75

ment resulted in better preparation and consequently better teaching.

Stephen Leacock had the wisdom, apparently unusual in a scholar of his stature, to recognize the limitations of the student. He frequently advised his staff to "bite off a small piece of your subject and chew it well." Leacock was easy to work for and he was extremely loyal to his staff, defending them to administration and students alike when necessary. He tried to choose his faculty so carefully that no defense would be required, although in B. K. Sandwell he found himself disappointed. Sandwell knew his subject, and he evidently had the self-discipline, but he did not have the knack for teaching. He resigned rather than embarrass Leacock, and, although he went on to become Professor of English at Queen's, he found that instruction was not his province. Sandwell soon entered the professional side of literature with great success, distinguishing himself as editor of the Toronto *Saturday Night*. Such difficulties were rare, and J. P. Day, first Leacock's student and later a member of his faculty, said, "We prided ourselves—and the credit was his—that we were the happiest and most harmonious Department in the University."[11]

The third big event in 1908 for Leacock, the purchase of the place in Orillia, was the fulfillment of an early dream. While sailing his boat around Lake Couchiching in the early 1890's he had picked, as the most picturesque, the spot where a brewery had stood earlier. He determined then that if he were ever able and it were available he would own it. In 1908, his future reasonably

assured, he bought the place—thirty-three acres for sixteen hundred dollars.[12] He promptly christened it The
Old Brewery Bay and declared, "You can judge your
friends by that name. If they don't like the sound of it
they aren't your friends. On the other hand, I've known
people to grow thirsty as far off as Nebraska just thinking about it."[13] When he and his brother, Charlie, with
their own hands built a one-room shack right down on the
lake, he started a project which never saw an end. After
this it was to take all summer to effect the plans he had
made all winter. It was not long until the small house had
grown to a larger one, where Stephen and Trix could
more comfortably entertain their increasing circle of
friends.

Both Leacock and his wife liked entertaining, and
there was a kind of casual elegance about any party they
gave. They would invite a dozen people for dinner and
then be the last ones to show up; at The Old Brewery
Bay, Stephen might be still out fishing; in Montreal,
Beatrix would arrive glowingly from her ski club, and
Stephen would come in from a late class or perhaps a stop
at the University Club. George Leacock recalled one
evening when dinner, never a prompt affair, was unusu-
ally late. The conversation was brilliant and everyone
was having a good time, but finally at midnight George,
exercising his rights as a brother, asked why dinner had
not yet been served. Trix without the least anxiety explained that the turkey had not been delivered on time,
had in fact been very late, and was still cooking but "it
will be far enough along in an hour for us to start the

first course." Nothing disturbed the Leacocks, and they were such good company that nothing disturbed their guests.

Leacock by this time had gained some stature and recognition as an active scholar. To the American Political Science Association he had submitted a paper which he was asked to read at their meeting in 1908.[14] The following year the same body elected him to a two-year term on the Executive Council which served while Woodrow Wilson was president of the Association.[15] Although Leacock, the scholar, was becoming firmly established, scholarly publication did not pay, and his salary of four thousand dollars, while offering security for the future, was not sufficient for the kind of life he wanted to live.

It was only natural that Leacock, casting about for some way to increase his income, should think of his previous publications. Leacock, a man who could not tie his own tie so that it would stay, was always very methodical about his paperwork. He liked the business-like air of a good filing system, and, as his life and affairs became more complex, he needed the help such a system gave him. He might turn to anyone who was close and say, "Bring me my glasses," having no idea where they were, but his publication, his business, and his teaching were in perfect order. As his correspondence grew, it required rather elaborate classification—investments, taxes, lectures, contracts, personal letters, movie rights, and so on—and he had one folder carefully labeled LETTERS FROM DAMN FOOLS. Although his files were neither so

elaborate nor so extensive, of course, in 1909, he had kept a record of what he had published, and it occurred to him that more money might be made from these early pieces without further effort on his part.

Beatrix and Mrs. B. K. Sandwell, with the help of Stephen's journal, started going through the files of the magazines in which he had published.[16] Sandwell, who had been a student of Leacock's at Upper Canada during the time of his first publication, had come to Montreal as a reporter on the Montreal *Herald*. The two wives found enough to constitute a small volume, and Leacock edited the material and sent it off hopefully to Houghton, Mifflin, the publishers of his book on political science. At this point an editor pulled one of those magnificent boners that make publishing history fascinating. He refused one of the funniest books of its time because humor "was too uncertain."[17] This rejection might easily have been the end of Leacock the humorist. The manuscript had been compiled and submitted as an exuberant gesture or a prank as much as anything else. Still he did have a manuscript now. Sandwell, who had earlier tried to persuade Leacock not to publish such trivia, redoubled his efforts. He would ruin his reputation as a professional economist. His position as a scholar was not yet secure enough to stand such a display of frivolity. As a teacher he would take on the aspect of a "character." To all this Leacock could easily have added that nobody seemed to want the stuff anyway.

One evening early in 1910, the Leacocks were entertaining Sandwell and his wife while George Leacock,

Stephen's younger and favorite brother, was in town. As a convivial evening progressed, Stephen showed George the collection and told him of its rejection. Although this was not the first time George had read the material during the ten years or more since its publication, he had not realized that there had been such a body of it. George chuckled his way through it, exclaiming once, "Oh, hell! These are good." When he had finished, George displayed the brash imagination which might almost be called a Leacock trait. "Steve, why don't you publish these yourself?" Stephen impishly replied, "Hell, why don't you?" George, not to be outdone, said, "Well, hell, I will."

The next day George visited the Gazette Printing Company in Montreal to arrange for publication of the manuscript. Looking over the material, they determined that the only successful way to produce the book was in a paper-board bound edition to sell for thirty-five cents. This edition would allow a profit of about seven cents which Stephen and George agreed to split—five cents for George the publisher and two cents for Stephen the author. Having made these arrangements, George, who was traveling as a salesman of electrical supplies at the time, left town, but a short time afterward he received a letter from Stephen. Stephen said that, after considering it, he did not feel it was right for George to be burdened with a book which might or might not sell, particularly when the risk should be his anyway; he enclosed a check for fifty dollars, the amount George had deposited with the printing company. George had not

been unhappy with his bargain, but he was not unhappy either to be relieved of such an uncertain investment as an untried book.

Stephen Leacock took the chance. To the manager of the Gazette Printing Company he wrote:

Dear Mr. Larkin

I understand that in accordance with the memorandum which I append to this, the copies of my book are to be delivered to the news company at a cost to me of 15 1/3 cents per copy for which sum I am to make payment three months after delivery. The number of copies to be delivered to the news company is 3000 and 100 copies at the same rate of charge are to be sent to me at my house.

I thought it best to put this in writing before delivery.

Very sincerely
Stephen Leacock[18]

Because the Gazette Printing Company was not really a publishing house, Leacock had to handle the distribution of the book himself.

The Manager,
The Montreal News Company,

Dear Mr. Tanguay,—

Pursuant to our recent conversation, I propose to place with you for sale 3000 copies of my book, "Literary Lapses," now being manufactured by the Gazette Co.

It is understood that you are to pay me 23 cents each for the books sold, and that they are to be put on the retail market at 35 cents. I am to pay you 3 cents a pound for such books as you send out and are returned to you unsold. I will also supply you with 200 paper placards and 100 placards in cardboard to be used as advertisements in stores and book stands.

You will make payment to me of my share of receipts at intervals of three months after the first receipt of the copies from the printer, the first payment being made at the end of three months, the second at the end of six months, the third at the end of nine months, and a fourth and final payment at the end of a year when unsold books shall be returned and our transactions closed.

This arrangement carries with it the exclusive right of sale of the present 3000 and of all copies issued in the same form and the offer of the agency of any other edition on terms to be arranged. This refers only to Canada.[19]

The whole edition sold in two months, making him a modest profit of two hundred and thirty dollars.[20] More important was the happy accident which placed one of the three thousand copies in the hands of a man returning to England. John Lane, the British publisher, having completed some business which had necessitated his visiting Canada, casually picked up a copy of *Literary Lapses* at a newsstand to serve as light reading on his return voyage. Since John Lane's business was books,

undoubtedly he would have heard of the book anyway. But the humble format Leacock had chosen made the discovery more spectacular. Lane cabled an immediate offer to bring the book out in a regular trade edition; Mark Twain had died earlier the same year and Lane saw in Leacock a writer who could replace him, contemporarily at least. Stephen cabled back, "I accept with thanks."[21]

Literary Lapses, the book which introduced Leacock to the world, foretold almost the whole scope of Leacock's humor of the next fifteen years. Besides encompassing the literary forms which Leacock was to use for the first part of his career—forms about which more will be said later—*Literary Lapses* displayed his basic approach to humor. The mark of Stephen Leacock's humor was his sympathy for man. Leacock found much of his fun in the little man beset by advertising, fads, convention, sex, science, cussedness, machinery—social and industrial—and many other impersonal tyrannies. And in every case he aligned himself on the side of humanity. Swift would have ridiculed the little man in "My Financial Career" who could not manage his own checkbook; Leacock took him to his heart, implying that no bank had a right to frighten such an unassuming little fellow, and allowed him the final small but real triumph of declaring that now he kept his money in an old sock.

Even in "A, B, and C" this humanitarian attitude was evident. Leacock started with the usual old arithmetic problem of *A* who could run a mile in six minutes, *B* who could run the same distance in ten minutes, and *C* who

required fifteen minutes. But Leacock envisioned *A* as a bully who was running *C* to death simply because he could always beat him. What chance had man against science which went too fast for him? In "How to be a Doctor" Leacock said, "Just think of it, a hundred years ago there were no bacilli, no ptomaine poisoning, no diphtheria, and no appendicitis. Rabies was but little known, and imperfectly developed." Of course! It was the last phrase, "imperfectly developed," which turned the responsibility back on impersonal science. In "Men Who Have Shaved Me," the little man was badgered by the supercilious barber to let the ends of his hair be plugged up with sealing wax, to let his hair be singed up close to the follicles, to let his eyebrows be squirted with lemon juice; when he refused he was thrown out of the shop. But he had refused, and his dignity was intact, even though injured.

All these examples appeared in *Literary Lapses*, but this respect for human dignity which marked the early humor of Stephen Leacock was to continue throughout his career. He saw man so systematized that he could no longer fix his own shoes, shave his own face, keep his own money, or catch his own fish; but Leacock made fun of the system and not the man who struggled against it. He found something noble about the little man who refused to become a cog in a social machine, who insisted on being an individual. Leacock scanned man with the searching eye of the humorist, and he liked what he found; he liked what made man human.

The humor in *Literary Lapses* was cast in many forms

but one of the most prominent was the sketch, dear to the humorist perhaps because of its lack of definition. The sketch encompasses monologues, letters, descriptions, nonsense for its own sake, and casual comments on life as the humorist sees it. Stephen Leacock used them all. "A Model Dialogue" and "A Christmas Letter" indicated by their very titles the types of sketches they were. "A Study in Still Life" was a nostalgic description of a passing institution, the country hotel. In "Winter Pastimes," Leacock invented nonsensical indoor games, and in "The Force of Statistics" he rightly observed that man was awed by figures, whether the figures were right or not. In another book, people, in "The Marine Excursion of the Knights of Pythias," boarded the *Mariposa Belle* and:

> hunted for a place out of the sun and when they got them swore they weren't going to freeze to death to please anyone; and the people in the sun said that they hadn't paid fifty cents to be roasted. Others said that they hadn't paid fifty cents to get covered with cinders, and there were still others who hadn't paid fifty cents to get shaken to death with the propeller.[22]

None of these nonfiction pieces had the development of thought to be called essays. Much of Leacock's humor was sheer nonsense, on more than a score of different subjects. The forms which Leacock employed in the sketch he might have learned from earlier humor—which he had undoubtedly read—or from his contemporaries. At any rate, Lane advertised him as "The Canadian

Mark Twain," letting fall on Leacock's shoulders a capacious mantle. Even if the mantle was too big, there was certainly no one else more qualified to bear it. An impressively successful first book (printed twenty-two times by John Lane alone),[23] *Literary Lapses* was a good introduction to Stephen Leacock, since it displayed many kinds of humor—short stories, essays, parodies, sketches, and even verse.

V

1911–1914

THE versatility which was found in Leacock's first book of humor was simply an extension of the man. Early in his life Leacock became interested in a great many things, and the number increased as he grew older. He played billiards as he played cricket, with great enthusiasm and some skill. He had a phenomenal memory, seeming never to forget anything he had ever read, and there seemed to be nothing one could ask him that he did not know something about. He was one of three professors at McGill, including Herman Walter, chairman of the German department, capable of reading theses written in German. A copy of an Anglo-Saxon reader in his library reveals by inscription and notes in his handwriting that he acquired a reading knowledge of Old English. He built his own boat, cutting and sewing the sail himself. He played chess so well that when he and his companion went to the University Club for dinner they sat in the reading room and called out the moves to each other rather than have a board prepared for so short a

time.[1] When Wallace Goforth, first a student and then a teacher under Leacock, found Leacock "a *genie* in the real French meaning of the word" he was not exaggerating. Leacock frequently spread his genius thin because of his many interests and the humorist's distrust of the specialist. Few men were better founded in economics than Stephen Leacock, but he chose to be more than an economist.

In 1911, the same year he was appointed a member of the Fleming Electoral Reform Commission of Quebec,[2] Leacock became active in politics. Always calling himself a Conservative, another of the Victorian touches in his life, he became concerned when the Liberals proposed reciprocity with the United States. Traditionally a college professor is supposed to stay out of politics, but Leacock was outspoken when he thought something should be done. He stumped the East Simcoe riding, where Orillia is located, in favor of the Conservative candidate, W. H. Bennett. Orillia and environs was and is traditionally Liberal territory, but with Leacock's help Bennett won a Conservative victory, rare in that district.[3] Leacock could never bring himself to become a candidate in any election, though he was frequently urged to, but he always maintained an active interest and frequently involved himself in political issues through his speeches and influence. He had, of course, a political stake in two provinces: Ontario, where he spent the summers, and Quebec, where he lived during the school year. He had the distinction of campaigning for John Hackett, Q. C., of Montreal and seeing him elected the

only Conservative Member of Parliament from Quebec.

Leacock, a sound political science scholar, enjoyed a clever political move as well as anyone, but his participation in campaigns was not because they were fun; Leacock did not like to make speeches for a political cause. He took his politics seriously, but his audience, knowing him to be a funny man, expected to laugh. Leacock had to take his choice between entertaining them while he sneaked in his endorsement of the candidate or having them laugh at a serious speech. For all his partisanship, he never allowed his politics to interfere with friendship; he had close friends among both the Liberals and the Conservatives, and one of his friends—Vincent Massey—became the Governor-General who represents the nonpartisan Queen. More than one of his former graduate students enlisted themselves, to Leacock's dismay, in the socialist C.C.F. party.

It was in this year of his political activity that Leacock formed one of his strongest friendships with a student. Actually Stephen Leacock had met Gladstone Murray two years earlier, in 1909. Murray had just come to McGill; perhaps he had come too soon, for he soon exhausted his funds. Leacock saw him in the McGill Union and, noting the woebegone look on his face, said, "Something wrong, young man?" "Yes, sir," replied Murray, "I'm broke." "Well, here, take this," said Leacock and, handing him ten dollars, he turned away. He was not rich; his first really successful book would not come out until the next year, but Stephen Leacock was a kindly man. Murray and Leacock occasionally ran into each other on campus and

the following year began playing billiards together with some regularity. It was Leacock's suggestion, in 1911, which cemented the association into a lasting one. Leacock declared that he was tired of these "unrelated and insignificant encounters"—the professor was regularly the victor—and he challenged young Murray to a game of 20,000 points. Leacock's estimate of a duration of twenty years for such a game was short; at his death the score stood 18,975 for Leacock and 16, 793 for Murray, but the game had covered the globe. Whenever the two met, the contest was resumed, and they played from Vancouver to Monte Carlo, from Edgbaston near Birmingham to New York.[4]

Murray went on from the tutelage of Leacock to become a Rhodes scholar, editor, executive of the British Broadcasting Corporation, and ultimately chairman of the Canadian Broadcasting Corporation. Finally he became head of a public relations company dedicated to private enterprise. How this warmed the Conservative heart of Stephen Leacock! Years later an artist painting Stephen's portrait remarked that he chattered the whole time, and Gladstone Murray was one of the men he talked of most.[5]

Just as *Literary Lapses* had overshadowed his scholarly article, "The Union of South Africa," in 1910, *Nonsense Novels* in 1911 made most of Leacock's friends and contemporaries forget his four serious articles on political science. Four such articles, however, constituted good scholarly production, even for one who was not trying to write popular humor at the same time.

In *Nonsense Novels,* Leacock showed himself to be a parodist of very superior skill. The book, much like Bret Harte's earlier *Condensed Novels,* contained ten short parodies of almost as many different kinds of novels. Some of them were burlesques of particular authors. "Maddened by Mystery; or the Defective Detective," whose Great Detective kept half a bucket of cocaine and a dipper at his elbow, was an obvious parody of A. Conan Doyle. "The Man in Asbestos; an Allegory of the Future" was easily identifiable as a parody on Edward Bellamy's *Looking Backward.* According to Leacock, the man whose future Utopia was socialistic would need an asbestos suit because it would be hell. Robert W. Chambers's tricky historical novels were caricatured in "Gertrude the Governess; or, Simple Seventeen"; it was in this selection that Leacock's most famous line occurred: "Lord Ronald said nothing; he flung himself from the room, flung himself upon his horse and rode madly off in all directions." Others parodied were Marie Bashkirtseff, writer of heart-rending confessions, Upton Sinclair, and Sir Walter Scott. The rest of the contents burlesqued the sentimental novel, the gothic tale, and the medieval romance, the latter being so good that at least one teacher, Professor McClelland of the University of Pennsylvania, used it to teach the characteristics of the romance.

As a parodist, Stephen Leacock showed himself to be an astute student of literature. He copied structure; he copied style; he copied mannerism of character. With a practiced eye he picked the weaknesses in a style or

genre, and these weak points became the strong points of his humor. Leacock used no new techniques of parody; almost all parody depends on exaggeration of weaknesses or improbabilities for its success. Good parody differs from poor parody in the acuteness and accuracy of its analysis of the original. Leacock did not make fun of Scott's long-windedness; this was a weakness of the time, not of Scott. Instead, Leacock pointed the finger of criticism at Scott's insistence on using Scotch dialect and terminology where English would have served as well or better. Leacock did not bother with the garrulous style of *Looking Backward;* that was not the big fault. He made a logical extension of Bellamy's socialistic Utopia until it became so perfect and dull that its citizens wanted to die. For Leacock the major weakness was in the theory; in actuality, the little man did not want his life run by a big machine.

Leacock's parody was not confined to literary subjects. Some of the finest burlesque he ever wrote was in "Back to the Bush," a travel brochure extolling the virtues of Lake Owatawetness, where:

the air is loud with the lowing of moose, cariboo, antelope, cantelope, musk-oxes, musk-rats, and other graminivorous mammalia of the forest. These enormous quadrumana generally move off about 10:30 p. m., from which hour until 11:45 p. m. the whole shore is reserved for bison and buffalo.[6]

He even parodied a mathematical theorem in "Boarding House Geometry":

Definitions and Axioms

All boarding-houses are the same boarding-house. . . .

A single room is that which has no parts and no magnitude.

The landlady of a boarding-house is a parallelogram—that is, an oblong, angular figure, which cannot be described, but which is equal to anything.

A wrangle is the disinclination of two boarders to each other that meet but are not in the same line.

All the other rooms being taken, a single room is said to be a double room.

Postulates and Propositions

A pie may be produced any number of times.

The landlady may be reduced to her lowest terms by a series of propositions. . . .

The clothes of a boarding-house bed, though produced ever so far both ways, will not meet.

Any two meals at a boarding-house are together less than a square meal. . . .

If there be two boarders on the same flat, and the amount of side of one be equal to the other, each to each, and the wrangle between one boarder and the landlady be equal to the wrangle between the landlady and the other, then shall the weekly bills of the two boarders be equal also, each to each.

For if not, let the one bill be the greater.

Then the other bill is less than it might have been
—which is absurd.[7]

In his career Leacock parodied almost every form of
writing possible. Among his burlesques were found
obituaries, drama, novels, slick magazine fiction, do-it-
yourself articles, scholarly articles, memoirs, verse, guide-
books, outlines, oratory, and journalism. Since Bret Harte
and Mark Twain, parody had formed an important part
of the repertoire of the North American humorist; among
those writing at the same time as Leacock, Franklin P.
Adams was turning classics into newspaper jargon,
George Ade was finding material in the fable, and
Benchley was solemnly adding a page and a half of foot-
notes to one line of Shakespearean text or tracing the
etymology of the word three:

> One, two, three
> Buckle my shoe.[8]

Called by one critic the equal of Bret Harte or Thack-
eray,[9] Leacock did some of his best writing as a parodist.

In *Nonsense Novels* Leacock tried something he
seldom tried again in his writing career. He wrote a
book; that is, the contents of the volume had never appeared elsewhere and were written expressly for book
publication. The author-economist soon found that this
method was not the most profitable and aimed after
this at periodical publication first and book publication
later. In spite of his lack of foresight, *Nonsense Novels*

was a huge success and exhibited the lasting qualities that only really good humor can hope for; it required thirty-six printings by 1950.

Prodded by his success, Leacock started to work in earnest. He had always been a hard worker, and now he set for himself a schedule which would have been too confining for most but was merely stimulating for him. He was always up by five o'clock to start writing or working. In Orillia he wrote in the study above the boathouse, built over the lake. In Montreal, he did his work in his study, an attractive room with books all the way to the ceiling and a huge window the width of one side of the room. Here he could look out over the city and the harbor. Such early hours required a reasonably early retiring hour. He was almost always in bed by ten unless a lecture date or special entertaining made it impossible. Leacock tired because he did everything so intensely. He was strong and healthy, but the speed at which he lived left him exhausted at the end of the day. When he had guests, he entertained them jovially and enthusiastically until time for bed; then without any self-consciousness at all he excused himself, leaving his friends to his wife, his niece, or someone else who would be responsible. Stephen Leacock was early aware that his professional stature depended on good writing and his constitution dictated the early hours as his most productive time.

In these morning hours when he was alone, he wrote swiftly and evenly with a broad-nib pen, on rare occasions abbreviating when his mind worked too quickly for the pen. Like the story about Einstein's being unable to

make change, the legend has grown that there were only two secretaries in Leacock's whole life who could read his manuscript.[10] Stephen Leacock no more had copperplate penmanship than he had a copperplate personality; his handwriting had character, but it was legible. He became a very professional writer in time, telling his agent once, "I can hit 3,500 words to the syllable, knowing it beforehand. . . ."[11] During the morning work Leacock would brew himself a pot of tea to sustain him until breakfast and then settle down to whatever had to be done. Even when he had no publication to work on or when "real" writing would not come, he would work busily at letters, lectures, schedules, or bookkeeping.[12] Out of such industry Leacock expected to get good books; neither he nor his readers were disappointed.

For the third straight year, Leacock wrote a best seller. *Sunshine Sketches of a Little Town* of 1912 has been called Leacock's best book,[13] and it might well qualify; it is certainly one of the most charming. This series of stories and sketches about a small Canadian town was, in a way, the result of his having proved himself a good writer. Lord Atholstan, publisher and owner of the Montreal *Star*, asked Leacock to write something about Canadian life.[14] To know the pieces were sold before he wrote them was a new experience for Stephen, but one he relished. *Sunshine Sketches* first appeared as a series of twelve separate articles in the *Star* from February 17 to June 22, 1912. Following their success there, they were gathered with little change into the book published two months later.

The six short stories which made up the volume were
some of the best writing he ever did. The nostalgic essay,
"L'Envoi: The Train to Mariposa," which concluded the
book, made clear where the real appeal of the work lay:
North America was still a land of small towns, and even
the people who had left home remembered the little
towns with pleasure and affection. *Sunshine Sketches*
made gentle fun of the business, the church, the romances, the social life, and the politics of a little town.
In "The Speculations of Jefferson Thorpe," Leacock drew
the barber who realized forty thousand dollars paper
profit on a fourteen-dollar investment in a land specula-
tion scheme. Inevitably the forty thousand was put into
bogus Cuban banana plantations, and the barber finally
returned happily to shaves and haircuts. Leacock wrote
of the little church with its bazaars, its "whirlwind campaigns," and its debt-ridden new building. The Rev. Mr.
Drone muddled the finances of the church into a hopeless
condition, only to be saved by the burning of his heavily
overinsured church. "The Foreordained Attachment of
Zena Pepperleigh and Peter Pupkin" burlesqued the
courting customs of a small town and the romantic ideals
of a village maid. "The Marine Excursion of the Knights
of Pythias"—an excursion complete with shipwreck in
three feet of water—served to show the quiet social life
and the mild spirit of adventure. Politics was deftly
handled in "The Great Election in Missinaba County";
Josh Smith, owner of the local bar, campaigned and won
on a ticket of total prohibition. *Sunshine Sketches* was

quieter humor than Leacock had done before, but its touch was sure.

Leacock's source for *Sunshine Sketches* was for some time a matter of academic interest, but there was no doubt in Orillia; Orillians saw themselves too clearly. William Arthur Deacon, literary editor of the Toronto *Globe and Mail,* declared that Orillia never forgave Stephen Leacock, "its only internationally famous citizen for having laughed at the local politics, the social distinctions and the ornate costumes of the Knights of Pythias' Band."[15] In his preface Leacock protested, "Mariposa is not a real town. On the contrary, it is about seventy or eighty of them,"[16] but it did no good; Orillia knew. The *News-Letter* and the Orillia *Packet and Times* he had combined into the *Newspacket* and he had changed editor Russel Hale's name to Hussel, but of course they were not fooled. Jeff Thorpe, the barber, was their own barber, Jeff Short. Josh Smith, the hotelkeeper, was really Jim Smith, who ran the Daly House on Mississaga Street. And Leacock had not fooled them by changing names between serial publication and book publication. George Popley in the *Star* was George Rapley, even if his name was finally Mullins in the book. Judge McCosh, Orillia police magistrate, had been called McGaw at first, though it was changed to Pepperleigh now. Horace Bingham claimed he did not really object to appearing in *Sunshine Sketches* as Golgotha Gingham, the undertaker, but he wished Golgotha were not so concerned with "business."[17] There was really no doubt, but Leacock settled it for sure years later in a

letter explaining why some of the names were changed. According to his account, his very good friend Judge Tudhope had written him a letter righteous with mock indignation, threatening to sue him on behalf of the town of Orillia. Leacock enjoyed the letter, but the publishers grew cautious and made him change the names.[18]

The little town of *Sunshine Sketches* was playing an increasingly important part in Leacock's life as Old Brewery Bay and his boats drew him back to the lake and Orillia. Sandwell said he "always left McGill a few days too early and came back a few days too late to suit the university authorities,"[19] because of his love of fishing. Stephen Leacock did like fishing—frequently employing as his guide Jake Gaudaur, former champion oarsman—but fishing was not the only lure the lake had for him. He liked to sail his own boat, and he enjoyed watching the excursion steamers with their happy crowds. One of the three steamers—the *Sconscie*, the *Islay*, and the *Enterprise*—was surely the original of the *Mariposa Belle*. Professor Lower has identified it as the *Enterprise* out of the neighboring town of Barrie,[20] but it was the *Islay* which, like the *Mariposa Belle*, foundered while skirting the shore. And when the *Islay* called for help the *Enterprise* hurried over to steam around her in tight circles, hooting the foghorn derisively until a tug rescued her. Orillia became more than a place to spend the summer; it became home too. When Orillia dedicated its famous Champlain monument, it was Leacock who proposed the toast to the Queen, and he spoke at the opening of the bridge at the juncture of Lake Simcoe

and Lake Couchiching. As he wrote his books, he gave the public library copies of them. He counted among his closest friends some of the citizens of this little town: Harold Hale, with whom he played cricket; Judge Tudhope; Dr. Edward Ardagh, his Orillia billiard crony; John Drinkwater, a fishing companion. Stephen might have objected if he had overheard, as someone else did, an Orillia farmer point out Leacock to his wife and say, "There's Stephen Leacock, the craziest man in Orillia," but neither would he have wanted the man to be awed by him. It was with real appreciation that Leacock laughingly told of being introduced at an Orillia dinner as "One of the foremost humorists of East Simcoe."[21] At home a man wants rest, not reputation; he wants friends, not fans.

Of fans he certainly had enough. From 1910 on, his mail was filled with letters from those who admired his books: people who saw their neighbors in his humor, young girls who wanted his autograph, struggling young writers who were drawn to his style or wanted his advice, lawyers, housewives, students who were writing book reports. Leacock was evidently appreciative of these notices, for the letters from fans which remain in his files almost all bear the notation in the corner "Ans"—answered. Perhaps a good example is the one he received the middle of July, 1913:

Dear Sir:

My patient, Mrs. Emanuel Cohen, wishes me to express to you her sincere thanks for the delightful res-

pite afforded her from "sadness of the heart and suffering of the body" by your delightful *Nonsense Novels*. No doubt others like her have read it and have been grateful to the author. Mrs. Cohen suggests that the "Grand" operas—such as *Die Walkerie, The Huguenots, Lucia, Aida*—would afford good material for a companion piece to *Nonsense Novels*.

I might also add that while the sudden and uncontrollable out bursts of laughter of Mrs. Cohen caused me an endless amount of anxiety I am pleased to say that she has improved physically and mentally since we read your good book.

Yours Respectfully,
J. B. Morley[22]

This letter bore the familiar *Ans* up in the upper left corner, but the answer had not evidently been a simple one. The next letter reads:

My dear Mr. Leacock,

I appreciate your kindness in sending me *Sunshine Sketches* which Miss Morley has just handed me after having prepared me for a delightful surprise. I told her not to give me a surprise that would only make me weep. She replied, "no this will make you laugh" and the first chapter has done that already.

I think I am now "robust" enough to hear your delightful humor and nimble wit without serious results, and I can bear even the delicious Prefaces without more than temporary disturbances.

It was the Preface to Nonsense Novels that

prompted me to express my appreciation of that rare bit of drollery. Your wish that it might help one in trouble impelled me to tell you that it helped me.

With appreciation of your kindness as well as of your literary skill, fine humor and delectable insight

I am Gratefully Yours

Nina Marcus Cohen

per Julia B. Morley

P.S. I wish also to thank you and express my appreciation of your kindness. By telling you that as a nurse I shall always use *your* delightful *remedys* [sic] which has [sic] afforded so much pleasure to both

Patient and nurse

Sincerely Yours

J.B.M.[23]

Leacock's patience and sympathy with the people who wrote him seemed to stem from his innate kindness, not merely from the knowledge that these people bought and read his books.

Perhaps it took Leacock's next book to show the world that Stephen Leacock was really going to be its jester for a while. *Behind the Beyond,* published in 1913, was his fourth book of humor in four years; the annual Leacock book was to become a custom. Some of its essays showed the strained humor that a professional funny man is reduced to at times. The title piece, a burlesque problem play, was high humor in the critical Leacock vein. "My Lost Opportunities" was second-rate humor:

Forty-five years ago,—a man at the club told me this
with almost a sob in his voice,—either Rockefeller or
Carnegie could have been bought clean up for a thousand dollars!

Think of it!

Why didn't my father buy them for me, as pets, for
my birthday and let me keep them till I grew up.[24]

But there was remarkably little poor humor in this volume, even though his fourth in as many years. From 1910
to 1946 there would be only four years in which Leacock
did not produce at least one book, but in 1913 his reading public had not been sure that Leacock would last.
His other three books—the first, a collection it had taken
him years to write, the next two, books which had exhausted their subjects—might have indicated to the
reader that Leacock had written all he had to say. *Behind the Beyond* proved to a host of enthusiastic readers
that more would continue to come. It was not his best
book, but *Behind the Beyond* required six printings in
five years and, in 1913, raised his income above ten
thousand dollars for the first time.

As his success indicated, Leacock was gaining more
and more recognition. Instead of his having to submit
most of his material for the consideration of the cold
editorial eye, he began to receive requests from the
magazines themselves. From England came an interesting letter:

Dear Sir:
    Could you let me have a short story or humorous

sketch for an annual that I am editing for next year. I should appreciate this immensely. Could you do an analysis of a cinema play or perhaps better still a grand opera as you have the problem play? But not more than 4000 words. And could I have it by Febry 15? I want the annual to be . . . humorous, gay and charming.

Believe me Yours faithfully
E. V. Lucas[25]

Leacock replied that he would be glad to write the sketch, and when his contribution was received, Lucas wrote back enthusiastically:

Dear Mr. Leacock
Your burlesque is exactly what I wanted. No one on this side can do anything like that. Thank you very much. A proof will go to you very soon. What *Metheun's Annual* wants is serial rights & for America too although I doubt if there will be more than a very small sale there. I am yours faithfully

E. V. Lucas[26]

About the same time Paul Wilstach of the London Theatre Company wrote Leacock about a play which he hoped Leacock would write.[27] Fredrick Eckstein of Doubleday Page suggested to Leacock early in 1914 that his company would be happy to receive Leacock manuscripts in case he should become dissatisfied with his current publisher.[28] And Frank Crowninshield, of *Vanity*

Fair wrote Leacock concerning an article commissioned by his magazine:

Dear Mr. Leacock:—
We are entering you for a check for forty-five dollars for the "Survival of the Fittest." It is little enough, I think.

I have planned a party for you, and you must be sure to come on to New York and go through with it like a man.

Mrs. Longworth, daughter of the late, lamented Theodore Roosevelt, cherishes a nameless and unwholly passion for you. The affection which the lady in Mr. Gilbert's poem cherished for Mr. Reece, Commander of the Mantlepiece, was a slight and Virginal one compared to Mrs. L's for you.

Yours ever,
Frank Crowninshield

Excuse the lady stenographer! For "wholly"—read "holy."[29]

Such accolades indicated Leacock's success in his writing career.

Leacock had not, however, neglected his academic profession when he became a highly paid humorist. He had published seven articles since the publication of *Literary Lapses,* two of them in 1913, the year of his fourth book. Both of these articles indicated the bent of his scholarship. "The University and Business"[30] was a discussion of the relationship of the humanities and business, indicating that economic institutions are morally

responsible for the support of noneconomic ones. The other, "The Canadian Senate and the Naval Bill,"[31] was concerned not so much with political science, though that was its field, as it was with political action—how the human being acted as a political animal. Perhaps it was his concern for the practical side of his subject that prompted the mention of his name when Ottawa proposed a cost-of-living study. It was even suggested that he head such a team. In an interview before the commission was appointed, Leacock turned down such a suggestion on the grounds that there were better-known scholars than he for the job, and put forward the name of Professor Mavor as the logical one to head any such study.[32] Mavor had crossed Leacock at the University of Toronto and had rejected Leacock's application for a job in 1901. He was later to say to Henry Janes, bearing a letter of introduction from Leacock, "That fellow Leacock, I knew he'd never amount to anything." But Stephen Leacock was too competent a scholar not to recognize Mavor's worth and too big a man to allow personal feelings to influence a professional decision.

In 1914, Leacock achieved one of his biggest publishing years. In addition to one of his best books of humor, he published three volumes of history. He had been honored by being asked to write the first, second, and twentieth volumes of a new series, "The Chronicles of Canada." Though they appeared together rather abruptly, these histories had probably been in preparation since his success with the 1907 volume. For the series he wrote *The Dawn of Canadian History*, the story of

aboriginal Canada; *Adventures of the Far North,* the story of early explorations; and *The Mariner of St. Malo,* Jacques Cartier's contribution to Canadian history. His was the kind of history he liked to write. In spite of his interest in political science, he preferred the history of adventure to the history of politics.

Arcadian Adventures with the Idle Rich, published the same year, has been called one of Leacock's three best books, the other two being *Sunshine Sketches* and *Literary Lapses.*[33] In one way, *Arcadian Adventures* was a companion volume to *Sunshine Sketches.* Mariposa of *Sunshine Sketches* was a typical small town; the location of *Arcadian Adventures* was a typical metropolitan center. It exposed completely the falseness of the things they of the city lived by, showing the city dwellers to be really the same people he had found in Mariposa. People did things on a bigger scale in the city, but they did the same things. If any distinction was to be made, the small town was the kindlier, less cold-blooded place. In place of Jefferson Thorpe's forty thousand, *Arcadian Adventures* had Tomlinson's quarter of a million a day. But Tomlinson's gold mine turned out to be salted, and his profits, too, disappeared. Dean Drone had his counterpart in the Reverend Edward Fareforth Furlong, who, when threatened by the increasing popularity of the Presbyterians, formed a merger along strictly business lines. The terms of the contract declared that "no form of eternal punishment shall be declared valid if displeasing to three-fifths of the holders of bonds."[34] The romance of the city was that of Peter

Spillikins, the victim of a money-hungry widow with four grown sons. Social life in the city was depicted in "A Little Dinner with Mr. Lucullus Fyshe"—a dinner party given for purely financial purposes—and in "The Yahi-Bahi Oriental Society of Mrs. Rasselyer-Brown"— a society woman's search for adventure in an empty life. In "The Great Fight for Clean Government," the campaign resulted in a change of personnel, but no change of tactics. Perhaps because the city was more impersonal, the satire in *Arcadian Adventures* was more biting than any other he ever wrote.

Leacock had been somewhat disappointed in *Sunshine Sketches;* he had wanted it to be a novel. He had intended the love story between Zena Pepperleigh and Peter Pupkin to be a central theme to unify the story. It had not developed that way; the book was, in spite of its title, more than sketches, but it was no novel. It was, instead, a group of short stories about the same people, like O. Henry's *Cabbages and Kings.* In *Arcadian Adventures,* Leacock succeeded in doing the job better, though he had not been trying so hard. The book about the City at least managed an overlapping of the several short stories. This unity was generally achieved by cross references, but occasionally the personality of a character was understood only after several stories. The reader knew the full character of Dr. Boomer, the president of Plutoria University, only after reading "A Little Dinner with Mr. Lucullus Fyshe," "The Wizard of Finance," "The Arrested Philanthropy of Mr. Tomlinson," "The Rival Churches of St. Asaph and St. Osoph," "The Minis-

trations of the Rev. Uttermost Dumfarthing," and "The Great Fight for Clean Government," six of the eight stories which constitute the book. The character of other people in the book was revealed in the same manner; Peter Spillikins appeared in every story, though his was a minor role. Even with unity so closely knit, *Arcadian Adventures* was not a novel; there was no single story, there was no single development of an important character. Each story still had its own climax and its own denouement. Like many humorists, Leacock was not a good novelist. *Vanity Fair* and *Huckleberry Finn* notwithstanding, most humorists see the foibles of the world in sharper flashes than the novel allows. The best Stephen Leacock could do in fiction was the humorous short story.

Leacock should not have been disappointed; the short stories which made such a substantial part of his humor were good ones. The real charm of the stories, it is true, lay in their humor and not their fiction. Sometimes their plots were a little obvious, but they served admirably to carry the humor. In *Literary Lapses*, "The Awful Fate of Melpomenus Jones" was not a complex story. Melpomenus Jones was a young curate, only twenty-three, who could not get away from people. He was "too modest to tell a lie, and too religious to wish to appear rude."[35] The day before his much anticipated two-week vacation began, he made what was to be his last pastoral call. After tea he rose to leave, but when pressed could not think of a valid reason for not staying to dinner; for the same reason he stayed after dinner, and then spent the

night. Two weeks later he had still been unable to tear himself away and had fallen into a fever because of his frustration. Finally he died and, with a smile on his face, murmured, "Now I really must go." In terms of plot this was not a story that Hawthorne or Poe might have been proud of, but the overtones of tragedy certainly prevented its being simply a humorous anecdote. The purpose was still humor, as Leacock's sly "too modest to tell a lie, and too religious . . . to appear rude" indicated. His technique was not that of the short story which used humor, but that of humor which used the short story.

In both *Arcadian Adventures* and *Sunshine Sketches*, Leacock as a fiction writer obviously owed something to the earlier local colorist in his choice of material. He had claimed that Mariposa was not a real town but was seventy or eighty of them. It was not really even that. It was all the little towns in North America. The one Main Street, the undertaker who was viewed as a professional man, the barbershop crowd that discussed baseball scores, and the participation of everyone in both Orangemen's Day and St. Patrick's Day were as familiar to the Americans as they were to Canadians. Perhaps Leacock owed to the same source his method of subordinating plot to other considerations. Local color writers were as concerned with explaining the environment as with developing individual characters. Even protagonists were frequently well-drawn types of local people instead of individual personalities. Leacock dealt with his characters as Mariposans or residents of Plutoria Avenue first, and as individual people second. His real purpose, laugh-

ing at inconsistencies in all people everywhere, was achieved by extension of the local color method. Leacock's locale was the world, and his local people were humanity. He was not, then, a local color writer, although the proportionate importance of his exposition and action allied him with that school.

Perhaps the fiction of Stephen Leacock indicated still another literary debt. In "O. Henry and His Critics," a critical essay, he had defended the writer on the grounds that those who attacked his work so severely were those who criticized him as a short story writer. He was not basically a writer of short stories, said Leacock, but a writer of humor. And furthermore, insisted Leacock, he was funny.[36] Leacock undoubtedly read O. Henry while he was publishing his hurried stories, and Leacock recognized in his own work something of the flavor of O. Henry. On rare occasions he used the typical trick ending of O. Henry. The writers were more similar, however, in their quick appreciation and varied use of humorous situations. Stephen Leacock had been trained too well in the literatures of more than one language to fall into the slipshod plotting habits of O. Henry. A man who had been taught better could not use the long arm of coincidence as O. Henry did. Leacock was too much a conscious literary artist to copy bad art, but he did produce humor that was similar to O. Henry's. In "The Errors of Santa Claus," akin in theme and structure to "Gift of the Magi," two fathers, Jones and Brown, had bought trains for their sons, while the mothers had bought dolls for the daughters. The sons had got their fathers cigarettes for Christ-

mas, and the daughters had decided on playing cards for
their mothers. The whole Jones family was giving Grandfather a Bible. Grandfather had selected gifts also:

> There was a beautiful whiskey decanter, with silver
> filigree outside (and whiskey inside) for Jones, and
> for the little boy a big nickle-plated Jew's harp. . . .
> But the next day . . . indeed by ten o'clock, Brown
> and Jones were playing with the train, and Mrs. Brown
> and Mrs. Jones were making doll clothes, and the boys
> were smoking cigarettes, and Clarisse and Ulvina
> were playing cards for their pocket money.
> And upstairs—away up—Grandfather was drinking
> whiskey and playing the Jew's harp.[37]

The literary debt which Leacock owed to O. Henry
probably had to do with resemblance rather than influence, and it was not a great one. But it was an honest
debt, and Leacock paid it by his defense of the maligned
writer.

The city in *Arcadian Adventures,* while not the one of
O. Henry's *The Four Million,* is not as easy to identify as
Mariposa. It was not New York, for people came there
from New York. It was not, a Canadian city, for
Canadian currency is referred to as foreign. Although
gold was found in the Canadian bush by Tomlinson,
another of the characters, Mr. Boulder, had a hunting
camp in Wisconsin. Some of Leacock's friends seem to
remember that he suggested to them that the town was
Montreal. Toronto has also claimed the honor, but
Montreal is probably the better choice. The Mauso-

leum Club, situated just where the residential section ended and the business section began, was surely Leacock's own University Club. Plutoria University, beginning with little Concordia College and becoming a university with the addition of the science buildings, was undoubtedly McGill. The geography of the town was not as plainly indicative of Montreal as Mariposa was of Orillia. Everything of any importance in the city was on Plutoria Avenue; this corresponded in general to College Street in Montreal. The answer probably lay in Leacock's intention. He had written *Sunshine Sketches* for Canada and had found it popular all over the world, particularly in the United States. Evidently he wrote *Arcadian Adventures* purposely for a wider audience, intending that it would serve as a satire on all large cities. Leacock enjoyed being a humorist, but he wanted to make money at it. When he found that America, like Canada a land of small towns, had appreciated *Sunshine Sketches,* he made that country consciously a part of his audience. And the audience accepted him; after only five years of publication, Leacock might consider himself a humorist of international reputation.

VI

1914–1921

As HIS literary prestige grew Leacock continued to live the sedentary life he loved. He spent the winter in Montreal at McGill and his home, 3869 Cote des Neiges Road, and the summers at The Old Brewery Bay in Orillia. He wryly offered sympathy later to whoever might be his biographer, saying, "I haven't moved around enough." Leacock was not a traveler. Though he did take some trips he preferred to stay home in Orillia and Montreal.

At The Old Brewery Bay he kept a host of employees busy, most of them on a part-time basis. The one man he depended on most was Bill Jones. Jones, whom he referred to as "our Mr. Jones," was a retired British army sergeant out of India who now served as a gardener. George Leacock recalled a time when Stephen decided to raise wheat. He and Jones planted about an acre, and it came up beautifully. About the time Leacock got really proud of it, the crows came. Leacock was beside himself; for days anyone who visited him was pressed

into service as a scarecrow. When it got too much for him, he took time for a fishing trip with his brother. He stationed Jones in the field and, said George, gave him "a case of beer, a shotgun, and instructions to shoot any crows that came near." When they returned, the beer, the shotgun, and Jones were gone and the crows were feasting. Jones's principal job was gardener, but at various times during the summer he might be asked to act as carpenter, valet, fishing companion, butler, or mechanic.[1]

Leacock liked Bill Jones because he could do more than one thing; so could Leacock, and they worked together. When there was gardening to be done, they could do it; when the place needed a tool shed, they built it; when a boat needed to be built or painted or sailed, they could build it or paint it or sail it. It was true that Stephen was inclined to stand back and let "Mr. Jones" carry dirt and then speak of how "we filled in this marsh"—a characteristic he made fun of in Edward Newberry in *Arcadian Adventures*—but Stephen Leacock could still drive a nail straighter than could most gentlemen.

At McGill, Leacock was proving himself to be a most popular professor with his humor and his high interest in his work. He would announce to his class at the beginning of each term, "There is only one good book in political science. That is my book, *The Elements of Political Science*. I make seventeen cents off each copy. But I don't want to make money off my own students, so when you buy the book, come by the office and I'll autograph it and give you the seventeen cents." When stu-

dents, thinking to play a joke on him, did turn up at his office to collect, they found him ready. He signed his name with the characteristic flourish of his broad pen and then, from a stack of pennies already on his desk, gravely counted out seventeen cents. Such refined buffoonery, however, was not the only appeal that Leacock had for his students. He was dedicated to his teaching, and pupils finishing his courses felt that they knew economics.

In 1915 Leacock published *Marionette's Calendar,* a production distinguished only by his kindness in doing it to help the illustrator, A. H. Fish. Miss Fish had started her career in professional art by doing a set of illustrations for *Nonsense Novels* sometime after its publication. Thinking they were good, she took them to John Lane, Leacock's London publisher. He liked them so much that he had a special edition run using the new illustrations. A short time later she was chosen to illustrate *Behind the Beyond.* She had still not reached the peak of her success when Lane suggested that she draw some pictures for an engagement book and that Leacock write verses to go with them. Leacock, as the established artist of the two, had the unquestioned right to ask that his poetry be written first, that the illustrations follow the verse. But, wishing to see young artists make progress, he genially allowed Miss Fish to do the pictures first. The production was certainly more beneficial to A. H. Fish's standing than to Leacock's, the caption verse being little more than doggerel, but the kindliness fundamental

to the writer dictated that he help the young Miss Fish build her own reputation.

Leacock drew the admiration of more than one young literary artist. In 1913 he had received a letter from a young lady who was just beginning to write:

My dear Stephen Leacock:

You are a most illuminating and enchanting person.— I have been devoted to you ever since a happy introduction to Nonsense Novels. Marie and Otto filled my waking hours with chortles of pure joy—this was some two years ago. I nearly married the man who gave me that book out of gratitude. (Of course, some people, knowing me might change the term *gratitude* to *revenge;* but that would be casting aspersions on you and myself.)

It may be of some interest to you to learn by the medium of my atrocious penmanship coupled with a poisonous pen, that I introduced your delightful Great Detective to the man who created the part of "Sherlock Holmes" on the stage and wrote the play. And I assure you that he enjoyed it as much as I did which is saying a great deal in a few well chosen words. I am sure that you will perceive that I possess an abnormally keen sense of humor when I tell you that my years number twenty and that I endite *serious* verse! And this is even funnier—get them accepted by editorial gentlemen totally devoid of humour. Also I have recently completed a poetic drama in several thousand acts, which I hope to get produced—provided I can

find a manager much more than usually a ripe candidate for some institution for the Particularly Feeble Minded.—

I suppose the thing that most interests the ordinary run of humans about your work is the fact that you are a professor—this they cannot reconcile with your more or less literary output. They do not realize as some of us do that it is merely cause and effect.— And that a prof. may even have bestowed upon him the saving grace of humour that amuses and delights while it does not wound.—

Yours cordially,

Faith Baldwin

P.S. I trust you will not make copy of me in an article entitled "Occasional Letters from Occasional and Irrational Readers."[2]

Another admirer wrote from Princeton:

My Dear Mr. Leacock:

As imitation is the sincerest flattery I thought you might be interested in something you inspired. The Nassau Literary Magazine here at Princeton of which I'm an editor got out a "Chaopolitan number" as a burlesque of "America's greatest magazine."

The two stories I wrote "Jemina, a story of the Blue Ridge Mountains, by John Phlox, Jr." and "The Usual Thing by Robert W. Shamless" are of the "Leacock school" of humour—in fact Jemina is rather a steal in places from "Hannah of the Highlands."

119

I'm taking the liberty of sending you a copy—needless to say it increased our circulation & standing in undergraduate eyes.

Hope you'll get one smile out of it for every dozen laughs I got from the Snoopopaths.

Very appreciatively yours,
F. Scott Fitzgerald[3]

When Kenneth Roberts—though somewhat older than the other two, still a beginning writer—wrote Leacock, he did not even mention his own writing:

I have often intended to write you of the enjoyment which I have taken in your writings since the evening when I borrowed "Nonsense Novels" from a friend (A voice: "Why didn't you buy the book, you piker?") to read on a long street-car ride, and disgraced myself in the eyes of a number of gelid fellow-Bostonians by my snickerings and whoopings. Had it not been for the fact that Cornell professors of Political Economy naturally encourage the study of their own books by their students, I might have studied your books on Political Economy and thus become a Leacock fan at a much tenderer age. For this I shall never cease to blame Professor Jeremiah Whipple Jenks.

As I said in starting, I have often intended to write you. Please multiply the sentiments in this note by fifteen or twenty, and consider that the result faintly expresses the pleasure you have given me.

I hope that some time in the near future I may have

the pleasure of meeting you and buying you a glass of the true matzoon or something.

> Very sincerely yours,
> K. L. Roberts[4]

Each of these letters was carefully answered, and even the short, pleasant reply which Leacock must have sent surely served as some encouragement to the beginners.

Also in 1915, Leacock published *Moonbeams from the Larger Lunacy*, containing what was now thought of as the usual Leacock mixture: a few parodies, an essay or two, a short story, and humorous sketches in various forms. The parody of a novel, "Spoof; a Thousand Guinea Novel," was a burlesque of prize-winning novels; "Ram Spudd: the New World Singer" was a parody, one of his most soundly critical, on modern poetry; "Aristocratic Anecdotes" was a striking burlesque of the usual pointless story whose only distinction is that it is about a celebrity. He poked fun at buying and selling in "The Reading Public; a Bookstore Study," a neat piece of satire in which the salesman sold the same book to different people as light summer reading, as a book suitable for a sixteen-year-old daughter, as a very erotic story, as a tragedy, and as adventure fiction. The salesman finally confessed that he had not read the book, never did read the books he sold. *Moonbeams* was not distinctive, but it was successful enough; reprinted eight times, it was certainly a financial triumph, though by this time Leacock and his publishers expected such a sale.

In the summer of 1915, Stephen and Beatrix returned

to Montreal early. The birth of their first child was expected the latter part of the summer and they were not a moment too early. Stephen wrote his mother:

My dear Mother—

Young Stephen was born at a quarter to three this afternoon. He is a fine big boy, in fact a regular corker, and weighs eight and a quarter pounds. Beatrix had made an error about the date of his birth, but thank Heaven, we left Orillia in time or the journey might have been too much for her. He had a close run for his life as he had decided to throw himself into the world wrong end first. We had the three best men in Montreal and four nurses. Peters told me that without those SEVEN people working at it, there would have been no chance. Beatrix was taken ill at 6 this morning and I drove her over to the maternity hospital. She had a bad time but it is over now & she is resting & doing fine. The baby looks just like Barbara and little Stephen and me and all the rest. Beatrix was awfully well right up to the end except that she had a bad fall two days ago. But Peters says that the baby is not a premature baby being if anything over developed. Beatrix will have to stay where she is for some time, I don't know how long, two weeks I should think. How soon can you come down? We must take up the arrangements for the christening right away. I want my friend Mr. Symonds the rector of the cathedral to do it.

I need hardly say that your journey down is of

course to be at my expense. If you haven't the ready money wire or write me & I'll send it.

I sent a wire to George today. Will you please tell Charlie and the rest. Teddy is probably still with you. . . . I gave the telegraph company a dollar to take the message from Sutton to the Grange. So don't let them charge you for it. . . . I could only stay with Beatrix for a little while this afternoon as they wanted her to sleep but I am going over after dinner and we'll see the baby together. I never yet saw a baby that looked so complete, so all there, so little like a red monkey as Stephen does: indeed he seems to me a most remarkable child. Please write and tell Carrie that her present hit it just right because it arrived at the very hour that he was born. I'd write to her myself but I have no address. Beatrix won't be able to write for some days. Be sure to let me know right away just how soon you can come, and come as soon as you can.

Your loving son

(Old) Stephen Leacock

P.S. Tomorrow I am going to make my will and appoint trustees, guardians, and a staff of godfathers, godmothers, proxies, and assistants. We have decided that from the boy's birth there shall be no extravagance on him. We got from Eatons a plain basket for him to sleep in,—there—I guess this is as much as it is fair to inflict in one dose.[5]

This was the first child born to one of Agnes's sons and she recorded the event in her diary:

September 5, 1915

It is a long time since I have written anything but letters, and a great event has taken place. My first Leacock grandchild was born on the 19th of August, Stephen's boy. He and Beatrix have been married a long time and this longed for child has taken up all my thoughts of late. I hope very soon to see him; at present he and his mother are in the maternity hospital, and it's not much use for me to go to Montreal till they get him home to Cote des Neiges, as one can see so little of people in hospital, but Stephen writes often of the boy and he's a chip off the old block I'm sure—like Stephen and my father. He is to be called Stephen Lushington.[6]

Stephen Lushington proved to be the only child the Leacocks were to have. It was not until some time after his birth that it became evident to Stephen and Beatrix that the growth of Stephen, Jr., was not progressing as it should, but this lack of development may have influenced their decision about other children. When they first noticed the slowness of growth, however, it was not immediately certain that it was a serious problem.

Stephen Leacock continued his diversified publication in 1916 with one article of literary criticism and two concerning political science. "Is Permanent Peace Possible?" he answered with a qualified yes[7]: in "Let Us Learn Russian," he said, "The Russian Empire and the Russian people are destined to play a great part in the world in the century that is opening."[8] This was on September 23,

1916, six months before the fall of the Czar and a full year before the Bolshevik revolution. Both articles stood well the test of time.

In the same year he published two volumes of humor. *Further Foolishness* contained the more usual ingredients, largely parodies and sketches. Besides "Humor as I See It," one of the best bits in *Further Foolishness* was his parody of slick fiction, "The Snoopopaths or Fifty Stories in One." The characters, he said, were always The Man and The Woman:

The Man is always detailed as if he were a horse. He is said to be "tall, well set, with straight legs."

Great stress is always laid on his straight legs. No magazine story is acceptable now unless The Man's legs are absolutely straight. Why this is, I don't know. All my friends have straight legs—and yet I never hear them make it a subject of comment or boasting. I don't believe I have, at present, a single friend with crooked legs. . . .

Then comes The Woman of the snoopopathic story. She is always "beautifully groomed" (Who these grooms are that do it, and where they can be hired, I don't know), and she is said to be "exquisitely gowned."

It is peculiar about The Woman that she never seems to wear a *dress*—always a "gown." Why this is, I cannot tell . . . I wear a gown myself—at night. It is made of flannel and reaches to my feet, and when I take my candle and go out to the balcony where I sleep, the

effect of it on the whole is not bad. But as to its "revealing every line of my figure"—as The Woman's gown is always said to do—and as to its "suggesting even more than it reveals"—well, it simply does *not*. So when I speak of "gowns" I speak of something I know all about.[9]

Though a successful book, *Further Foolishness*, in some straining for effect in the political humor, showed the difficulty under which the author was working. Leacock, concerned about the war his country was fighting but, at the age of forty-six, too old to get into it, struck a more serious note in *Essays and Literary Studies*. The semi-serious essay, to be discussed later as a regular part of his technique, were still humor in that they were good-natured, friendly, and clever, but it was a humor which pervaded serious discussions of literature and education, interpretation of history and morality. Its more sober quality foreshadowed the next year when he produced no book of humor at all.

It seems at first incongruous to find that Leacock had no time to write a book during the war year of 1917 because he was busy giving humorous lectures. However, this first lecture of the humorist was undertaken for the benefit of the Commission for Relief in Belgium. Leacock had been for some time a popular speaker, but his lecture career had not properly begun. He had given individual speeches suitable to the occasion. Now, during his lecture tour through central Canada, he had one lecture which he delivered again and again at different places.

His announced subject was "Frenzied Fiction," a title he was soon to appropriate for one of his books. The lecture was a quasi-serious discussion of literature, using Leacock's own parodies instead of the literature itself. Though he was making no money, because he donated the proceeds to the sponsoring charity, he was learning the technique of the professional funny man on the stage.

This apprenticeship was obviously not his purpose: Stephen Leacock was a man of intense patriotism and, with a regard of soldiers bordering on reverence, probably would have liked joining the fight himself. He watched carefully the war careers of the men he knew— he was proud when Gladstone Murray became one of the world's first flying aces—and he gave unstintingly of his own talents as a lecturer, teacher, and humorist.

During this war year, Leacock received a letter which he valued greatly. From Oyster Bay came a note:

I am sending you the Metropolitan with an article by me dealing with Canada's great record in this war.

All my family, including myself, owe you much for both amusement and instruction. When you are next in New York, do let us know. If you have leisure, I'll get you out here for dinner.

Theodore Roosevelt[10]

It had been while Roosevelt was President that he had added extra fame to Leacock's name when, in a political speech, he had quoted the famous line from "Gertrude

the Governess" about riding "madly off in all directions."

In 1918, shortly before the war was over, Leacock published *Frenzied Fiction,* containing a pleasant alternation of Leacockian sense and nonsense. The pieces ranged from a parody of the journalist's problem column to the half-serious and very cogent "Father Knickerbocker; a Fantasy," which treated of the spirit of America once awakened to the war. In many ways the best of the group was "My Revelations as a Spy," a parody which returned to the glorious nonsense of his earlier work:

> In many people the very name "spy" excites a shudder of apprehension; we Spies, in fact, get quite used to being shuddered at. None of us Spies mind it at all. Whenever I enter a hotel and register myself as a Spy I am quite accustomed to see a thrill of fear run around the clerks, or clerk, behind the desk. . . .
>
> The death of a certain royal sovereign makes it possible for me to divulge things hitherto undivulgible. . . . When more sovereigns die I can divulge more. I hope to keep on divulging at intervals for years. But I am compelled to be cautious. My relations with the Wilhelmstrasse, with Downing Street, and the Quai d'Orsay, are so intimate, and my footing with the Yildiz Kiosk and the Waldorf-Astoria and Childs' Restaurants are so delicate, that a single *faux pas* might prove to be a false step.[11]

A short story or two, some burlesque interviews, half a dozen other parodies, and some other sketches made up

the rest of the volume, the contents of which was similar in nature and about equal in quality to that of *Behind the Beyond*.

In 1919 *The Hohenzollerns in America* represented Leacock's war humor, written as if to prove the war was really over and the German family could be laughed at now. In this volume he laughed at the false modesty of the returned veteran, the confusion of war reporting, the armchair enthusiasm of civilians who followed the war in the news, and the war sacrifices of Mr. Spugg, who personally sent two chauffeurs and a valet. "War and Peace at the Galaxy Club" was one of Leacock's best examples of extravagant humor. The Galaxy Club's first efforts for Belgian Relief resulted in a loss of two hundred dollars. "Some of the ladies of the committee moved that the entire deficit be sent to the Belgians, but were overruled by the men." The next attempts resulted in deficits of four hundred and fifty, then sixteen hundred and fifty, and finally five thousand dollars. The Armistice was signed just after it was decided to clear the whole loss by one big War Kermesse. Undaunted, the club changed to a Peace Kermesse and lost fifteen thousand dollars. The good ladies voted to send sixty per cent of the total deficit to Belgian Relief, and fifty per cent to the Red Cross, the remainder to be put into war bonds. At this point the men dissolved the Galaxy Club. Stephen Leacock's inventive imagination was still strong in 1919; the quality of his humor was unimpaired by the war.

The war had not stopped his serious writing either. Stephen Leacock's interest in the war was patriotic and

humanitarian, but also sociological. The phenomenon of war moved him to write; in 1919 he produced a greater number of serious articles than any other year. He wrote a series of six articles for the New York *Times* in which he proved himself a social scientist who ranged from moderate to moderately conservative.[12] The six articles, which he turned into a book the next year, constituted a study of the postwar social and economic conditions.

In his other articles of 1919, Stephen Leacock, the man who said, "I like to mix with millionaires; I like the things they mix," demonstrated his fear of something else he saw resulting from the war—prohibition—and he argued against it as an invasion of personal liberty in "The Tyranny of Prohibition" and "The Warning of Prohibition in America." The eight articles which Leacock wrote this year were a very large number for a man who was also writing some of the world's best humor and teaching a full course at McGill.

In this same year, Leacock found in Robert Benchley the only real literary disciple he ever had. The formal salutation of the first extant letter between them indicates that it was very close to the beginning of their friendship:

Orillia, Sept 18 19

Dear Mr. Benchley

Here is a little compliment from "a [sic] unknown lady" that I should have sent you long ago.

V—— truly

Stephen Leacock[13]

What the compliment was, or who the lady was, is lost. But the next letter, written the same year, began on a more familiar footing. It contained an advertising card which Leacock called to Benchley's attention. It is not hard to see why Leacock wanted to share it with Benchley:

UNDER THE DISTINGUISHED PATRONAGE
OF THEIR EXCELLENCIES
THE GOVERNOR-GENERAL AND DUCHESS
OF DEVONSHIRE

Private Lessons given in "WHAT TO DO" and
"WHAT NOT TO DO"
when meeting

H. R. H. PRINCE OF WALES
by

PROF. FRANK NORMAN, Sr. (the original)
STANLEY HALL, 92 STANLEY STREET

who has prepared thousands for COURT PRESEN-
TATION and has had the unique honor of Dancing
before
HIS MAJESTY THE KING

Prepare now for the CIVIC BALL to be given by taking a few PRIVATE DANCING LESSONS at Stanley Hall, (Lady Assistant) FIVE of Prof. Norman's pupils have already been honored in Canada with a command to Dance with His Royal Highness.
"There's a reason."

DANCING CLASS FOR ADULTS MONDAY,
WEDNESDAY 8 P.M.,
CHILDREN MONDAY, THURSDAY 4.30

Telephones Uptown 5168–1231
Circulars mailed on request[14]

The covering letter explained rather fully what Leacock
had in mind:

Dear Benchley,
I think you'll appreciate the enclosed. It is quite
genuine. Like so many other things it is so damn funny
it can't be satirized.
It doesn't quite become me as a loyal subject to get
too funny about kingship. But I wonder if your nimble
wit couldn't do something about this new coming of
the King to America. The Prince & Albert no doubt
presently followed by Tino and Ferdinand, & lots more.
You'll have to have a new code to deal with them.
Some hotels will have notices (*Kings not admitted*),
others will cater to the king trade.– I see a title like
Kings Wanted or *What Shall We do with our Kings*.
Imagine for instance a steel magnate appealing to
another & saying, I wonder if you could help me get
something for a king; we've got three already at our
plant & we can't take on any more. etc.
–Possible openings ought to supply you with plenty
of ideas. Go to it.

Stephen Leacock[15]

A search of Benchley's literary production, however, dis-
closes no use of the ideas which the older man sent him.

A letter from Fredrick Lewis Allen evidently gave an added impetus to a natural attraction between the two humorists.

Sunday, Nov. 30, 1919

Dear Robert:—

Notable epistolagrapher that I am, I seldom write you, but when I do it is because I have something to say. We have had here as our recent guest one Stephen Leacock, who was lecturing at the Union and being dined by Lampy and lunched by signet, and being vastly enjoyed by all; and Professor Stephen expressed great admiration for your stuff, and said you should put out a book.

He said for one thing, that your ideas for pieces were first-rate; that when he saw the title "How I Improved My Memory," for example, he cried, "Why, of course!"—and wished he had thought of it. Of Vanity Fair, he said he didn't read much of it except what you wrote. And he argued that you ought to collect your skits into a book, because then you would be able to write with subsequent book publication in mind, and the result would be remunerative.

So much for your information from the conversation of a very genial and lovable man, whom you should meet. Why don't you clip together a sheaf of your things and approach some publisher with them—say Douglas Doty at Harper's, or anybody at Doran's or Doubleday, Pages. Tell them that Stephen Leacock's *Nonsense Novels* sold more in the past 2 years than in the 1st 2 years of their existence—and dangle the

analogy before them. Not so ridiculous after all, that idea. . . .

Goodnight, Robert.

Ferdinand[16]

Ferdinand was the name Allen had carried since he had been Ibis (vice-president) of the *Lampoon* when Benchley was president, both as Harvard undergraduates. Allen at the time of the letter was Secretary to the Corporation at Harvard, a position he held from 1919 to 1923.

As a matter of fact, Benchley had already started work on such a collection. A little over three months before, on August 26, he had been dining at the Harvard Club with Henry Holt's representative, Lincoln MacVeagh, where they had discussed the possibility of book publication.[17]

When a few years later John Lane brought out the British edition of Benchley's first book, *Of All Things,* Leacock was asked to write the preface. Leacock readily complied, ending the preface by saying:

I will only state as the measure and indication of Bob Benchley's personality, charm, gift of conversation, ease of social movement, that he is one of *my* friends. That ought to cover the whole case.[18]

In gratitude Benchley sent his benefactor a copy of the New York edition, elaborately autographed:

To Stephen Leacock
who certainly *ought* to like

most of the stuff in this book
as he wrote it himself first.

> Gratefully
> Bob Benchley

"So teach us to number our days
that we may apply our hearts unto
wisdom."

New York
February 22*, 1922

*no offense[19]

Far from denying his literary indebtedness, Benchley seemed to enjoy admitting it. When he was asked later to offer some criticism for the preface of a Leacock anthology, he wrote: "I have enjoyed Leacock's work so much that I have written everything he ever wrote—anywhere from one to five years after him. . . . P.S. In case the proof-reader thinks that I meant 'I have *read* everything he ever wrote,' please tell him I really meant 'written.' "[20]

Such adulation as Benchley offered Stephen Leacock might easily be dismissed because of its extravagance as a kind of practical joke between two men of Puckish spirit. Various critics, however, have noted the resemblances in the work of these two writers. The foremost Canadian literary judge, Professor Pelham Edgar, in discussing *Literary Lapses,* said that it indicated "the future Leacock and Robert Benchley."[21] Another found "that on

this continent a distinctive type of humor is being evolved. In the shaping of it, Leacock has played a big part. If he received the tradition from men like Bret Harte [and O. Henry, one might add], he inspired disciples like Robert Benchley and S. J. Perelman."[22] The character that Benchley made famous, the little man in an incomprehensible world, was foreshadowed from the beginning of Leacock's work in "My Financial Career," which, incidentally, was Benchley's favorite piece of Leacock humor. As Leacock did in "My Revelations as a Spy," Benchley liked to prolong an explanation until it had lost all point. Benchley played his own fool in his humorous writings, just as Leacock frequently did. If Robert Benchley's position was so secure that he did not have to acknowledge any debt, it was secure enough that he could give credit anywhere he chose. He chose Leacock. When Leacock was compiling a collection of American humor, he requested permission to include a selection from Benchley without payment of royalty. Benchley wired back:

ANYTHING OF MINE THAT YOU MIGHT WANT TO USE IN YOUR BOOK WAS YOURS IN THE FIRST PLACE.[23]

In 1920 Leacock put together some of his pieces into a book he called *Winsome Winnie*. When his publisher expressed some doubt as to the advisability of producing the book except as a favor to Leacock, Stephen immediately objected. He was a hardheaded businessman, but he showed the same flair for effective language

in his business letters that he did in his professional writing. There was a bit of intentional bathos in his letter to Jefferson Jones, managing editor of Dodd, Mead:

My dear Jefferson.

I was sorry indeed to learn from your telegram that you had refused my offer. Your publishing at a loss will, of course, be a disastrous thing for me as your interest and mine will be exactly opposed, and you will have no incentive to advertise or to push the book. In other words, it bids fair to be strangled in its cradle, whereas I am quite convinced that it is the best book I have done since *Nonsense Novels,* and that with energetic and enterprising handling it could have been a great success.

Following this, Leacock, knowing he could not push them too far, made a compromise offer of reduced royalties on the second and third lots of five thousand copies, retaining his original high 15 per cent on the first lot.[24] Two days later Jones accepted the terms and the book was published.[25]

Winsome Winnie was another volume of burlesqued novels. Though perhaps not quite so good as *Nonsense Novels, Winsome Winnie* was still highly competent humor. The title story displayed Leacock's skill at verbal humor:

"Alas," said Winnifred, wringing her hands, "I am, then, alone in the world and penniless."

"You are," said Mr. Bonehead . . . "and let me ask

137

you in what way do you propose to earn your liveli-
hood?"

"I have my needle," said Winnifred.

"Let me see it," said the lawyer.

Winnifred showed it to him.[26]

The same piece showed that Leacock could still achieve
outrageously good puns:

"Nay," cried Mordaunt, leaping now to his feet, "your
birth is all right. I have looked it up myself. It is as
good—or nearly as good—as my own. Till I knew this,
my lips were sealed by duty. While I supposed that
you had a lower birth and I an upper, I was bound to
silence."[27]

"The Split in the Cabinet; or, The Fate of England" was
a neatly done burlesque of the kind of English society
novel which employed complicated English politics as
its background. His parody of detective fiction, "Who
Do You Think Did It? or The Mixed-up Murder Mystery," did not equal his own earlier standard, but in
"Buggam Grange; a Good Old Ghost Story" he was again
at his best. This book, returning to one of the earliest
forms of humor used by Leacock, indicated no loss of
critical faculty, no lessening of wit. In spite of Jefferson Jones's objections to it, it ultimately required eight
editions. Stephen Leacock not only knew his publisher,
he knew his market.

Leacock's fan mail kept him assured of the devotion
of his following. From London he received a letter:

Christmas, 1916

Dear Sir—Your book of Nonsense Novels is so damn funny, & has made me laugh so immoderately, that I feel myself greatly in your debt. I am by profession a portrait photographer & will at any time give a sitting and one dozen photographs to any sitter chosen by yourself.

Laughter is so rare these days, that one cannot remain unappreciative of your effort.

Yours very truly,
Maud B. Davis[28]

Sometimes such a kind gesture was a reciprocal action for a previous kindness on Leacock's part. From the president of a Massachusetts bank came a letter one Christmas:

Two years ago at Christmas, you extended a fine courtesy to my young son, Jack. You sent him an autographed copy of one of your books refusing to receive any pecuniary return for the value of the book. We have never forgotten this courtesy and intended last year to send some little thing to your own boy, but, we hit upon a rather confused situation just at Christmas time and it was not attended to.

When my boy, Jack, was about the age of your boy, he had no end of fun in making different designs out of blocks. We have sent you, therefore, by post a little box of blocks, worth less in themselves, but which perhaps may give that boy of yours, of whom you wrote me at the time, an occasional hour of pleasure. If it

serves him for an hour's pleasure, I know it will to some measure serve you as well. I trust the boy is growing in a fine way.

I note with pleasure that you are to be at our City Club in Boston Dec. 30 and regret exceedingly that I have a speaking appointment at a club at Pawtucket, R.I., that very evening and cannot possibly hear you and have the pleasure of meeting you. I intend, however, to have Jack there with some other friends of mine and shall tell him to "foot-ball" his way up to you sometime in the course of the evening and make himself known. You never had a truer disciple than Jack. He reads every sentence that you write, if he can get hold of it, and much of it many times over.

Again thanking you for your courtesy of two years ago and for the pleasure you have given to both Jack and myself through your books, I remain

Very truly and sincerely yours,
Charles A. Littlefield[29]

On occasions, of course, the communications were less flattering to his literary skill but still indicated his spreading fame.

Dear Mr Leacock

I saw a pretty Novel which I sure enjoyed reading it that you wrote in a copy of a Boston paper I got somewhere the paper said that you are a professor in McGill University. You must be a great gentleman when you are a professor I am sending you this watch case I made. I made it I thought some gentleman here

would buy from me and give me little money for I
wanted to buy a Cap of Velvet for myself I wanted
awful bad but I cant get it because I am so poor I got
no money my parents are dead Mama died a year ago
There is no nice gentleman here all are old farmers
they dont care for a watch case. Please excuse me for
bothering you best wishes.

Ella McLean[30]

These letters, of course, are a tribute to the humanity
of the man as much as to his ability as a writer or to his
fame as a personage.

In 1920 Leacock wrote his first political science book
since 1906. To an economist, *The Unsolved Riddle of
Social Justice* indicated by its title where his interest lay,
but Stephen Leacock interpreted justice much more
liberally than did his companion Conservatives. Leacock
was deathly afraid of socialism because he thought it un-
workable, but he declared in *The Unsolved Riddle* that
if the employer did not take care of the evils of the current system, the government would have to. To argue a
case for his kind of justice, Leacock discarded some of
the basic tenets of economics. The theory of values, so
dear to an academic economist, said that a man's wage
was indicative of his productivity. Nonsense, argued
Leacock; a man's wage was indicative only of the selling
price of the product and the availability of labor. It was
a reverence of "immutable" economic laws, he said
further, which had held off most social legislation. The
war turned almost the total productive power toward

things economically useless, proving that our productive power had been misdirected toward luxuries most of the time, directly contradicting the theory that a sound economy depends on utilitarian production. Here was one economic law gone.

> The war brought with it conscription—not as we used to see it, as the last horror of military tyranny, but as the crowning pride of democracy. . . . But conscription has its other side. . . . If every citizen owes it to society that he must fight for it in case of need, then society owes to every citizen the opportunity of a livelihood.[31]

Undoubtedly Leacock was a Conservative, but even in 1920 he sounded as liberal as the mid-century Conservative, flatly declaring the necessity of social security, minimum wage laws, and legislative shortening of working hours. Theories had not solved the riddle of social justice; action would be required. He wanted individualism—a much better term, thought Leacock, than capitalism—more than he wanted anything resembling socialism, but most of all he wanted "real" justice, not the poverty-ridden "natural" justice that economic law had provided.

General Sir Arthur Currie came to McGill in 1920 to take the position of principal. Sir Arthur had been Commander-in-Chief of the Canadian Corps in France and had acquitted himself admirably. When Leacock, as a member of the faculty and head of a department, went into Currie's office to pay his respects and welcome him to McGill, he carried with him the deep admiration he

had for the military. He could not restrain himself from saying, "I think, General Currie, I must have had the honour of teaching you when I was a teacher in training at Strathroy in 1888." Sir Arthur looked at him quizzically for a moment and then answered, "I recognize you now; you were the young man to whom Jimmie Wetherell, the principal, said that he admired your brains more than your manners."[32] On this note began a friendship that lasted until Sir Arthur's death. General Currie had been selected for the job because he had demonstrated administrative ability; he knew little about the academic structure of the institution. His salvation was that he knew he did not know. He came to depend on Leacock, among others, of course, for common-sense solutions to university matters. He often came to Leacock to confide in him and to ask his advice. In 1931 he wrote a letter to his friend beginning "Dear Stephen" and asking his advice on the best way for McGill to help Canada's floundering agricultural industry.[33] Stephen Leacock's affection for the general was just as great, and he learned to depend on his honesty and integrity.

Both Leacock's attitude and his technique made him popular also with his students at McGill. He would come into his classroom, escorted by Bill Gentleman, custodian of Arts Hall, with an impressive kind of quick dignity. There was nothing pompous about Leacock in the classroom, but he was impressive. He wore his ragged gown with all the aplomb of a little boy playing baseball in torn trousers. He knew the condition of his attire; he just did not care. He was there as a teacher, not a fashion

plate. Besides, the familiar garment was comfortable now. One year a class that became particularly fond of him bought him a new robe. He thanked them generously, and thoughtfully wore the gown the next day, but it was not the same; it rustled. When he appeared the second day in his old robe, the class was not surprised and neither he nor the class ever mentioned it again. He had a commanding appearance before his class, though he was not a large man. Of average height, he seemed larger because of his deep, full-bodied voice and his magnificent head. His unruly, gray hair grew low and dropped even lower over his wide forehead. His mustache was as shaggy as his hair—George always said, "Stephen would have liked to get a haircut; he just never thought of it." His gray, twinkling eyes were set wide in a ruddy, mobile face. He was not a heavy man, one hundred sixty-five pounds for his height of a little less than six feet,[34] but he carried himself with an air of impressive assurance; here was a man who knew what he was doing, and he would get it done. The ring of hearty laughter was always in his voice and the gleam of joy in his eyes.

In 1919 Leacock had been granted an LL.D. by Queens University, Kingston, Ontario. In 1920, the same degree was conferred three times upon the famous humorist. From Dartmouth he received his honorary degree in the distinguished company of Herbert Hoover and Major General George W. Goethals. Brown University and his alma mater, the University of Toronto, likewise honored him. For a professor these distinctions were

great; he appreciated academic honors because he knew
what they meant. Leacock was proud of his humor, and
he was pleased to accept the degrees offered for his
literary efforts.

If 1920 had been a big year for Stephen Leacock, the
next one was equally exciting. Leacock published no
books in 1921, though his popular *Elements of Political
Science* required revision, a task he finished early in the
year. Late in the summer Leacock gave a small dinner
party for three of his writing friends at the University
Club. Murray Gibbon, sometime journalist and public
relations director for the Canadian Pacific Railway, B. K.
Sandwell, and Pelham Edgar were always glad to join
Leacock for any occasion, but this meeting proved
particularly interesting.[35] During dinner and the brandy
which followed, the conversation was animated with concern over a recent change in the Canadian copyright law.
According to William Arthur Deacon, later president of
the Canadian Authors Association, a printer-publisher
named Rose had found a way the copyright law could be
changed slightly to give a great advantage to Canadian
publishers. Because of the Berne Convention, Ottawa
could not pass a law affecting the reciprocal rights of
foreign authors. The Dominion parliament could, however, take legislative action concerning their own citizens. The Copyright Act of 1920, instigated by the lobby-
ing of Rose, required Canadian writing by Canadian
authors to be published in Canada before being eligible
for Canadian copyright. Books by foreign authors might
still be published anywhere. Leacock and his guests were

not against profits for their publishers, but they did not like to see native authors penalized. The four men around Leacock's table were of sufficient literary stature, particularly Leacock, that their reputations might protect them, but there were many others who would certainly suffer. They decided to organize a protest dinner.

The dinner was set for December 7, 1921, and all known authors, by blanket and personal invitation, were invited to attend. The date unfortunately conflicted with a lecture tour for which Leacock had already contracted, and he could not be present, but the idea was partly his from the first, and he lent his name to the invitations. The response to the proposal was remarkable; all the major writers—Frank Packard, the detective story writer; Charles W. Gordon (Ralph Connor), the novelist; Bliss Carmen, the poet—proved themselves in sympathy with the protest movement. The originators of the idea were agreeably surprised and even astounded that they had to seat a hundred authors at the dinner. A protest was drawn up which they endorsed with such singleness of purpose and convivial feeling that the idea of a permanent association was inevitable. No such purpose had been foreseen in the call for the meeting, but most of the guests had come such a distance that they had planned to spend the night anyway. If someone could manage to draft a constitution during the night, they could meet immediately after breakfast to adopt it. In a party as convivial as this it was hard to find anyone who wanted to spend the rest of the night drawing up a constitution, but B. K. Sandwell and Murray Gibbon

offered to try it. Murray Gibbon always claimed that they took the constitution of a fishing club he belonged to and spent the night changing the word "fish" to "book," "fisherman" to "author," and "fishing" to "writing." In any case, the following morning when most of the hundred met again they adopted the constitution of the new Canadian Authors Association, making themselves and Stephen Leacock charter members. Once established, the association grew in prestige. Finally almost all important Canadian authors belonged to it, and it was given the job of judging and granting the Governor-General's Awards for Literature.

The Canadian Authors Association was not the only protest group which Leacock joined this year. In 1921 he gave a public address, "The Case Against Prohibition," for the Citizens' Liberty League of Toronto, in which he made it clear that he was opposed on both theoretical and practical grounds. Theoretically, it was an invasion of private rights; the law could not declare two million people criminals. Practically, since the law would not be obeyed—witness the United States—it would breed crime.[36] Later the same year he announced, "I will write articles against prohibition at any time for any paper for nothing."[37] Yves Guyot, editor of France's *Journal des Economistes,* praised Leacock for his stand on prohibition and sent a copy of his own book, *La question de l'alcool.*[38]

As indicated by his activities and his humor, much of it about drink and drinking, Leacock liked his Scotch and soda. To the question, "Temperate or intemperate?" on a

questionnaire he was once required to fill out, he answered simply, "I drink every day."[39] His niece remembers that his flask was the first item to be packed when Leacock went on a lecture tour.[40] He had once planned the adventure of his life; he was going on a polar expedition with Vilhjalmur Stefansson. He wrote Stefansson that he did not want to be a drain on the meager grant which was financing the exploration; he would pay his own way entirely. "I'll even bring my own whiskey." Stefansson replied with gratitude, but told him the expense for whiskey would be unnecessary since liquor would not be allowed on the trip. With great regret but equally great speed, Leacock canceled his berth on the voyage.[41] Leacock's first words to a guest entering his house were, "How about a drink?" It had probably been a long, hard trip, and besides, as he once told George, "They might think it was a temperance house and be suffering." In spite of the overwhelming evidence of Leacock's insistence on liquor, not one of his acquaintances would say that they had ever seen Leacock when he had had too much to drink. The reason was fairly obvious; Leacock was as intelligent about his drinking as he was about the rest of his life. He had a drink or two in the afternoon; after dinner he might and probably would have more, but he was in bed by ten, before the heavy drinking started. Leacock was a temperate man; he did not approve of too much of anything, and that included drinking.

In 1921 Leacock made his first professional lecture tour. Since his success in the lectures for Belgian Relief,

his speaking engagements had multiplied rapidly. He, with Pelham Edgar, had been asked to attend the Lowell Centenary at Columbia University in 1919, and he had spoken to the Pilgrim Club while there. Regularly and with increasing frequency, he had been addressing such diverse groups as the Montreal Housewives League, McGill Alumni Clubs, Conservative Party meetings, and Rotary Clubs. With a kind of chauvanistic stubbornness, he refused to charge for speeches in Canada, though he accepted payment for addresses made in the States. England, loving him as if he were still the Britisher he was born, soon demanded that he be heard over there. Christy and Moore, Ltd., agents and promoters, asked Leacock to consider a speaking tour under their direction. Leacock was ever ready to visit the center of his beloved Empire and agreed to lecture in the British Isles from October until Christmas. Without much difficulty, McGill was persuaded to grant Leacock his second leave of absence in twenty years, and Stephen, Trix, and Stephen, Jr., sailed for England on the fourteenth of September aboard the *Metagama*.[42] They reached London the twenty-sixth and the next day Leacock was given an accolade any true British citizen would appreciate; the London *Times* itself called him "a master of satire."[43]

VII

═══════

1921-1925

THIS was Leacock's first trip to England since his
Rhodes tour in 1907, before he had begun his career
as a humorist. Christy and Moore had assured him that
the visit would be successful, but they had not prepared
him for the reception he got. Although Leacock knew
that his books had been selling well in England, he was
still surprised. These people were not like Canadians
dealing with their own prophet; they thought of him as a
writer, a man of letters, not just a funny man. After opening the tour with a lecture at Thirsk in Yorkshire on October 4,[1] Leacock made his way to London. Leacock's
first London lecture, on October 17 at Aeolian Hall,[2] was
introduced appreciatively by the editor of *Punch,* Sir
Owen Seaman:

> Ladies and gentlemen, this is Mr. Stephen Leacock.
> Mr. Leacock, this is the flower of London intelligence—
> or perhaps I should say one of the flowers; the rest are
> coming to your other lectures. . . .

I will . . . tell you a thing or two about Mr. Leacock. In the first place, by vocation he is a Professor of Political Economy, and he practises humour—frenzied fiction instead of frenzied finance—by way of recreation. . . .

Farther, Mr. Leacock is all-British, being English by birth and Canadian by residence. I mention this for two reasons: firstly, because England and the Empire are very proud to claim him for their own, and, secondly, because I do not wish his nationality to be confused with that of his neighbours on the other side. For English and American humourists have not always seen eye to eye. When we fail to appreciate their humour they say we are too dull and effete to understand it: and when they do not appreciate ours they say we haven't got any.

Now Mr. Leacock's humour is British by heredity; but he has caught something of the spirit of American humour by force of association. This puts him in a similar position to that in which I found myself once when I took the liberty of swimming across a rather large loch in Scotland. After climbing into the boat I was in the act of drying myself when I was accosted by the proprietor of the hotel adjacent to the shore. "You have no business to be bathing here," he shouted. "I'm not," I said; "I'm bathing on the other side." In the same way, if anyone on either side is unintelligent enough to criticise Mr. Leacock's humour, he can always say it comes from the other side. But the truth

is that his humour contains all that is best in the humour of both hemispheres.

Having fulfilled my duty as chairman, in that I have told you nothing that you did not already know before—except perhaps, my swimming feat which never got into the Press because I have a very bad publicity agent—I will not detain you longer from what you are really wanting to get at; but ask Mr. Leacock to proceed at once with his lecture on "Frenzied Fiction."[3]

Leacock spoke in London three other times the same week, introduced on the nineteenth by J. A. Spender, editor of the *Westminster Gazette,* on the twentieth by Sir Campbell Stuart, editor of *The Times,* and on the twenty-first by J. St. Loe Strachey, editor of the *Spectator.*[4]

Stephen Leacock's tour was planned around two lectures, "Frenzied Fiction," and "Drama as I See It." Both lectures were syntheses of his previously published parodies. Although he would have, perhaps, felt ill at ease delivering someone else's material, he used his own, and his platform manner was one of great informality. He spoke in a mature voice which had retained its mimic mobility from his youth. And, as he read, he laughed. His lecture technique might have been called a conspiratorial one: it was never really that of a performer; rather he maintained the attitude of a raconteur who wanted to share an amusing experience or some clever ideas he had happened upon. Since his lectures purported to be discussion and criticism of literature, he was able to adapt

his regular teaching technique to the public platform. His unaffected, intimate style won the hearts of his English audiences.

Stephen Leacock never went anywhere without making friends. Cyril Maude, the actor, took him to see Sir James M. Barrie. Following an eccentric custom, the playwright, then sixty-one, received them lying on a couch in a darkened room. He was, Leacock found, quite listless until Leacock mentioned O. Henry. Barrie raised up quickly, and the discussion sparkled until Leacock left.[5] About the same time Leacock met E. V. Lucas, the English critic and humorist, with whom he got along famously. Lucas accompanied him on an off day jaunt to Bury Lodge, family seat of the Butlers, his mother's family. Here Leacock showed him the fire screen still covered with scores of some of the first cricket matches. Leacock recalled that Lucas was more impressed by Leacock's relation to the origin of cricket than by his reputation as a humorist.[6] An indication of the companionship between these two humorists remains in a letter Leacock wrote Lucas:

My dear E. V.

I may be the worst correspondent in the world but I'm the best friend. . . . I have drunk whiskey with you in a car for 80 miles. . . . Let me therefore hear no more complaints out of you on the mere ground of not writing.[7]

From London, Leacock moved north, lecturing regularly. He interrupted his tour in order to return to Lon-

don for the first meeting of the newly formed Canada Club, on the twelfth of December.[8] During the same break in routine, he addressed the London Society, describing his impressions of London.[9] Leacock's lecture series carried him to Edinburgh and finally on December 23, to Bournemouth, Hampshire, where his tour ended. It was with regret that he said to the Bournemouth audience:

> As far as I know, it is not very likely that I shall have the opportunity to be free from my college work to come back again, but I leave with very great regret. I have met with such extraordinary kindness and such generous appreciation from the audiences who have heard me all over England and Scotland, that the experience is one which I shall long cherish. I am afraid that when I go back to Canada, and say how I have been treated, it will let loose upon these shores a flood of Canadian humorists and economists. I hope, for my sake, that they will be treated as I have been treated. From my experience here, I am convinced that all the good old jokes about the lack of humour in the British people are pure myth. I have made during the last three months a very good livelihood out of the British sense of humour, and I am properly grateful for it.[10]

Leacock wrote Christy that he was well pleased with his last lecture and the whole tour.[11] The trip had obviously been a success; even without his annual book of humor, Leacock's income was a little over twenty thousand.

After spending a few days in Paris, arranging for the translations of some of his work, Leacock sailed with his family from Le Havre for Montreal January 14, 1922.

Returning from his success in England to 240 Arts Hall, his office at McGill, Leacock entered again in the life he loved most. He walked the hall of the building as if it were home, striding surely with a heavy step, banging his cane along the floor just because he liked the sound of it. His deep voice rang pleasantly from the walls as he greeted students, faculty members, and his favorite, the janitor—Bill Gentleman. He liked to call out to the janitor by name because when he said "Good morning, Gentleman," everyone always answered.[12] It was Gentleman who helped him into his tattered gown just before he went into his classroom. Bill Gentleman had retired from the British army in Afghanistan before he became one of the "characters" at McGill. One day, passing Leacock's door, he overheard the professor say, in connection with a discussion of Indian currency, something about the rupee. With no hesitation he stepped in and challenged the accuracy of the professor's statement. Futhermore, Leacock had to admit the correction (*doit s'incliner devant la mise au point*).[13] Stephen Leacock never liked to admit that he was wrong, but he did like the freedom of thought that the interruption stood for.

Leacock put his English lecture tour to good use in his next book. *My Discovery of England* contained largely humorous impressions of the British Isles, and gave opportunity for him to exercise a kind of tongue-in-cheek irony. He told of his trip to England, the "brutal" way

the English customs officials had treated him—"the strap of one [trunk] was rudely unbuckled, while the lid of the other was actually lifted at least four inches"[14]—and the carelessness of the immigration officials:

"Let me tell you . . ." I said, "that I am an anarchistic polygamist, that I am opposed to all forms of government, that I object to any kind of revealed religion, that I regard the state and property and marriage as the mere tyranny of the bourgeoisie, and that I want to see class hatred carried to the point where it forces every one into brotherly love. Now, do I get in?"

The official looked puzzled for a minute. "You are not Irish, are you, sir?" he said.

"No."

"Then I think you can come in all right," he answered.[15]

With an experienced and humorous insight, he discussed the possibility of prohibition in England, the English and American newspapers. He wrote as a tourist:

No visitor to London should fail to see . . . [the Tower of London, the British Museum, and Westminister Abbey]. Indeed he ought to feel that his visit to England is wasted unless he has seen them. I speak strongly on the point because I feel strongly on it. To my mind there is something about the grim fascination of the historic Tower, the cloistered quiet of the Museum and the majesty of the ancient Abbey, which

will make it the regret of my life that I didn't see any one of the three. . . .

Each day, after the fashion of every tourist, I wrote for myself a little list of things to do . . . :

1. Go to bank.
2. Buy a shirt.
3. National Picture Gallery.
4. Razor blades.
5. Tower of London.
6. Soap. . . .

I was able at times both to go to the bank and buy a shirt in a single morning: at other times I was able to buy razor blades and almost find the National Picture Gallery. . . .

I actually stopped the taxi. "Is that the British Museum?" I asked the driver. "I think it is something of the sort, sir," he said. I hesitated. "Drive me," I said, "to where I can buy safety razor blades."[16]

"Oxford as I See It," Leacock's most anthologized essay, was a clear-eyed analysis of why Oxford, so out of date in physical facilities and teaching methods, succeeded in really educating men. Leacock's answer was threefold: the tutors who smoked at their students; a leftover mediaeval belief that a professor is a really learned man and that a student is one who wants to learn; and the residence halls which required men to live together as well as learn together. *My Discovery of England* was a cogent, charming book, and showed what a glorious visit the Leacocks had enjoyed in England.

In 1923 Leacock published *College Days* and *Over the Footlights*. Publishing his own juvenilia in *College Days* was about as close to conceit as Stephen Leacock ever came. It was primarily an accumulation of pieces he had written for the *Varsity* and other college magazines. There were one or two good things in the book, but most of the contents, much of it poetry, was too localized and dated to have the usual appeal of Leacock humor. The reader had to know of Leacock's connections with the University of Toronto and McGill University, as well as know of the standing rivalry between the two institutions, to understand properly "Toronto and McGill":

The object of this poem is not very hard to get onto,
Since it is intended all through as what is called
   a poem on Toronto.
I don't deny, have not and never will,
My debt of gratitude to old McGill.[17]

In the same way, one needed a knowledge of Canadian geography and an affection for Canada for thorough appreciation of:

I need not sing your praises, every word
Of mine, New Brunswick, would appear absurd,
Beside the melody that freely pours
From out the polysyllables of yours.
   Where Chedabudcto roars and bold Buctouche
Rivals the ripples of the Restigouche;
Or where beneath its ancient British flag
Aroostook faces Mettawamkeág.
   Oh fairy-land of meadow, vale and brook,

Kennebekasis, Chiputneticook,
Shick-Shock and Shediac, Point Escuminac,
Miranachi and Peticodiac.
This is no place to try poetic wit,
I guess at least I know when to quit.[18]

"A Little Glimpse into the College Future" was a prose burlesque commencement address for Harvard in the future. The speaker, evaluating the advances education had made, recalled that at one time only four years of college was enough; now a man could stay in school until he was sixty-five, and it was being proposed to the trustees at the next meeting that a Harvard man be allowed to spend all of his life at the university. The trouble with even the best of *College Days* was that it appealed only to those who understood the internal workings of the university system of the moment.

Over the Footlights, published the same year, was a better book; in it Leacock returned to parody. He took to task the collegiate production of Greek tragedy in "Oroastus." "The Soul Call" was:

An up-to-date Piffle Play. Period, 1923. (In Which a Man and Woman, Both Trying to Find Themselves, Find One Another)

It is named by such a name as *The Soul Call,* or *The Heart Yearn,* or *The Stomach Trouble*—always something terribly perplexed, and with sixty per cent of sex in it. It always deals in one way or another with the Problem of Marriage. Let it be noted that mar-

riage, which used to be a sacrament, became presently a contract, and is now a problem. In art and literature it used to constitute a happy ending. Now it is just the bad beginning.[19]

In Leacock's parody of historical drama, Napoleon went around pinching his generals on the cheek, murmuring endearments like *"Mon vieux paquet de linge sale."* A burlesque of Russian drama listed its cast:

THE CAST OF (WANT OF) CHARACTERS

Stylipin	*A Thief*
Yatschscha	*His Wife*
Patch	*An Imbecile*
Hootch	*A Homicidal Maniac*
Itch	*A Paragoric*
Pravda (aged eighty)	*An Immoral Woman*
Prybiloff	*A Murderer*[20]

"Cast Up by the Sea," the best of a good selection was a burlesque of the rousing melodrama of the 1890's.

In 1923, both *Over the Footlights* and *College Days* contributed to Stephen Leacock's most financially successful year. This year his income reached almost forty thousand dollars,[21] of which only five thousand represented his academic salary. This was fifteen thousand more than his average income, but the large figure in 1923 was occasioned by a number of things. He published two books instead of the usual one; the previous year he had reissued six of his books, and he was drawing royalties from those; five more books required reprinting in

1923; he had recently revised his *Political Science,* and its earning power was revived. Yet Leacock was not the wealthy man that legend made of him. One commentator extravagantly reported that Leacock in the early twenties made sixty thousand dollars a year in royalties alone.[22] His friends recall hearing him say that his salary at McGill would not even pay his income tax. Since his academic salary never exceeded fifty-five hundred, this may be true, but Stephen Leacock was always capable of exaggerating to heighten the dramatic quality of an illustration. Besides, Stephen would have laughed heartily at anyone who was disappointed to find that he made "only" forty thousand in his biggest year.

In addition to his financial returns in this period, Leacock received other recognition. Stephen Leacock was included as a subject in the "Makers of Canadian Literature" series, and his first paper was accepted by the Royal Society of Canada, to which he had been elected a fellow in 1919. The presentation of a paper to the Royal Society was the height of scholarly endeavor. "On the Grain of Truth in Popular Economic Fallacies" was a typical Leacock study, indicating at the same time his belief that economics was an inexact science and that man, even untrained, was not such a fool as the pedant tried to make him out. Leacock's volume in the Makers of Canadian Literature series was written and compiled by his old friend Peter McArthur. McArthur had known Leacock since, as editor of *Truth,* he had accepted some of Leacock's first attempts at humor. Besides a small anthology of seven sketches, *Stephen Leacock* contained a short

biography and a critical essay by McArthur. The critic's appraisal was just and the honor was deserved, though perhaps a little premature since Leacock was to continue to make Canadian literature for another twenty years.

For some years after his successful tour of England, Leacock continued an active lecture schedule. He spoke on "Education and Democracy" at the fiftieth anniversary convocation of the University of Iowa.[23] He began to speak quite often in the United States, where he was in great demand at conventions of every kind from meetings of educators to meetings of electricians. Americans were a convening people who were willing to pay lecture fees as high as five hundred dollars. In 1925 he made a tour through the South, which his agent found prosperous enough to suggest that they try it again.[24] Leacock had made the tour with the same two lectures he had used in England. The trip was not so extended: his lecturing was now confined to holidays and weekends when he would not have to miss school. Even this restricted schedule helped boost his income in 1924 to thirty-two thousand dollars above his McGill salary. Such activities made great demands on his time and vitality, but Leacock, as he became a professional, realized the value of publicity to an author. His speeches sold his books just as his books sold his speeches.

Continuing his annual publication, Leacock wrote, in addition to an article on business which *Harper's Magazine* took, *The Garden of Folly* in 1924. This volume contained the same sort of scattered tomfoolery that Leacock had made his own during the fourteen years he

had been publishing humor. Pieces like "The Human Mind Up to Date" and "The Human Body: Its Care and Prevention" were not quite the quality to which Leacock's readers were accustomed. But "Romances of Business" and half a dozen burlesque letters were very creditable humor.

In the preface to this book, Leacock expressed the basis of much of the humor of his initial literary career:

> Humour cannot exist alongside of eager ambition, brisk success, and absorption in the game of life. Humour comes best to those who are down and out, or who have at least discovered their limitations and their failures. Humour is essentially a comforter, reconciling us to things as they are in contrast to things as they might be. . . .
>
> I have no doubt that this theory, like most things that I say in this book, is an overstatement. But I have always found that the only kind of a statement worth making is an overstatement. A half truth, like a half a brick, is always more forcible as an argument than a whole one. It carries further.[25]

This statement, though brief and guilty of oversimplification, declared the basis of both his philosophy and his technique of humor. His fun was neither low nor condescending, but it was for everyone, and most, certainly, had experienced varying degrees of failure. And his principal tool, under many guises, was overstatement. In Leacock's case, overstatement most often took the form of simple exaggeration or an involved, frequently in-

correct, extension of an obvious statement or figure of speech. Both technique and philosophy of humor will be discussed in more detail in connection with his own books on those subjects.[26] *The Garden of Folly*, an unsuccessful volume in terms of Leacock's usual sales, was one of the few books Leacock ever wrote which did not have to be reprinted. Although it was an undistinguished production, it was still funny, and Leacock had no reason to be ashamed of it.

The next year Stephen Leacock received the tribute of being parodied himself. C. K. Allen's *Oh, Mr. Leacock!* was a heavyhanded attempt at satirizing Leacock's style as a humorist. The book demonstrated two things: it is difficult to parody humor, and Mr. Allen did not understand Mr. Leacock. Had Allen been unsuccessful only at writing parodies of Leacock's parodies, his failure might be more understandable, but his attempts to parody the other forms of Leacock's humor were equally ineffective. Leacock was a master in the use of exaggeration, but when Allen chose to amplify Leacock's hyperbole, the result was simply overexaggeration. The end product was not parody of Leacock's style; it was merely poor humor in the Leacock style. The second fault of the book lay evidently with Allen's sense of humor. He took Leacock's humorous gibes too seriously. He resented humor at the expense of Parliament, "the Mother of government," without realizing the complete absence of malice inherent in all of Leacock's work. He took offense at the flippancy toward society that he found in a man who was a far more competent sociologist than he. Allen

placed himself in the peculiar position of laughing at Leacock because he was laughing at something else; the real difficulty, of course, was that the rest of the world was laughing *with* Leacock.

If being chosen as the subject of a parody indicated Leacock's success, his relations with his publisher indicated the same thing. Stephen Leacock could demand more of his publisher than a less profitable artist could; but, like almost all other interpersonal relationships in Leacock's life, the link between Leacock and his publisher was one of mutual consideration. In 1923 Dodd, Mead and Company, at Leacock's request, turned all dramatic rights on the works back to the author.[27] And when he wrote in 1925, asking that the second serial rights of his material be returned to him, Dodd, Mead answered that, in view of the fact that the rights had netted over four thousand dollars in the last two years, it would not seem a wise business move to relinquish their contractual control, but they would release them anyway.[28] It was certainly not a one-sided arrangement; there was faith and understanding on both sides. This same year, when the publisher wanted to offer one of his books to Grosset and Dunlap to produce in a seventy-five-cent edition, Leacock, knowing that Dodd, Mead would look after both his interest and theirs, agreed to the contract without even knowing which book would be chosen.[29] Raymond T. Bond, vice-president of Dodd, Mead and Company, recalls that no author was easier to work with than Stephen Leacock.

Leacock's writing continued to appear in magazines

during the early part of 1925. But when the time came for the preparation of his usual book—his books generally were published in time for the Christmas trade—he was absorbed in the tragedy of his wife's fatal illness.

After leaving the stage, Beatrix Leacock had given herself over to domestic duties, dinner parties, club meetings, and such activities as befitted the daughter of R. B. Hamilton and the wife of Stephen Leacock. She and Stephen enjoyed many things together, but a large part of her life was devoted to her own interests. Though in no sense a collector, she was fond of antiques and used them extensively to decorate and furnish both Old Brewery Bay and the Cote des Neiges residence. She liked dining frequently with her close friend and neighbor Mrs. H. T. Shaw, known to Trix as May. She liked running up to Ottawa with Stephen for amateur theatricals at the Governor-General's. In spite of her slight appearance and almost electric beauty, Trix was not a small woman. She was as strong and as vital and as interested in everything as Stephen himself. Then, beginning in 1924, she found her energies depleted, so that faculty teas and other social functions were a burden. Finally, accompanied by May Shaw, she went to her doctor in late 1925.

Mrs. Shaw recalls her as she came out of the doctor's office—white but calm—she was a brave woman and an actress. She had been told she had cancer. Science knew little about the disease in 1925, and, without any appreciable sign to her, cancer had eaten away her breast. Leacock's sympathy with human weaknesses

had made him a great humorist; now he found himself suffering from these same weaknesses. In a state near panic, he rushed to combat a condition already diagnosed as hopeless. Research's newest cancer remedy was the lead treatment being offered in Liverpool. Stephen made immediate plans for getting Beatrix there.

When Sir Edward W. Beatty, chairman of the Canadian Pacific Railway, learned of Leacock's plan, he ordered that one of the CPR ships be made ready for Beatrix's removal. The walls separating three staterooms were knocked down to make a floating private hospital for her. Measures were taken for keeping it sterile and for providing quarters for a nurse, her mother, and Stephen, who accompanied her. Late in November they sailed for Liverpool, having been advised already by the specialist there that the journey was probably useless.[30]

The doctor had been right; it was hopeless. Beatrix was so weak on her arrival that the Liverpool authorities could neither operate nor start the lead treatment. On December 15, Trix died. Typical of the messages which poured in was Sir Arthur Currie's: "Courage, Stephen, we are all with you."[31] Stephen, shocked, arranged for her cremation and then started home with her ashes. On the thirty-first, the day after his birthday, Stephen Leacock buried the ashes of his wife in the St. James Cemetery in Toronto.

Years later in the midst of a humorous essay, he interpolated the poignant words that must have reflected this tragedy of his fifty-sixth year:

The real adoring husband overtalks his wife, over-dominates her, pays with unexpected presents for easy forgiveness of his ill temper, and never knows that he adored her till it is too late, because now she cannot hear it.[32]

VIII

1926–1928

LEACOCK turned to his writing and teaching with
renewed intensity, but the death of Beatrix had
been a shock to him. He had liked planning special, fancy
meals, only half aware that it was Trix who would see
that they reached the table. He used exorbitant amounts
of clean linen, but it was Trix who had managed to see
that they were always available. He had indulged in
the small luxury of losing his temper at the servants,
leaving her to soothe injured feelings. He had enjoyed
having someone at breakfast to listen to his latest manuscript after he had been writing for three hours; Trix
had always listened. Beatrix had done all these things,
and he had accepted them. The acceptance had not
been thoughtless; he had loved his wife extravagantly if
not passionately. He had not considered the possibility
of her dying. She was only forty-six years old; she had
been well until shortly before her death. Suddenly, without warning, the stability of his life was gone. Of all
his activities, his writing and teaching were the least

affected. These things he had done by himself from the beginning, and in them he found his salvation.

Leacock's next book, published in 1926, was put together, in a great measure, out of material he had written in the early part of 1925. *Winnowed Wisdom* was perhaps a better book than *Garden of Folly* and was certainly a better one than *College Days*. Some of the pieces were as good as anything he ever wrote. "How We Kept Mother's Birthday" has often been reprinted. The deft touch of the master was in "The Give and Take of Travel": "I am aware that there is a class of persons—women mostly—who carry away spoons and other things deliberately as souvenirs. But I disclaim all connection with that kind of thing. . . . I would never take a valuable spoon, unless I happened to be using it to open the back of my watch, or something of the sort. But when I sign my name on the hotel book I keep the pen. Similarly and in all fairness, I give up my own fountain pen to the telegraph clerk."[1] One of Leacock's most hilarious parodies was "How My Wife and I Built our Home for $4.90"—"Owing perhaps to my inexperience, it took me the whole morning to dig out a cellar forty feet long and twenty feet wide."[2] The volume could not, however, maintain such a level of quality. The preface, in which he dedicated the work to the average man, was written after his wife's death and indicated best how that event had affected him:

The average man is not, by statistics, a great traveler. The poor fellow has been only sixty-two miles away

from home. He owns nine-tenths of a Ford car, punctures a tire once every twenty-two days, and spends, in the course of his whole life, a month and a half underneath his car.

. . . .

I would like ever so much to start a movement for getting above the average. Surely if we all try hard, we can lift ourselves up high above the average. It looks a little difficult mathematically, but that's nothing.[3]

This humor, though it was still funny, had not the light touch that Leacock had achieved before. It was too carefully done. Here was not the man pushed around by statistics; here was a man pushing statistics around. It was the best he could do at the time. And, though it did not have the sale that some of his books enjoyed, it helped maintain Leacock's income at a high level, twenty-four thousand eight hundred dollars this year.

The same year Stephen Leacock wrote two serious articles. "Quebec Liquor Laws" was, as its title indicated, an explanatory essay, clarifying the rather jumbled local option and piecemeal legislation which the traditionally, and still practically, wet province had on its books.[4] The other, "The Work of the University,"[5] was a serious, professional discussion of the aim of any university. Should it try to train everybody? Stephen Leacock believed that a college should produce, not a man who could do something, but a thinking man who could learn to do anything.

The middle of the 1920's was a golden period for the Department of Economics at McGill. Leacock, partly to compensate for his wife's death and partly to develop his graduate students of this time, threw himself into his work more vigorously. With this extra effort he helped three students to become Rhodes scholars and other young men toward other forms of success. One of his students became president of a public relations company;[6] another, after extended graduate work, became executive editor of the Montreal *Herald*.[7] Still others, J. P. Day and later John Culliton—probably Leacock's favorite—eventually joined his staff.

Culliton had done some good work and Leacock had his eye on him. He was always quick to spot a graduate student who was willing to do more than the minimum and who seemed to be able. Leacock did not know all of his students; he was far too popular for that to be possible, but he took a close, personal interest in those who showed real promise. One day he found it necessary to get in touch with the boy. He called John's boarding-house and asked for John Culliton, the student. "Student," said the shocked landlady, "he told me he was a night watchman."[8] This was enough of a character reference for Stephen Leacock. John Culliton was a man after Leacock's own heart; he was a good student, but he knew how to live too. They became close friends, and when Culliton became a member of the faculty he gradually became Leacock's assistant. Later he helped Leacock with some of his books, served as a companion when Leacock needed him, and became almost a second

son to the professor. It was John Culliton who frequently had to take over when Leacock went to bed early. He did not strenuously object to this; he was Leacock's kind of man. But occasionally Stephen thought it was fun to make John go on the wagon. He would leave Culliton in charge of a convivial party which he knew would last until the small hours of the morning. Then at five o'clock he would wake him so they could "get right to work." Three days of this treatment were usually enough, and Stephen and John would return to their regular habits.

Stephen Leacock felt his responsibility as a teacher very strongly. He regularly read all the pertinent journals in his field and kept himself thoroughly up to date in his scholarship. With the same caution, he kept a close eye on his faculty. When he found that any member of his staff had allowed himself to lose track of recent developments in economics or political science, he gently but firmly warned him. The students were going to receive the best, whether they understood it or not. But Leacock made his students understand it. Although he was not a clown in class, he believed that the teacher who did not keep his students interested was not likely to teach them much. As his written humor indicated, he was a master of the clever turn of phrase. Such a technique does not destroy the effectiveness of a lecture, it enhances it. He used humorous illustrations, but they were accurate ones. Because of his ambition to fire the interest of the student, he founded the McGill Political Economy Club,[9] the total expense of

which he paid himself during the twenty years he sponsored it.[10]

One of his faculty members of that time, Wallace Goforth, recalls that before the opening meeting of the Political Economy Club each year Leacock invited his staff to a stag dinner at his home. They were gay affairs with Leacock playing to perfection the role of host that he loved. Leading the way in the dinner talk, he used a salty vocabulary and a select store of stories, both of which he reserved for such gatherings as this one. Retrospect reveals, however, says Goforth, that not one of the stories could be called in bad taste. They were neither vulgar nor coarse. It was his custom to have at these dinners a guest of honor whom he drew out in conversation after dinner. Because of his own experience, he could never inflict real after-dinner speaking on any man. To one preclub dinner he invited Edward Peacock, director of the Bank of England and formerly his teaching companion at Upper Canada College. Not all of his guests, however, were so distinguished; Leacock in an almost uncanny fashion sensed which young men were going to make something of themselves. As one of his guests he had young Graham Towers, a minor bank official; in less than ten years Towers had become governor of the Bank of Canada and later was honored by the offer of an appointment as president of the Bank of America. Knowing that most of his students were not going to be academic economists, Leacock wanted to give them the opportunity of hearing and meeting men who were at work in the world they would enter.

When Stephen Leacock held a departmental meeting, he would abide none of the pedantry and stuffiness that frequently goes with such meetings. Though they were real academic sessions, there was a charm about them that his cohorts looked forward to. The staff exchanged ideas freely without wasting time discussing such nonsense as whether it would be all right for fourth-year men to write their exams in pencil. The meetings were efficient, unhurried ones, and they slowed down almost to stopping when there were questions which had to be deliberated, such as the separation of the honor students from the pass students. Stephen Leacock never mistook pleasantry for work.

One of Leacock's statements most often quoted in biographical sketches came from the preface to *Sunshine Sketches:*

> The writing of solid, instructive stuff fortified by facts and figures is easy enough. There is no trouble in writing a scientific treatise of the folk-lore of Central China, or a statistical enquiry into the declining population of Prince Edward Island. But to write something out of one's own mind, worth reading for its own sake, is an arduous contrivance only to be achieved in fortunate moments, few and far between. Personally, I would sooner have written "Alice in Wonderland" than the whole Encyclopaedia Britannica.[11]

This statement, perfectly honest on Leacock's part, distracted his public for the rest of his life from the fact

that he was a contributor to the Encyclopaedia Britannica, indeed one of its important contributors. He was first asked to write for the thirteenth edition (1926); in this edition five articles bore the signature, SLEA: "New Brunswick," "Nova Scotia," "Ontario," "Prince Edward Island," and "Quebec." To these were added others in later editions until the 1950 editions carried eight additional sections: "Alberta," "British Columbia," "Canada" (in part), "Humour," "Manitoba," "Montreal," "Northwest Territories," and "Saskatchewan." The editors of the 1954 edition found his articles still sound enough that they simply added material to bring them up to date and, Leacock would have been proud to note, they allowed the section on humor to stand as it was. It was still good criticism and good analysis.

When Beatrix died, Stephen had to make some sort of arrangement for maintaining a household in Montreal. There was a young son to take care of, a house to run, and entertaining to do. Shortly before the tragedy, he had employed a new secretary, Grace Reynolds. She was only eighteen, but he asked her to take over the management of his home. She was given complete care of the housekeeping, buying, banking, and entertaining.

Professor Leacock was not, Miss Reynolds remembers, a hard man to work with, but he insisted that the household be conducted according to his rules. They always dressed for dinner; Leacock wore a loose dinner jacket and an old-fashioned dress shirt with a pleated front. His tie, he never managed; it either hung in a

very loose bow or was simply wrapped into an overhand knot with the ends dangling.[12] Practicing one of the little economies he delighted in, he wore the dress shirt to classes the next day with an ordinary collar. Soup, which he wanted almost every evening, had to be served in a tureen. Leacock, of course, continued his accustomed early rising. After he had been up for an hour or so, he would make tea for Grace and Stevie and about six o'clock would wake them. They would have tea in the study with Leacock, and then, in good weather, they might accompany him for a walk around the mountain. Good weather or not, Leacock went on his hike.

He had returned from his jaunt one day and before going to school asked his housekeeper for pocket money. She asked him what he had done with the ten dollars she had supplied the night before in answer to the same request. Leacock reluctantly admitted that on his walk he had met a cleaning woman who had lost the address of the house she was to go to. "She was crying," said Leacock, and he had given her the ten dollars. "I didn't have anything any smaller."

About the middle of October of 1926 Stephen Leacock received a rather strange letter from V. C. Clinton-Baddeley, a history don of Jesus College, Cambridge. Clinton-Baddeley had adapted Leacock's parody "Behind the Beyond" for dramatic production in his amateur stage group. It had been accepted with such acclaim that he wanted to try to place it professionally. As the correspondence ran well into 1927, Leacock agreed to

the collaboration and wished him well. Clinton-Baddeley was, of course, quite pleased when St. Martin's Theater accepted "Behind the Beyond" as a curtain raiser for *Berkeley Square,* and he prophesied to Leacock that it would run for two weeks and maybe three. Both men were pleasantly shocked when the little play was held for eighty-four performances, paying Leacock sixty-one pounds. Something over two hundred and fifty dollars was hardly a windfall for Leacock, but it added to the success of an already successful book. And the triumph came at a time when Leacock needed the boost.

By 1927, Leacock had written a great many books and was, of course, in almost continuous correspondence with his publishers. In addition to books he was planning, Leacock was concerned with the details of reprinting his old books. This year, for example, Leacock wrote Dodd, Mead and Company a short note on the small, neat, black-edged stationery he was still using, accepting reduced royalties to keep *Essays and Literary Studies* in print.[13]

Stephen Leacock by this time had become a social lion, and he was entertained as often as he had guests himself. He did not enjoy being lionized, but he felt his responsibility as a guest and tried not to be a disappointment. Many of the dinner parties that he went to were huge affairs of nearly a hundred guests. Since this was the kind of occasion that would have thrilled his young housekeeper, Leacock, an understanding person, as his humor showed, reported each evening what

the women had worn, who was there, and what had happened.

He needed someone to see that Stevie took his medicine on time. "It never occurred to Dr. Leacock that he could do it himself," said Miss Reynolds. Leacock also engaged a governess for his son; his real companionship with the boy was not to come until later. It had become increasingly evident that Stephen, Jr., was not growing as he should. He was under the care of the best pediatrician in Montreal, but Leacock heard of a doctor in New York who was very hopeful of endocrine gland treatments that he was giving. Dr. Goldbloom, Leacock's Montreal doctor, was advised by the secretary of the New York Medical Association that the gland specialist was too enthusiastic, that he gave parents false hopes.[14] Nevertheless, on May 6 Leacock and his son went to New York, where the specialist prescribed a series of hormone tablets.[15] Sometime later Leacock, the man of vision, the man who could see this year's garden where last year's weeds were still standing, wrote, "I think he's growing. But I hate to measure him."[16] As a matter of fact, the growth he wished so desperately did not come until much later when, almost suddenly, Stephen, Jr., reached a short but normal height. For now, however, the medical world recommended sunlight and sea air. Florida was covered by the dry blanket of prohibition, and Leacock chose Europe.

Leacock, Stevie, Grace, and some Montreal friends sailed for England the first of May, 1927.[17] Once on

the boat, Leacock thoughtfully arranged for a stewardess to take care of Stevie so that Grace might be free
to enter the social life on board. He gave a cocktail
party for Grace, helped her enter into the shipboard
activities, and chaperoned her meetings with the young
electrical engineers aboard. As a chaperone, he kept
popping up out of stairways and from around corners,
talking about the ship or phosphorescent fish. Then he
would turn to Grace and say, "You know the hours
before twelve are more valuable than those after."

When they reached London, Leacock, between re-
newing old friendships and visiting with his son, took
Grace to see the London Tower, Westminster Abbey,
the changing of the guards at Buckingham Palace, and
all the things a tourist was supposed to see. Then one day,
trying to make her content with a responsibility she was
tiring of, he said, "Grace, there are lots more places in
London you ought to see, but I'm too old to take you.
You ought to see some of the supper clubs." All his life
Stephen Leacock was a manager; this was just one more
little drama to work out—besides, he did not like supper
clubs. He wired one of the young engineers from the
boat to have dinner with him. The three of them had
hardly started their soup when the waiter came and, as
he had been carefully coached, called Leacock away,
leaving Grace and the engineer to tour the clubs.

When the summer really started, they all went on to
Biarritz where the sea and sun were supposed to do
wonders for young Stevie. Leacock felt at home in
France; his knowledge of French was still superb and

he had kept in practice in Montreal, where his closest friend was René du Roure, head of the French department. Miss Reynolds, speaking no French and getting more homesick, soon returned to Montreal with much regret at leaving the Leacocks and their friends but none at abandoning the situation at Biarritz. Throughout the trip Leacock had demonstrated his kindliness, and she was always to remember the gentleman who was so considerate. The Leacocks made a short trip into Spain and then returned to Montreal, where his niece took over Leacock's affairs. Barbara Ulrichsen, the daughter of Stephen's sister Carrie, became the manager, personal secretary, friend, and companion of Leacock until after his retirement. The bond between them grew until it was one of the strongest in Leacock's life.

The visit to Biarritz had precluded any real publication for Leacock in 1927, though he had written a little essay "On Literature" for *The Times* while he was in London.[18] When he returned from Biarritz, Stephen Leacock lent his name to a new fight, that for the control of cancer. He had early entered the struggle when he addressed the New York society shortly after Beatrix's death.[19] In 1928 he began in earnest. He invited Dr. John C. A. Gerhster of the American Society for the Control of Cancer to speak at McGill.[20] His correspondence, as preserved in his files, was heavy that year with letters of appeal to influential members of his own as well as other faculties. He ran an advertisement in the *Star* at his own expense on "The Problem of Cancer."[21] He distributed posters and spoke before civic

groups. He even wrote, printed, and distributed "A Proposal for a Montreal Association for Cancer Control and Cancer Research," a single sheet which he sent out by the hundreds. He waged a fight to set up a cancer research program at McGill. But it was before the days of applying advertising methods to national welfare problems in Canada, and the university authorities turned him down. The extent of his failure or the irony of it could not be seen until his death.

IX

1928–1931

LEACOCK returned to publication in 1928 with *Short Circuits*. This volume, one of his largest—more than three hundred thirty pages—was the poorest single book of humor he ever wrote. Undoubtedly his bereavement diminished his motive for writing, but the major reason was the pace he had set for himself. He was writing too fast and too much in the limited time he had for composition. One or two pieces, like "Old Junk and New Money," could stand beside his previous production, but most of the fifty-odd selections were mere strained suggestions of fun, never developed properly. The reader started "Literature and the Eighteenth Amendment," and found that "since the Eighteenth Amendment . . . writers of fiction, poetry, and drama have found themselves under a handicap. In the stories of today they are unable to give their characters a drink. . . . When we realize how much of our literature . . . for centuries past has depended, rightly or wrongly, for conviviality on the drinking of toasts and healths,

on wassail and on Xmas, on stirrup cups and Auld Lang Synes—we can see how hard it is, in literature, to do without it"; this beginning foretold high humor. Then the reader went on to find what Leacock did with the idea:

> As the pea soup circulated freely, a new animation seemed to come to the guests. Lord Dangerdog, already at his second plateful, smiled across at Lady Angela . . . while the young girl herself hid her blushing face in her soup to avoid the boldness of his eye.
>
> "Come," said the host, turning to his English guest, "let me pledge you in another stick of celery," and, suiting the action to the word, he held aloft a magnificent bunch of Kalamazoo celery, and with the words, "Let us eat to our English visitor," he devoured the entire bunch in a single mouthful.
>
> Then beckoning to the noiseless butler to whom he passed at the same time the key of the cellar, "Meadows," he said, "fetch me up some of the old soup: it's in the fourth trough on the left.[1]

This was not without humor, but it was not as funny as it should have been. With his usual fine critical eye Leacock had seen where the humor lay, but he could not bring it off this time. There had been some evidence of Leacock's straining for humor since *Behind the Beyond:* the death of his wife could not be counted the total reason for the lessening in power. Stephen Leacock was working too hard at being a funny man, and it was the hard work showing through which ruined

the fun. His humor had always seemed spontaneous and fresh; now it seemed labored. Perhaps, too, the increased time he was giving his students turned his mind to more serious topics.

Certainly two of his best articles were written in 1928. The St. Louis *Post-Dispatch,* planning a semicentennial anniversary edition, asked Stephen Leacock to comment on the future of American humor. He answered with gusto and distinction, displaying, as he had in previous essays on the same general subject, a wide reading in the earlier humorists.[2] The same year he submitted his second paper to the Royal Society of Canada. On the same program during which he read the paper appeared B. K. Sandwell, whom he had nominated as a fellow in 1925.[3] "The Economic Aspect of Aviation," a timely paper, merited publication in the proceedings of the society, a distinction by no means granted to all papers read before the body.[4]

Stephen Leacock was continually importuned, recalls his son, to join the exodus to Hollywood about this time. Douglas Fairbanks and his Toronto-born wife, Mary Pickford during their frequent visits to Canada in the late 1920's, almost pleaded with him to come write for their company, United Artists Corporation. At the same time Charlie Chaplin was bidding for his services. Both sources were offering salaries which seemed magnificent even to a successful writer like Leacock, but he was forced by his own foresight to refuse. He liked the life of a professor, which he would have had to give up. Besides, he said, his training as an economist told him

that the man who had a secure position was going to be the lucky one; a break was coming in the current economic high standard. Later, of course, the whole world knew it.

Stephen Leacock was not all business; at the same time he was refusing big money because of the impending crash, he was accepting small checks from a little magazine called the *Goblin*, just because he liked the editor. The *Goblin* had started in 1921 as a college magazine with twenty-four associate editors and no business manager. No such publishing venture has ever succeeded, and the comic magazine eventually fell into the hands of one of the original editors, Joe McDougall. By 1928 the *Goblin* had no connection with the University of Toronto where it started, but Leacock persisted in pretending that it was still a college publication, because this allowed him to accept the reduced rate with a clear conscience. When McDougall sent him a modest check for an article he had written and expressed the hope that he might find time to write something every month, Leacock graciously answered, "You're too generous but I'll help."[5] Leacock, of course, did not need the money; this year his literary efforts had paid him more than twenty-one thousand dollars.

At Orillia, Leacock finally found time to do something he had intended to do for some time. He discovered that the house he had built at Old Brewery Bay was too close to the lake. There would be a better view, and the house itself would appear to a better advantage if he moved it back. He had considered build-

ing a new house similar to the old one when he arranged for a firm of architects, Wright and Nixon, to draw up plans in 1922,[6] but he decided to move the original house up the hill. The construction men he called in to do the job had to tell him as tactfully as possible that, while it was a fine house where it stood, he and Bill Jones had not built the house so that it could be moved. Leacock exploded, "Well, by God, you can knock it down, can't you?" and he ordered another house built a hundred yards up the slope from the lake.

The new house, the one presently operated as the Stephen Leacock Memorial Home, was designed by Leacock, who, himself, drew the first rough plans for it. A nineteen-room, hospitable-looking lodge, it incorporated several features which suited Stephen Leacock personally. His own wing was carefully separated from the rest of the house, and the glass-enclosed gallery running along the back of the house was the kind of bright, cheerful room Leacock meant it to be. The walls throughout the house were paneled in mellow Norwegian fir, which glowed as dusk made it necessary to turn on the lamps along the walls. The basement, besides a wine cellar and two furnaces, housed a large billiard room with its own fireplace. George had evidently arranged for the equipment, because Brunswick-Balke-Collender Company wrote Leacock shortly before the table was delivered:

Acknowledging your second wire as follows, "Will pay $575.00 just the same, you and my brother split

the difference." We are mailing you two copies, which you will note are made out for that amount, and we would greatly appreciate your signing and returning one copy, keeping the other copy for your records.

The Factory is already working on the Table, and we will have delivery of same made before the 18th of this month, as you desire.

The writer earnestly hopes that you will find this table to be everything he promised, including extra heavy slate, steel rails, Rex cushions, and several first class features, and looks forward to hearing from you after you and your friends have used same for two weeks or so.

We have no doubt that your brother has many charities to which he can devote the $25.00 which we will mail him when everything is happily delivered. . . .[7]

This was a house Leacock and his friends could be comfortable in.

The new house was a more fundamental alteration of the estate than usual, but it was simply a part of the pattern of perpetual change. Leacock never stopped working on the estate, though the annual expansion was likely to be more on the order of the sundial he erected the next year. Like the other changes, too, the sundial bore the mark of the writer. The dial itself was a common cast-brass design with a Browning inscription, "Grow old along with me, the best is yet to be," but in the cement around the base Leacock scrawled:

HORAS BREVES ANNOS LONGOS

HIC
SOL
ILLUMINET
AD MCMXXIX

If there was not the sundial to put up, there was the tennis court to line off, or the garden to plan, or a walk to lay out, extravagantly wide and straight as the eye could make it, right to the boathouse. Of course there was fishing to be done too. Leacock, not content with fishing in the lake, leased a trout stream from his friend John Drinkwater. He dammed up the stream to form a good pool, and, to complete an angler's dream, stocked it with fifteen thousand dollars' worth of speckled trout.[8]

Whatever Stephen Leacock did, he did it enthusiastically. He liked to put on plays with the children, staging them in the living room or on the lawn, when they were presented at his house. Frequently he merely helped Mrs. Shaw, his neighbor around the bay. And, indeed, probably more of the little dramas were produced on her lawn than elsewhere. But when he worked up one of his plays for the children, he had programs printed at the *Packet-Times* office:

The Old Brewery
Players
present
RED RIDING HOOD
UP TO DATE

After a cast of characters which included Stevie, Peggy Shaw, and anyone else he could find, including Mlle. Castillon, Peggy's governess, down at the bottom of the sheet appeared:

Stage Management by Captain R. du Roure
Costumes from Northway
Lighting Effects from the Orillia Power Commission
Refreshments from Barrie[9]

The wolf became Lord Wolf, "*Son and Heir of the Marquis of Snarl*," who was dangerous only because his father had disinherited him. To her Grandmamma, Miss Riding Hood took *pâté de foie gras, champignons aux truffles*, and a pint of Pommery. Another play, "Beauty and the Boss," presented New Year's Eve, had at the bottom of the program:

The Road not being passable for motors, a sleigh will be at Anderson's Livery at 3:30 P.M. very sharp. Tea, Refreshments and Cold Buffet Supper 5–7 P.M.[10]

Though clever, the plays were simple enough; but, when Leacock touched them, they turned into extravaganzas.

Something of this characteristic *élan* was evident in his relations with the library at McGill. One observer remembered that Leacock always came in just before class, with "giant and hasty strides,"[11] to get books for immediate use in his classes. Perhaps his own well-ordered life made him impatient with waiting on other people. His gruff chiding of the slow feet of the stack boy, however, was always accompanied by the twinkle

in his eye. His book orders to Redpath Library at McGill were extensive—sometimes marked advertisements, sometimes short notices, and sometimes carefully evaluated lists of books. In answer to what was evidently an announcement of budgetary difficulty, he wrote the librarian:

> Dear Lomer,
>   Yours 19th. I propose to go on sending in lists of books that ought to be ordered. If the college can't buy them that's too bad. But list is necessary anyway.
>   Please buy in arrears. Wait till the money comes in and then spend it.
>   1 a.m.[12]

Leacock was a familiar figure in the library, visiting it often and using it frequently. Goforth remembered walking with Leacock between the shelves of new acquisitions in the library. They carried on an engaging conversation, nodding pleasantly at the books occasionally. Finally they became engrossed in a fine point of theoretical economics, on which Leacock expounded in eager tones. When they reached the end of the stacks, however, Leacock broke off the discussion momentarily to dictate to the attendant half a dozen titles which he wanted placed on reserve for his students. While he had never missed a word of the conversation, he had quietly picked out and stored in his capacious mind titles of the books he needed.

One day Wallace Goforth brought into Leacock's office a skit by an English humorist. He had enjoyed

reading it so much the night before that he wanted Leacock to read it. Stephen picked it up and began to chuckle as he read the first paragraph; then laid it down and said, still chuckling, "I know how the rest of it goes. I see how the man's mind works." He went on, developing the idea in the same line as the original article. He stopped once and said, apologetically, "There's really nothing to it. Once you know what you're making fun of, and for whom, it can only go one way." He continued with the sketch, frequently following so closely that it seemed a paraphrase and, once or twice, almost a quotation.

This was the way Stephen Leacock's mind worked. He had a highly developed faculty for analysis, whether he applied it to humor or economics or history or chess. He read enormously, though, as his brother George said, "You never caught him at it," and he never forgot anything he read. Though he cared little for statistics, he remembered them, insisting all the time that the figures were not the important thing but what the figures proved. He taught his classes with this idea in mind. He saw no practical value in spouting pages of data on tariff if he were going finally to have to interpret the figures himself. His advanced students learned to handle the statistics of trade balances and wheat futures as they were supposed to, but he did not press the ridiculous point with his undergraduate classes. Their first job was, as he saw it, to learn how the science worked; then they could learn to work it themselves.

His students came to appreciate the inexhaustible

vitality of the man who taught hard every time he met the class and still had the energy and understanding to put on a show occasionally. As Leacock became more of a legend, his class meetings drew more visitors; frequently the back row would be filled with students from other faculties who had free time and who liked to hear Leacock talk. It was not unusual for a visiting debate team or football squad to join his class as an anticipated part of their sightseeing. On these occasions, Leacock would come into his room, recounts Ted Harris, and, noting the visitors, would give his class a knowing look. Then he would launch into a real show: he would talk about economics, but he would play the funny man. It was two-edged humor; the guests were entertained outrageously, but the class was in on the real joke, that this was not the real Leacock at all. His students were not surprised when one day one of the most haughty of the faculty stuck his head into Leacock's room to get his attention. Leacock turned and when he saw who it was called out cheerily, "Come in, professor, and hear a decent lecture for a change."[13] His lectures were not all jocularity, and they were not always charming, but they were never dull. When he said, "That'll be all for today," his students, always filling the room because they did not cut his class, were not already on their feet. Stephen Leacock saw no reason why wisdom could not be combined with wit, and he dispensed his own masterful blend of the two for thirty-five years. The students came to regard him with such affection, one person noted, that

at a large student gathering "the entire audience rose and shouted with one voice, 'We want Stevie!' "[14]

Leacock carried the same charm for his public audiences that he did for his academic listeners. As his voluminous files of correspondence attest, whoever heard him became a hard-working publicity agent. Scores of letters begin, "Mr. Brown, who heard you speak in Pottsville, is very anxious that we should have you address our group." By this time Leacock was receiving as much as five hundred dollars for some lectures, and he had all the dates he felt he could take and still continue his university work properly. His lectures were widespread in subject matter, locality, and audience. He spoke to the YM and YWHA in Philadelphia on "Frenzied Fiction"; a short time later he addressed the Montreal Rotary Club on economic independence for Canada.[15] By now Leacock was quite familiar with his lectures, but he always made new notes, usually scribbling them on the stationery of the hotel where he stayed.[16] The outline did not always follow the same plan; it was typical of Leacock that he try to make the speech fresh for his audience. Another gesture which pointed up the innate kindness and graciousness of the man was his practice of sending an autographed copy of one of his books to the person who had acted as his host.[17] The token was not necessary, and the people had not expected it, but they loved him for it.

In addition to an essay on William Sidney Porter, in which he continued his defense of O. Henry, Leacock wrote one book in 1929. Like its companion volumes of

this period, *The Iron Man and the Tin Woman* was not the rich Leacockian humor of his earliest work, but it was certainly better than *Short Circuits*. *The Iron Man and the Tin Woman* was largely built around the idea of what the future held for society. Leacock projected the contemporary society of 1929 to ridiculous limits. "Life's Little Inconsistencies" was typical of most of the volume:

"Gee!" said the college professor of English to the farmer, "this is certainly a pretty layout. I'll say it is!"

"Yes," answered the farmer, "we like to think that this view from our veranda is really quite as beautiful as any landscape could be. My wife often compares it with Versailles. . . ."

"It's certainly a peach, all right," said the professor.

"I like it especially," the farmer went on, "when the sun sets and the twilight steals over it all. It gives one a sort of hushed feeling—I can't express it—but something almost reverential."

"I know what you mean," said the professor, "it gets your goat."[18]

As had been the case too often recently, Leacock had chosen a situation which had the basic incongruity to make good humor, but he did not take advantage of its natural quality. The piece was too studied and it had a false ring. A very important part of Leacock's craft had been his own obvious acceptance of the story he was telling. He told the tallest tale as if he believed it. Sometimes his attitude now seemed to be that nobody be-

lieved this story but let us all laugh anyway. On the other hand, "Further Progress in Specialization" was as clever as anything he had done in some time. In it the barber became Dr. Follicle, who "carried after his name the degrees of Cap. D. from Harvard, Doc. Chev. from Paris, and was an Honorary Shampoo of half a dozen societies." He accepted the incoming "patients" and his

trained gaze at once recognized a certain roughness in the skin, as if of a partial growth of hair coming through the surface, which told the whole tale. He asked, however, a few questions as to personal history, parentage, profession, habits, whether sedentary or active, and so on, and then with a magnifying glass made a searching examination of the patient's face.

He shook his head.

"I think," he said, "there is no doubt about your trouble. You need a shave."

The patient's face fell a little at the abrupt, firm announcement. He knew well that it was the expert's duty to state it to him flatly and fairly. He himself in his inner heart had known it before he had come in. But he had hoped against hope perhaps he didn't need it after all; perhaps he could wait; later on, perhaps, he would accept it. Thus he had argued to himself, refusing, as we all refuse, to face the cruel and inevitable fact.[19]

This was the Leacock of old; he believed society could come to this, and he was afraid of it. Several other sketches, such as "The Life of J. Correspondence

Smith" and "When Social Regulation is Complete," were equally good. In his mock correspondence course in "How to Come In Out of the Wet," his gibe at modern education had some of the sharpness of his old-time nonsense. The humorist proved that he could still write good humor, but in the same book he showed that he could not keep up the pace. However, in the last year of the boom economy, this book, with his other limited literary endeavors, earned Leacock about nineteen thousand dollars in addition to his five-thousand-dollar academic salary.

In spite of the publication of three books the next year, Leacock's income dropped below twenty thousand for the first time in fifteen years. The depression had hit, of course, and Leacock, who had been drawing extremely high royalties, was forced to accept a lower percentage. Even on *The Iron Man and the Tin Woman,* Frank Dodd had written Stephen that his usual twenty per cent was too high.[20] Leacock insisted on the regular terms, however, and Dodd acquiesced "because other elements than mere profit enter into business arrangements with authors whom we value highly, and with whom we have been associated for many years."[21] When asked to accept a royalty of ten per cent on the anthology on 1930, Leacock countered by telegram:

WILL ACCEPT TEN PERCENT ON FOUR THOUSAND AFTER THAT TWENTY.[22]

Frank Dodd agreed to the four thousand limit but offered fifteen per cent for all sold over that amount. Lea-

cock replied that he would accept those terms but added: "It is only fair to say that when I have a book to sale [sic] I think I can get 20% for it: but I may be mistaken."[23] Stephen Leacock came to see that the days of twenty per cent royalties were over, and his reduced income for 1930 was simply an indication of the times.

Still, seventeen thousand was no mean figure, and the two books of humor were not new volumes, but collections of his earlier work. Both *Laugh with Leacock*, published in the United States, and *The Leacock Book*, published in England, were anthologies of the best he had written, probably indicating that the publishers thought he was finished as a humorist. Publishers frequently resorted to anthologies to get the last sale out of a once-popular author. Both books had a good sale, the New York volume requiring six editions, and Leacock could count it a successful year in spite of the stock market crash.

His other book, *Economic Prosperity in the British Empire*, and the single article he wrote this year, "On Empire Trade,"[24] were on a subject dear to the heart of the author. Imperial preference had been proposed at the Imperial Conference at London in 1926. Because the theory stated that all goods produced by members of the Empire be given preferential tariff treatment within the Empire, Canada and Leacock were for it. England, who had been collecting duties on Empire goods, was against it. *Economic Prosperity in the British Empire* was a strongly argued case for imperial preference. As his publication had already proved, Leacock

was a practical economist; theory, as such, impressed him not nearly so much as the theory applied. He was not willing to sit in his office and write scholarly criticism and analysis of an interesting problem. Believing in imperial preference, he turned his pen to making it a reality. The reception of his book in England was about what might be expected. *The Times*, which had always been very kind to his humor—even his bad humor—said:

> It bristles with questionable epigrams, skates lightly over practical issues and waves aside both economic theory and statistical method. Few economists will be impressed with the shortcuts the author takes "through the jungle of statistics," or with his pieces of "financial magic in which something is made out of nothing."[25]

What *The Times* failed to see, or, perhaps better, pretended not to see, was that Leacock was not trying to convince economists that the move was the right one. The economists alone were not going to vote. Even the Orillia Board of Trade understood it better; they sent one thousand copies of a special edition of the book to England, one to every member of Parliament, one to each of the one hundred important editors, and the rest to others who they thought could help the cause.[26] Leacock was not even talking to people who understood very well the real use of statistics; he did not care whether they understood it or not. He had studied the statistics, he understood them, now he was trying to tell

the legislator and citizen what he saw as the truth. He did not want an argument; he wanted imperial preference. His two articles of the next year were concerned with the same problem, and he was to have still more to say on the subject.[27]

Wet Wit and Dry Humor in 1931 attacked Prohibition, a problem which Stephen Leacock felt almost as strongly about as imperial preference. The book was dedicated: "in friendly appreciation of Prohibition in the United States, the greatest thing that ever happened —to Canada." Much of the contents had appeared in others of his books first, but some of the new material shone with a brilliance not seen since his very earliest work. In "A Butler of the Old School," the narrator was conducted through the cellars of the 1860 house he was visiting. Here he found vintage Rain Water from the year of the Johnstown flood, and rare Ditchwater with just the right body—a cheap, commercial Ditchwater has "either got too much mud in it, or it's so thin it has no strength." He found "French Tap Water bottled in Paris, Pump Water from the town pump of the early nineteenth century, Trough Water from an abandoned New England farm, English Pond Water in stone bottles, and Dutch Canal Water in tempting square bottles with yellow and green seals."[28] The essay ended with an orgy as they swilled West Indian Bilgewater, a hundred years old. This clever bit was what he had been trying to do in "Literature and the Eighteenth Amendment." "Confessions of a Soda Fiend" was written from a condemned cell, though the author had been

warned that his time was short; the mayor had graciously granted permission to use the cell, but the contractors wanted to start tearing down the condemned lock-up almost immediately. He confessed that his downfall followed the classic pattern: drink—"soda water, pop, and even lemon sour"—women—the girl who lured him to Sunday school where the collection plate broke him—and song—gramophone records of "Old Black Joe" and "Onward, Christian Soldiers." The whole parody bristled with such nonsense as had not been since Gertrude's lover galloped off in all directions:

I was born of a family in comfortable, if not affluent circumstances, of parents of sincere, if not profound, convictions, in a home that was educated if not cultivated, in a house that was rough cast if not brick, with plumbing that was effective, if not open.

I often sat at my book still long after nine at night, even till nine-thirty or nine thirty-five. . . .

To my mind a good woman is one of the greatest things on earth, second only perhaps to a good child or a good man.

I had soon abandoned all attempts at serious study; spent my whole evenings hanging around Sunday School and choir practice.[29]

Other sketches, including "The Revised or Dry Pickwick," were almost as good.

Perhaps it was his concern for the subject that caused the temporary renaissance of unstrained humor. This

was not the first blow Leacock had struck at prohibition. He had seen prohibition begin in 1915 and take over Canada by 1918. By 1927 Canada had abandoned prohibition for local option. Stephen Leacock had won the battle but lost the war; Orillia went dry. Leacock's old friend, Harold Hale, had been active on the side of the local drys, and Leacock was so provoked that he canceled his subscription to Hale's paper, the *Packet-Times*. The two men remained fast friends in spite of Leacock's temper. And Leacock had to send ten miles to Barrie, Ontario, for his whiskey.

Because of his temper, Leacock had rather haphazard relations with his servants. He once fired all the servants in the middle of a dinner party because Rosie, the maid, got mad when he shouted at her. Both they and he understood the situation, because the next morning they were still there and he hired them back at increased wages. Such occurrences were an exception to Leacock's usual behavior. Generally his attitude toward those who worked for him was kindly. Tina Kelly, who came to cook for Leacock at this time would work for no one else until Leacock died. Barbara, his niece who ran the house for him, had hired Tina against her better judgment, knowing that her uncle did not trust a French-Canadian to handle the many telephone calls which his position required. For three days she did not allow Tina to speak and reveal her accent. Through the years, Tina would report to Dr. Leacock that she had a brother or sister who wanted work. Leacock always generously employed them and once had seven from her

family working for him at the same time. He always gave Tina and her husband, John, his car when she wanted to visit her mother, and more than once, when John could not go, Leacock paid her fare to her mother's home. People who worked for Stephen Leacock very long came to understand that he was temperamental, but his kindliness was truly magnanimous.

X

1932-1933

WITH *Back to Prosperity; the Great Opportunity of the Empire Conference* in 1932, Leacock returned to the fight for reduced trade barriers within the Empire. The reviews he received proved that the earlier argument, presented by others, of course, as well as Leacock, had accomplished something. Said one English reviewer, "[It] should be read by anyone interested in the welfare of the Empire."[1] Another declared it should be read by every delegate to the Imperial Economic Conference.[2] Again Leacock was not interested in economic legerdemain; he wanted action. The Conference met at Ottawa late in the summer of 1932, and the first grudging progress toward imperial preference was made. The part Leacock played in its acceptance was not immediately obvious, but a number of economists, including Wallace Goforth, attribute to him certainly a part of that success. England had listened to Leacock for a long time—his stature was higher there than in Canada. Undoubtedly, Stephen Leacock's popu-

lar economics had helped make possible the new trade treaties.

Because he could and would write popular studies, and for a number of other reasons, Leacock's professional reputation was not equal to his literary one. It was a standing joke in professional circles that economists thought Leacock was a humorist and humorists thought he was an economist. Harold Innis, of the University of Toronto, classed him as a competent social scientist but not a great one.[3] A lesser critic had observed that he showed a "surprising grasp . . ." of the significance and influence of "certain political events,"[4] but this opinion was hardly shared by most of his contemporaries. They generally viewed him as misguided and shallow at best and fraudulent and subversive at worst.

Conservative Leacock was too liberal for his contemporaries. This was not the contradictory situation it seemed; Leacock's liberalism was in the method and approach rather than the theory of economics. To most other economists, conspicuous consumption was an interesting variable; to Leacock, it was people. Leacock understood the complex mathematical economics that Irving Fisher was turning out at Yale; Goforth was present at a staff meeting where Leacock not only demonstrated his grasp of Fisher but pointed out some errors which were to become obvious later. Leacock, however, was unable to view economics as the exact science it had to be for Fisher. Though it was a series of experiments which might yet give an answer, it was

not precise enough for a science. In the later days of his teaching, he wrote a memorandum, presumably to himself: "Recent Standard Treatises trying, for what they are worth, to keep up Economics as a System."[5] Leacock could have stated his quarrel with economics and political science quite simply; if they were worth the study, they should try to solve man's problems, not merely give names to them.

Part of Leacock's difficulty with his fellow social scientists lay in his humor. He poked fun at economics and political science and made money at it; his contemporaries could abide neither the attitude nor its result. With an average income of over twenty-five thousand, Leacock was making at least five times what his academic companions were making. Because social science was not his bread and butter, his critics thought he had really abandoned the field when he said it was not difficult to make Conservatism out of the economics learned in his class; "as a matter of fact we merely needed to mix a pint of pure economics with a gallon of wash and strain through an old flag. For Liberalism, much the same, warmed over hot air."[6] The critics forgot that Adam Smith and Thorstein Veblen had, with telling skill, satirized the existing order. Touchiness about their own studies plus envy of Leacock's financial success caused the scholars to turn their backs on him and even falsely accuse him of charlatanry.

On the other hand, there was ample evidence of Leacock's economic grasp and professional ability. The success of his students, who always gave him credit,

attested to his knowledge of the sciences he taught. His own investments and speculations, adding to the already envied income, showed he was a skilled practical economist. For example, he had his bank buy mining stock, a risky business at best, with the specific provision that it was to be sold in two months. Precisely two months to the day the bank notified him that he had netted a hundred dollars on the sale.[7] After Wallace Goforth left academic economics for the financial world, he was working with Mr. Eden, a top executive in the rubber industry. Eden was thrilled to discover one day that his companion knew Stephen Leacock. It was one of his life's ambitions, he said, to meet the man whose humor he had enjoyed so much. Knowing Leacock's capacity for friendship, Goforth assured him that such a meeting could be arranged; as a matter of fact, he would call him up right then. "Of course, Wally," said Leacock, "have lunch with me at the club tomorrow." Leacock continued with his work, classes in the afternoon and a lecture in the evening, but, in spite of the press of time, he met them the next day at lunch. For the next two and a half hours they talked rubber, from the wages paid at the plantation to the comparative efficiency of manufacturing methods. After they had left Leacock, Eden turned to Goforth with a bewildered look on his face. "That," he stated flatly, "was the most amazing person I ever met. I've learned more about rubber in two and a half hours than I have the rest of the time I've been in the business." Leacock's schedule

had obviously precluded any quick study on his part; he just knew.

Leacock was generally ahead of his day in his economic and political theories. He had little or nothing to do with socialism, which seemed, it is true, then to be the progressive movement. Leacock was a lifelong Conservative, but he was ahead of the Conservatives of his day. In the twenties his convictions were those of the mid-century Tory. He saw that a degree of social control by legislation was practically necessary and morally imperative. Early in the depression he pointed the way to recovery by the reduction of gold in the dollar. Although he was derided for his insistence on imperialism, it was too often ignored that his imperialism was not jingoistic; Leacock did want to retain an empire system, but he wanted a new one, an Empire bound by good will and co-operation.

Leacock's professional position was perhaps best presented in *Contemporary Political Science*, a UNESCO report. Stephen Leacock, the authors declared, was one of the first political economists in Canada to break away from preoccupation with purely fiscal problems.[8] This stated Leacock's belief admirably. Government was not a budget; it was a service for its citizens, and citizens were people. Economics should not be a game of juggling the figures of supply and demand; it should be an attempt at foretelling the demand far enough in advance that it could be supplied, or of determining the supply in time to divert the demand. People, not

science, should be served by statistics. There were many things wrong with Malthus's theory, but Leacock objected most to his discussing humanity as if he were talking about ciphers. Leacock was always concerned with the man who consumed conspicuously, who supplied and who demanded, who was governed politically, whether scientifically or not.

In spite of his skepticism concerning the infallibility of his subject, Leacock viewed the study of economics and political science as a serious business. His students were trained along the classical academic patterns. He was likely to express indignation when someone tried to get around the rules:

> In regards to Mr. Douglas W—'s application to enter 2nd year Ph.D.
>
> Objections:—
>
> i   He is late in applying.
>
> ii   The rules demand that he should follow out a course of study as arranged & approved by us in advance, and arising out of his previous work. He has not done this (see his letter of Sept. 30). He only says that when he selects his courses he will let us know.
>
> iii It is my personal opinion that Mr. W—'s previous work and attainment would not justify him on entering in Ph.D. work unless he did so with a full realization that he might or might not attain to a degree. This is a hard saying but it is better to be candid.

iv   Mr. W— must realize that the whole test of the
McGill Ph.D. in economics as planned & the central & dominant idea in it is that the candidate
present a *printed book* on his topic of such merit
that the dep't is glad to accept it as a Ph.D. publication.

_____

Now:—

Mr. W— is at London anyway. He is taking the
courses anyway. We didn't send him: we didn't
advise him: we don't control him.[9]

Leacock was not a martinet, but he did believe that
graduate work was important study and was not to be
approached casually. This dedication to his work did
not, of course, appear either to the public or to his
scholarly contemporaries.

Stephen Leacock did, of course, get some recognition
in his profession. In 1931 the recently reorganized Canadian Political Science Association elected him vice-
president.[10] He was re-elected to the same position the
next year when he presided at a seminar on "Current
Problems of Political Science."[11] In 1933, the association honored him by electing him president.[12] In his
presidential address, "The Revision of Democracy," he
again spoke of the Empire and the democratic proc-
esses within it, and he warned his audience, "Scholars
who love minutiae deny everything."[13]

Besides *Back to Prosperity*, Leacock published two
books of humor in 1932, wrote a biography, and edited
a volume of history. Leacock was asked by Lawrence

Burpee, noted historian and author, to edit the discursive and sometimes fantastic journal of Louis Armand de Lom d'Arce, Baron de Lahontan. Though Baron Lahontan had a Baron Munchausen reputation, Leacock believed his account to be generally valid and took on the job. Graphic Publishers, with whom Leacock signed the contract, went bankrupt before the book was issued, and he got not a penny for editing it and writing the introduction and notes. Publication of the book had been started, however, before the company failed, and a few copies of *Lahontan's Voyages* had been bound. Much to Leacock's surprise they appeared years later in secondhand bookstores, having been sold with the rest of the stock as remaindered books. In spite of all his work, Leacock was never able to get a copy.[14]

His experience with the biography was happier. *Mark Twain,* a slim volume, was written in a popular style with Leacock's own wit evident in it. Perhaps, he said, Mark Twain had not invented American humor but "he at least took it over and made something out of it. He did for it what Shakespeare did for the English drama, and what Milton did for Hell."[15] The book was marred by its dependence on Van Wyck Brooks's exaggerated *The Ordeal of Mark Twain,* but otherwise it was what it was intended for, a familiar, chatty study of a man whom Leacock admired greatly. It played up the romantic qualities of Mark Twain's life, and in fact was but a charming story which offered no new critical appraisal at all. Leacock's interpretive eye was blinded by his affection for his subject. Whether he acknowl-

edged it or not—he never denied it—Leacock owed much to Mark Twain. The earlier author had made Leacock's kind of humor popular and socially acceptable. After Mark Twain, one could be both a funny man and a respectable citizen. A biography should have some reason for being written; if it does not offer new criticism, it should justify its existence some other way. The affection with which Leacock wrote was not new; Paine's work had been affectionate. What Leacock offered was sympathy. He understood Mark Twain's suffering when he spoke seriously and everyone laughed; Leacock had suffered himself. He appreciated the humor Mark Twain had found in the Bible; he had seen it himself, but like Twain he could not write it. As he said, "People who read the Bible don't want it made fun of, and the people who don't read the Bible don't see any fun to make of it."[16] *Mark Twain* was by no means an idolatrous book. Leacock found much of the humor outdated, as when he judged Twain's book, *Christian Science:*

> He could not see that Christian Science would . . . become . . . just a way of "going to church. . . ." "Christian Scientists" who call in doctors become like Methodists who dance and Presbyterians who don't go to hell. Mark Twain needn't have worried.[17]

It was such original humor as this plus the sympathy of one humorist for another that made *Mark Twain* an acceptable unit in the endless line of biographical studies of America's most native writer.

The two volumes of humor which appeared in 1932

were disappointing. *Afternoons in Utopia,* directing most of its humor against left-wing politics, was not far above the level of his worst work. Most of its contents was pointed at socialism and communism—a pair of targets which should have inspired Conservative Leacock—but "Utopia, Old and New" and "The Band of Brothers, Being the Memoirs of a Future Communist" were strained and silly. The other book, *The Dry Pickwick,* was little more than *Wet Wit and Dry Humor* done in an English accent. The first had been compiled expressly for prohibition-ridden America. *The Dry Pickwick* had to replace those pieces which depended on the Volstead Act for their fun, and the replacements were not as good as the originals. Such bits as "The Great War as Recorded by Mr. William Shakespeare" and "A, B, and C after Twenty Years" he had done before—and better.

Five books left Leacock little time for serious periodical publication, but the two articles he did write fitted the general scheme of his other writing. Leacock, who liked to waste nothing, applied the work he had done on the Lahontan book to an article for the *Canadian Geographical Journal,* about Lahontan's role in Canada.[18] In "If Gold Should Cease to Be 'Gold'" he again showed himself to be concerned with economic practice rather than theory. Economists tell us, he said, that we do not need gold as the basis of our money. Leacock's objection was that the economist had forgotten the difference between us and money. Money did not need gold; anything would do for a basis, but

man needed gold as a money base because too many
people were involved in gold as a business to take away
its reason for being.[19]

He followed this the next year with *Stephen Leacock's Plan to Relieve the Depression in 6 Days, to Remove It in 6 Months, to Eradicate It in 6 Years*. In it
he advocated reducing the gold in the dollar from
twenty-three grains to seventeen grains. Because gold
was material and could be controlled, the resulting price
rise could be controlled. It could be done, he said, with
"inflation" by unbacked paper money but it would be
"as hard to maintain as it is to keep a man one-quarter
of one per cent intoxicated under the Volstead Act."[20]
In "The Economic Analysis of Industrial Depression,"
published the same year, he reflected that Stephen Leacock's Plan was now being called Mr. Roosevelt's Plan
because it was going to be used.[21]

During its fiftieth annual meeting in 1932, Leacock
sent the Royal Society of Canada a note in which he
resigned from the Society on the grounds of "personal
economy." The chairman commented, with some confusion, "This seems to be a serious document."[22] His
confusion was understandable. Stephen Leacock's finances were in good condition, and, besides, one did
not resign from the Royal Society. Pelham Edgar's explanation was that Professor Mavor had attacked a
paper which Leacock had read to the Society, stating,
"It was an outrage that the Royal Society should have
presented to it a paper so inept and so lacking in the
fundamental principles of economic science."[23] Edgar

then explained that Leacock resigned, using economy as an excuse.

As dramatic as the story is—so dramatic that there must be some truth in it—evidence does not support it. The only paper Leacock read before Mavor's death in 1925 was "On the Grain of Truth in Popular Economic Fallacies," in 1923.[24] This was the kind of paper Mavor would have attacked, but his name does not appear in the list of those present at the meeting. More important, it is unbelievable that Leacock should have taken offense and resigned nine years later, after having read a second paper in 1928. Leacock's niece, who was with him at the time of the resignation, heard no criticism of Mavor, or any disturbance about the affair. Leacock was in the middle of one of his periodic economy drives, and he cut out his membership to the Canadian Authors Association and others at the same time. The fees were a drain on his income, and Leacock was determined to build up an estate to leave his son.

The word of an eminent scholar like Pelham Edgar is, however, not so easily disregarded. The solution must be that Mavor's name was accidentally left off the roll, and that he did launch the rather violent and ill-mannered attack against Leacock's paper. But evidently Edgar was more impressed by the outburst than was Leacock. In Leacock's situation, Edgar himself would have resigned, and in later years thought Leacock had. Leacock simply outlived his critic.

One writer, in 1933, suggested that Stephen Leacock should be knighted.[25] Because such appointments in

Canada were controlled by the Liberal Prime Minister, Conservative Leacock could not expect to gain knighthood unless he worked for it at least a little. Perhaps because of his early aversion to titles, perhaps for sake of pride, he made no such attempt, though he did remark later to his son that maybe he should have tried it, "It would have been so good for the sale of my books in the United States." Leacock understood his international reading public even better than they understood themselves.

This year Leacock lost one of his closest friends. Sir Arthur Currie, principal of McGill University for thirteen years, died in office. Sir Arthur's administration had been a good one for Leacock. He had found the principal a man of his word and had grown more fond of him through the years. In tribute, Stephen Leacock wrote in the Montreal *Herald:*

> It is as a great soldier that the world at large mourns General Currie today. It is right that it should be so. His great achievement was in arms. Those who know tell us that he was one of the great generals of the War; and that if the War had continued, his record, scarcely more than begun, would have placed him among the great captains of the ages.
>
> But there are those of us who were not privileged to know him in this wider horizon. Our memory of him is that of his thirteen years as our principal at McGill. There he sat in his college office room, ready and accessible to all of us. Beside him was his pipe

with plenty of strong tobacco and plenty of strong language to keep it burning.

There was a man! I have known many college principals and presidents,—a poor lot most of them, with a few brave exceptions here and there. But there never was one to match up to General Currie. College presidents, as a lot, must bow to the rich and fawn for benefactions. Not so General Currie. He thought no more of a plutocrat than of a ninepin.

College presidents must be careful what they say and how they say it. Not so General Currie. He said what he thought and he said it in his own way,— which was a forceful one. He knew some of the strongest words in our language. Nor was there ever such honesty as his.

For General Currie owed no responsibility to any man. For that he looked elsewhere. Never was there a man so deeply religious in the real meaning of the word. He lived, in peace as in war, with the consciousness of the imminence of death. For him life was but a pathway to something else, and he walked the path with a sense of its meaning and its end that never left him for a day. Beside him as he walked was the shadowed curtain of the infinite.

General Currie knew nothing of scholarship in the narrower sense of the term. His dusty, shabby professors were always a sort of mystery to him. He could never quite understand whether they were researching or loafing. When he first came to us, he im-

agined that the professors were always buried in the library, each lecture planned and prepared like Vimy Ridge.

Later on he was a little disillusioned. "Some of these gentlemen," he said, only that was not the name he used for them; he had a simpler one, "don't research at all." They were like hens that wouldn't lay. But disillusioned or not he was unfailing in the devotion of his leadership.

We never had the place in his heart that he kept for his generals. Nor had we the right to it. His generals were always there in his mind, all nicknamed and labelled, as General Currie loved to name people. But his professors had at least second place. Indeed as time went on, we too dropped into our nicknames and labels. No one but General Currie could think of a professor of seventy as "Bill." But he had to have it so. He could not bear a world of idle dignity and pretences.

There were those of us who served under him at McGill to whom there came during his principalship those dark hours that at some time must shadow every human life. And there General Currie was beyond words,—a tenderness of sympathy, an affection for those in distress that no language can present and that no gratitude can repay.

Now it is over. We have laid him to rest. Yet we who served with him at McGill can only hope that somewhere in the sound of the martial music and the

measured step of his soldiers, his soul might hear the shuffling feet of his dusty professors, out of step and out of breath, but following him,—as they had been wont to do these thirteen years,—as best they could.[26]

XI

1933–1935

L EACOCK'S only book publication in 1933 was
Charles Dickens, His Life and Work. It was a more
complete study than his *Mark Twain,* with much less
of the popular hodgepodge effect. He wrote the same
kind of humor that Mark Twain wrote and was in
sympathy with him. Dickens's humor was a different
case. Leacock could not write like Dickens, and the very
fact that he could not enhanced his respect for the
English humorist. The same reaction could be seen in
his treatment of Dickens as a lecturer. Leacock had
given funny lectures in the Mark Twain style, but he
could not draw the tears that Dickens had. Leacock,
however, did not allow his veneration of his subject to
color his interpretation of Dickens's character. When
he discussed the first unfortunate visit to America, he
found himself solidly on the side of the American.
Dickens, he said, was "a spokesman for the common
people, but now in a land where they spoke for themselves."[1] The book demonstrated a good critical appreci-

223

ation of the works of Dickens, but it was a book written for pleasure; it made no attempt to be scholarly. He placed his own study in its proper place when he said:

In John Forster's account of Dickens's visit to Montreal there occurs one of the few out-and-out errors to be found in that magnificent work. Misled no doubt by Dickens's handwriting in the letters he received, he says that Dickens and his wife stayed at Peasco's Hotel. This is incorrect. Recent researches personally conducted in front of the hotel (still standing, in St. Paul St.) show that the name (still legible) in Rasco's Hotel. All research workers in the history of our literature will find in this correction of a standing error a distinct contribution to our knowledge of the life and character of Dickens and an ample justification of the present volume.[2]

Leacock might have as well called the volume *An Appreciation* instead of *Life and Works*. The meaner side of Dickens's character did not escape Leacock. But, though he noted the conceit, the melodrama, the sentimentality, the envy, the very reason he had loved Dickens in the first place was the humanness of the man. Leacock did not like tin gods. He liked Mark Twain because he swore like a mule driver and because, in spite of the protestations of his wife, he could not stop smoking. He liked the author of *The Old Curiosity Shop* because, for all of the sophisticated veneer of the successful author, Dickens cried maudlin tears over Little Nell. The biography was well enough received

that the Dickens Fellowship of New York asked him
to speak at the annual dinner, an invitation which he
could not accept.[3]

The Dickens biography received such good notices
that Leacock's regular publisher, Dodd, Mead and Company wrote to congratulate him and to suggest other
books in the same line which they hoped to interest
him in. They suggested a biography of Lewis Carroll
or a book on Lincoln as a humorist. Leacock drafted
an answer:

> L Carroll   no   he had no life
> Lincoln have done a book—
>   have put in section on humour[4]

but he did get them interested in a book he had been
working on for some time—Napoleon as a Naval Strate-
gist. Leacock had a lifelong admiration of Napoleon as
a military man—even had a large portrait of the Little
Corporal hanging in his Montreal study—and he did
research on him off and on for most of his writing
career. But he never finished the book. Other, more
profitable work evidently got in the way.

In 1934 Leacock followed the Dickens biography
with *The Greatest Pages of Charles Dickens,* a well-
selected anthology of representative writings inter-
spersed with abridgments from his biography. In the
same year he published *Stephen Leacock,* a less well-
selected anthology of his own writing. This book, called
The Perfect Salesman in its American edition, was edited by E. V. Knox for the "Methuen's Library of

Humour" series. In 1933 there had been no book of humor by Leacock on his publishers' lists, and now came this made-over book. Leacock the funny man was running down. Leacock's situation as a humorist was evident. In the last eight years, since *Winnowed Wisdom*, only *Wet Wit* had been up to the quality of his early work, and even in it he had depended somewhat on pieces which had appeared elsewhere.

Oddly enough, Leacock's serious writing was maturing. The same year, 1934, he wrote *Lincoln Frees the Slaves* and *The Pursuit of Knowledge*. The latter discussed the relative merits of a restricted curriculum and the system of electives in producing the best-educated person. *Lincoln Frees the Slaves* was, said one critic, "a book of which its author may well be proud, and of which we . . . may be proud with him."[5] In form it was a historical essay; in penetration it was interpretative professional history, though its interpretation of the legal and ethical aspects was not new. Both its style and its point were well indicated by the flyleaf inscription he wrote in the copy he presented to May Shaw:

> With sincere apologies to Mr. Punch for recalling the form of his matchless poem of 1865; "You! lay a wreath on murdered Lincoln's bier, etc. . . ."

You! undertake to read a Lincoln biography,
Without even an working notion of American geography,
Who could not possibly define
Mason and Dixon's line,

For whom a Lincoln is a touring car
And Henry Clay the name of a cigar
Or Gettysburg a fatal day for France
And Robert Lee a Carolina dance!
Yes, even you! But let me first I pray
From certain misconceptions clear the way.
Lincoln was not the same as Washington,
No, he was not the man called Uncle Tom,
Oh, no, his soldiers never called him Stonewall,
The novel is quite wrong you got that from.
Your Grandmamma remembers when they hanged
    him?
I think she's got him mixed with poor John Brown.
What's that you say? It's all come back at once?
How silly to have spoken like a dunce.
Lincoln! Of course, how could one ever pause,
Lincoln! the Hero of the Southern Cause!
Now that you're qualified please take a look
And find your views supported in this book.[6]

The book, delving into the social causes and results
of the War between the States and the importance of
Lincoln in the action, was written with a sensitive appreciation of the strong convictions on both sides of
the conflict. Leacock found in Lincoln, as others had,
a nobility and humanity which fitted him to be one of
the world's historical figures. The work pointed out
strongly that Lincoln had understood the Southern temperament and belief, and that he would have saved the
South much degradation had he lived. Leacock's at-

tention was finely divided between sympathy for the South and devotion to human liberty. Sympathy for the South was an established Canadian trait—Canada in the summer being full, as one observer said, of Southerners who "wanted to summer in the North but wouldn't stop among the Damyankees."

Bishop's University, of Lennoxville, Quebec, conferred a Doctor of Civil Law degree on Leacock this year in honor of his contribution to Canadian letters. Perhaps it was in answer to this favor that he published the articles he did in 1934; at any rate they were, except two on American humor, Canadian writing about Dominion subjects. "Revision of Democracy" was about a dominion's status in a democratic empire.[7] "The Stirring Pageant of Canadian History" was a mildly chauvanistic reminder of the struggle for the settlement of Canada,[8] and the other two were concerned with the contemporary economic and social structure of his country.[9] His other two articles, "Two Humorists: Charles Dickens and Mark Twain"[10]—a critical appreciation—and "The Humorist who Made Lincoln Laugh[11]—an appraisal of Artemus Ward—obviously came out of his recent work.

The same year he published at his own expense a three-page pamphlet, *The Restoration of the Finances of McGill University; Suggestions Submitted to the Consideration of My Fellow Members of the University. 1. To Diminish the Deficit. 2. To Carry the Deficit. 3. To Remove the Deficit.* He advocated retrenchment, one of his proposals being a contraction of the staff, not

by firing, but by not replacing members who retired or resigned. Further, he said, those eligible for retirement should be retired.

Leacock always felt strongly that he had a special duty to assist his Conservative party when possible, and, because of his training and his popularity, that party turned to him often. He was asked to help the Prime Minister formulate a monetary policy.[12] Later when Mr. Bennett's radio addresses were to be published in pamphlet form, Leacock was invited to write a foreword.[13] He was pleased to accept and did his job so well that the editor assured him:

> The best expression I can give you is to tell you that we decided to print your preface as the foreword to the first radio speech so that it would have priority over all others.[14]

It was this same year of 1935 that Stephen Leacock received his highest commendation from his party. Prime Minister Bennett wrote him:

Personal and
Confidential

Stephen Leacock, Esq., B.A., Ph.D., Litt.D.
Orillia,
Ontario

Dear Stephen Leacock:
A number of our friends are extremely anxious that you should permit your name to be placed before the

Conservative Convention in the constituency in which you make your summer home.

I need hardly say that I am thoroughly convinced that you could render very conspicuous service to Canada in the next Parliament. Your wide knowledge, your great reputation, and your disinterested approach to problems affecting the welfare of the country could not but be of the utmost value. Won't you favourably consider this matter, and thereby give great satisfaction not only to those who know you in the community in which you live, but to thousands who have read your books with pleasure, as well as to one who subscribes himself, with high esteem and regard.[15]

Leacock did not, however, feel that he could accept the offer. He was far too dedicated to his teaching; he was busy writing, and there was at least one additional reason. His friend John Drinkwater was sure to be the candidate if Leacock did not make the race himself. It was with regret but also with considerable appreciation that Leacock declined.

Articles, honorary degrees, books, recognition, criticism—all made little difference to Leacock. He taught three days a week at McGill. He still walked to the university, down Cote des Neiges Road to Cedar Avenue and down Cedar to McGill. His students came to know Cedar Avenue as "Leacock's office," when they learned that the best place to catch him in the morning was there as he came striding down the flank of Mount Royal, pounding his cane along just for the fun of it,

his hat pulled down against the wind, his greatcoat flopping about his legs. Though he would sometimes come into his class a little late; after class, he would find his way to the University Club.

His friends at the club were many, but the closest one was Captain René du Roure. He was a professor and head of the French department, but Leacock never forgot a military title. Leacock's world was peopled with captains, majors, and colonels because, if a friend had ever been commissioned, he remained on active duty the rest of his life as far as Leacock was concerned; he always called du Roure *"mon Capitain."* Leacock always spoke French to René, just as he always addressed Herman Walter in German. They held long, lively discussions of all the things they shared an interest in—war, French classics, history, education— and they played equally lively games of billiards and chess. Professor du Roure was a Parisian Frenchman who retained much of the continental air and attitude which Leacock admired. With established habits and established friends, Leacock liked the life he led.

Breaking into the pattern of his life in 1934 came one of the world's new inventions, radio. Leacock liked listening to the radio—he thought Charlie McCarthy one of the funniest characters ever created—but he abhorred the idea of appearing on the medium himself. When his young editor friend McDougall, now in advertising, wrote him concerning a radio contract, Leacock did not even answer. McDougall recalls with glee his visit to Montreal to see Leacock; his company had thought

the idea so good that he could not back out now. Leacock told him grimly, "The thing for you to do is go to . . . [your hotel] room right now and sit down and write me a letter. In this letter state clearly to me the largest amount of money your firm is willing to pay for me to appear on your radio show, or whatever it is. I may tell you at the same time I don't think you're going to be able to offer me enough. . . ." With that Leacock walked out of his office followed by McDougall on his way to his hotel; the whole idea was smashed and he knew it.[16]

Halfway across the campus, Leacock turned to the young man. "You will deliver this letter to me, Mr. McDougall, at precisely one o'clock at the University Club. I will be sitting in the University Club at precisely one o'clock having a whiskey and soda. Do you know where the University Club is, Mr. McDougall? No, you are from Toronto. You probably do not know where any of the important ornaments of Montreal are. . . . I will take you there now so that you will know where it is." Having discussed their earlier connection, they reached the club and Leacock invited McDougall in. Very solemnly he said, "Mr. McDougall, I am going to have a whiskey and soda. Will you have a whiskey and soda, Mr. McDougall?" After their third whiskey and soda, consumed during an increasingly friendly conversation, du Roure came in. "Ah, mon Capitain . . . I want you to meet my old friend Joe McDougall. . . . You read nothing but periodicals from France. You would not have heard of the Goblin magazine and you probably

never heard of Joe McDougall. But, let me tell you, Joe McDougall is an old friend of mine and one of the brightest minds in Canada. He has come to Montreal to get me to go on the radio and you know what I think of that."

As the time neared twelve, McDougall suggested that he had better go write his letter if he were going to get it back by one o'clock. Leacock agreed, enjoying himself hugely. This was the kind of fun he liked; no one was getting hurt, but he had the young man thoroughly confused. "I suppose you are staying at some commercial hotel—the Mount Royal, for example. . . . The Mount Royal is not a suitable place for a writer, Joe. I think you would be more comfortable at the University Club. I will arrange for you to have a room." Finally, as McDougall started for his room, Leacock said, "Now, Joe, I do not want you to worry too much about this letter, because I may tell you that no matter what your offer is, I am going to do what you ask. . . . You go and write that letter."

Stephen Leacock readily agreed to the financial terms of the offer, but the contract was an odd one. Leacock insisted that the broadcast originate from Montreal, that Joe McDougall come to Montreal each week and attend a dinner party just before the broadcast, and that all the guests at the dinner party be permitted to go with him to the studio. He could not talk to a machine; his humor was for people. His friends looked forward to these parties, which were as entertaining as all of Leacock's affairs. He dominated the table, restraining René

233

from telling anecdotes "calculated to shock the pillars of Montreal society." In spite of the attending gaiety, Leacock never learned to be comfortable before a microphone. When he was preparing to move the program to Orillia for the summer he wrote:

> Dear Joe,
> Please see that the Broadcasting Machine used in Orillia looks like the one here,—a box on a stick—not a metal frame (1) this one begins to seem natural, (2) it all helps.[17]

Leacock gave sixteen broadcasts in all, fifteen minutes each on Tuesday and Friday nights around ten o'clock,[18] but trouble was developing and Leacock sensed it. The advertising agency found that the Leacock programs were almost complete disappointments. Few listeners enjoyed the show at all. Leacock had the habit of chuckling as he told a story; it was an infectious practice for those in his company, but on the air he sounded conceited—a judgment as far removed from the truth as possible. Before the thirteen weeks was up, Leacock asked for release from his contract, and both parties were relieved. In spite of a plea from his friend, Gladstone Murray,[19] Leacock never again appeared on the radio unless a speech to a large audience was being incidentally broadcast, in which case he ignored the microphone and spoke to the audience he could see.[20]

Shortly before Leacock had started his broadcasts, a matriarchy had come to an end. Agnes Leacock died

January 19, 1934.[21] She had been a woman of quiet courage and great strength. She had held together a family that had never been all under one roof at the same time. A woman of natural gentility, she had been able to get Indian servants when no one else could, and half the Indian population from "The Island" across from Sutton attended her funeral. She had almost anything she wanted after her children had begun to make money, but one of her ambitions was to reach ninety. At the age of seventy, she survived a cancer operation which cost her part of one foot. At eighty-nine her health began to fail, but she achieved the age of ninety, and fourteen days later she died.

The next year, 1935, was a big one for Stephen Leacock. He wrote a book, published five scholarly articles, and received the Mark Twain Medal. In 1930, Leacock had accepted an invitation to join the International Mark Twain Society, grantor of the medal, by means of the shortest letter in their files:

> Dear Mr. Clemens,
>   I will.
>   Sincerely yours,
>   Stephen Leacock.[22]

The Mark Twain Medal was not given just for distinction in humor, but for outstanding accomplishment in any field. Preceding Leacock as recipients of the honor were Guglielmo Marconi, Benito Mussolini, General John Pershing, Charles Evans Hughes, Oliver Wendell Holmes, Rudyard Kipling, Booth Tarkington, W. W.

Jacobs, Hilaire Belloc, Franklin D. Roosevelt, and Willa Cather. This was impressive company—a bit too impressive really. Leacock knew how easy it was to award medals for publicity purposes. But if the medal ever carried honor, it was in 1935, the year of the Mark Twain Centennial Celebration. On January 16, the same day he accepted the medal at a dinner in St. Louis, he addressed the University of Missouri. This speech officially opened the celebration.[23]

As if in honor of Mark Twain and as if determined to prove that he still knew what humor was about, though he seemed to have lost the touch for writing it, in 1935, Stephen Leacock published *Humor: Its Theory and Technique*. This was the first of two volumes on the criticism of humor. Because the second volume is more concerned with the philosophy of humor, and the first with technique, technique will be discussed with reference to the first volume and philosophy will be analyzed in connection with the second.

In his criticism, Leacock praised highly the humorous techniques of Charles Dickens and Mark Twain, but he made little attempt to treat his own humor. There was an occasional hint of personal analysis. He partly admitted the accuracy of one reviewer's discovery that his humor was an "ingenious mixture of meiosis and hyperbole." "I felt that, after all, all I needed was a can of meiosis and a can of hyperbole and go down to the cellar and mix them up."[24] Of the misuse of words, particularly words pushed along logical lines until they had illogical meanings, Leacock said of himself, "The

author of the present work (if I may with modesty call myself that) has probably made more extended use of this than any other person who has written so copiously."[25] When he spoke of parody he drew on his own work and mentioned several times, with justifiable pride, *Nonsense Novels*.

It may have been modesty, but it was not ignorance that prevented Leacock from dissecting his own humor; in the masterful and acute criticism offered in these two books, Leacock showed himself to be an able student of humor. He said, "Mark Twain was beyond anybody in the world a technical humorist. . . . He brings into play . . . the resources of technique,"[26] but he might have said almost the same thing of himself. Every technique which critics had found in Leacock's humor was to be found in Leacock's discussion of humor. Leacock knew what he was doing. He was not surprised to find that he was using meiosis; more than that, unlike most of his contemporaries—critics or authors—he knew that the word meant understatement. The reviewers might have called him an academic humorist except for the stigma attached to the word *academic;* he had certainly studied the field enough to be a scholar in it.

Leacock discussed exaggeration, particularly as a characteristic of American humor, but without once mentioning his own use of it,[27] but critics had already discovered it. One London *Times* writer called Leacock a "humorist in the American tradition dealing huge hammer blows of exaggeration and over-statement."[28]

Another, confused but chauvanistic, agreed as to his use of "American hyperbole" but thought it was "developed in English fashion as a rule, in a quiet and close-knit narrative which has none of the exuberance of the typical American humorist."[29] There was, however, an enthusiasm about Leacock's humor which denied this close tie to British humor. Very early he wrote:

> Yet Gertrude cherished the memory of her parents. On her breast the girl wore a locket in which was enshrined a miniature of her mother, while down her neck at the back hung a daguerreotype of her father. She carried a portrait of her grandmother up her sleeve and had pictures of her cousins tucked inside her boot, while beneath her—but enough, quite enough.[30]

This was nothing if not exuberant. In the same way that he heightened the effect of his own actions—pouring a tureen of soup out the window to indicate his displeasure at the kind being served—Leacock heightened the effects of his writing by exaggeration, and he did it everywhere: in character, in language, in situation.

It was in connection with exaggeration that Leacock used understatement to achieve his anticlimactic humor. Leacock recognized the anticlimax as an effective trick of humor, discussing the trait in both his books on humor.[31] Leacock's method of working to an anticlimax was, to some extent, distinctive. In "The Family at Football," when Ernest had just proposed, Leacock had the girl say:

And I said I didn't know what father would say and
Ernest said he didn't care a damn what father would
say (Ernest is so manly in the way he talks) and he
offered to break father's neck for me if I liked. So I
said I hadn't ever meant to get married but to be some
sort of a sister, but that if he liked, I would get
married this time for his sake.[32]

How priceless is "this time for his sake"! Leacock's
method of anticlimax was different from that of his
English counterpart. The English humorist was inclined
to wander desperately away from a climax. On the other
hand, Leacock extravagantly built toward a climax
which he proceeded to knock down with an empty or
trite phrase, not foretold by the buildup at all. Discussing his theatrical career, he said of his role in *Uncle
Tom's Cabin:*

My work was in the great climax scene, where the
fugitive slave girl, Eliza, her unborn babe in her arms,
is fleeing across the Ohio—leaping from one ice floe
to another in the swollen flood of the river. That's
where I acted—I was a chunk of ice in the Ohio,
the third one from the Kentucky side, working under
a blue curtain.[33]

The high excitement faded off in the useless knowledge
of stagecraft. Sometimes Leacock's anticlimax appeared
as a complete disintegration of reason, as if the idea were
simply coming apart. He managed this by using statistics or details followed by a completely unwarranted
and illogical statement—a technique he admired much

in Bill Nye's "There must be at least 500,000,000 rats in the United States: of course I am only speaking from memory."[34]

If Leacock formed his anticlimax by incongruously placing together exaggeration and understatement, it was merely a specialized extension of a concept which colored all his work. Incongruity, as all critics from Freud to Al Capp have declared, is one of the most important bases of humor. Stephen Leacock, of course, recognized this, and the concept of incongruity plays an important part in his discussion of humor throughout his two volumes on the subject. Leacock further recognized, however, that there were degrees of incongruity. He liked placing side by side things which did not belong together, making the difference obvious. He said, "The pleasing ingenuity—which lies in the juxtaposition of the incongruous . . . excites our sense of humor."[35] He found this trait to be particularly elemental to American humor.[36] His own use of the technique resulted in both verbal and physical incongruity —words that did not match and objects that did not belong in the same group. When used verbally, the technique was likely to produce a kind of intellectual nonsense: "I don't say . . . we can have the next war for this autumn. . . . Xmas is approaching and that's apt to bring along a nasty outbreak of good will."[37] Physical incongruity appeared in his parody of the promotional pamphlet:

The limpid waters of Lake Owatawetness . . . abound with every known variety of fish. Near to its surface,

so close that the angler may reach out his hand and stroke them, schools of pike, pickerel, mackerel, doggerel, and chickerel jostle one another in the water. They rise instantaneously to the bait and swim gratefully ashore holding it in their mouths. In the middle depth of the waters of the lake, the sardine, the lobster, the kippered herring, the anchovy and other tinned varieties of fish disport themselves with evident gratification, while even lower in the pellucid depths the dog-fish, the hog-fish, the log-fish, and the sword fish whirl about in never-ending circles.[38]

To the practiced eye of Stephen Leacock, there were many things in the world that did not belong there. He simply moved them closer together so that everyone might see the inconsistency. Even his parodies, with their strangely dissimilar, but strangely apt, silly ideas and high-sounding language, were a less obvious kind of incongruous juxtaposition.

Regardless of what other techniques he employed, part of Leacock's effectiveness came from his assumed air of unconsciousness. One critic called this "the assumption of simplicity."[39] Leacock commented on the value of artlessness in his own criticism.[40] He did not always use the innocent approach, of course; there was nothing artless about the bad puns to which he was addicted in his early work. In much of his work, however, he spoke as if unconscious of being funny:

Here is the Police Concert, one of the first. A policeman brought tickets for it to the door yesterday—

such a big fine-looking fellow—with a revolver. I took two tickets.[41]

This could not be very funny unless it seemed that the speaker did not see the relation between the revolver and the tickets. Leacock's favorite humorous character, the little man in the society too complex for him, had to be unconscious of his ridiculous appearance or he would have become a second-rate tragic figure. As it was, he preserved his dignity by continuing, in his ignorance, to act like a man. No man understood better than Leacock precisely what was funny: neither did anyone realize the importance of pretended innocence more than Leacock.

Just as Leacock was interested in the techniques of humor, he was interested in the language of humor. Besides the careful selection of language, said Leacock, humor demanded a "great 'naturalness' of language, the use of phrases and forms so simple that writers straining after effect would never get them."[42] He admired the easy flow of language which was Mark Twain's, and he said of Lewis Carroll's "The Hunting of the Snark," "the language is so 'damn' simple! A boy would say it just that way."[43] He might well admire such language; it was his own. Sandwell felt that one of the main reasons for Leacock's success was that his style was that of "a talker rather than a writer."[44] Another said that in Leacock "the style and the man were one. The style was consciously undistinguished, slippered, loose-buttoned, the very original of the fireside chat. He *talked*

to the world. And the talk was good. . . ."[45] Except when Leacock was consciously copying style for the purposes of parody, he did sound as if he were speaking to the reader. Even in his short stories, such as *Sunshine Sketches*, there was the ease of colloquial idiom:

> Why everybody's here. There's Hussell the editor of the Newspacket, wearing a blue ribbon on his coat, for the Mariposa Knights of Pythias are, by their constitution, dedicated to temperance; and there's Henry Mullins, the manager of the Exchange Bank, also a Knight of Pythias, with a small flask of Pogram's Special in hip pocket as a sort of ammendment to the constitution. And there's Dean Drone, the Chaplain of the Order, with a fishing rod (you never saw such green bass as lie among the rocks at Indian's Island), and with a trolling line in case of maskinonge, and a landing net in case of pickerel, and with his eldest daughter, Lilian Drone, in case of young men. There never was such a fisherman as Rev. Rupert Drone.[46]

Both the intimacy and the idiom were that of a man talking to his friend. Leacock identified the idiom once, saying that Canada had too much trouble with its two languages to make up any slang so they just used "English for literature, Scotch for ceremony and American for conversation."[47]

Thomas Masson had said in *Our American Humorists* that Leacock had "an astounding gift in the use of words and images that compel" laughter.[48] Leacock, himself, recognized this use of language when he said, "Com-

parison is the very soul of humor. . . . It is the discovery of resemblance and the lack of it that builds up the contrasts, discrepancies and incongruities on which . . . humor depends. . . . One is lost in admiration of such comparisons as, 'A face like a ham,' 'eyes like puddles of molasses.'"[49] Leacock did not mention the comic figure of speech as a part of his own humor, but it was there. He was a highly imaginative man who frequently wrote those poetic bits of humor that showed so much in so few words, as in:

> . . . the sudden backfire of Congress against the TVA decision of the Supreme Court—or, no, the other way —the backfire of the court—anyway, another explosion in Washington as sudden and arresting as the sound of a lamb chop blown up in a lunch wagon.[50]

Leacock seldom used an extended figure of speech, except as a parody is an extended metaphor. He preferred a short, pithy statement, frequently full of common sense: "A gradual change of spelling is as out of the question as a gradual stroke of lightning."[51] His writing is filled with the sparkle of quick comparison. Leacock's criticism had recognized all these characteristic techniques for good reason; he found them in his own writing as well as that of Bill Nye and Mark Twain.

Stephen Leacock's own humorous writing had declined in quality, in spite of his demonstrated knowledge of the genre. His total production from 1925 to 1935 contained only a small portion that could be called good humor. Perhaps it was the loss of the com-

panionship of his wife, turning him toward academic pursuits, which had isolated him in a scholastic ivory tower; at any rate, he seemed to have lost touch with the world. His contemporaries were doing well. But Leacock loved humanity too much to write the cynical humor of Ring Lardner or the popular, acid commentary of Dorothy Parker. His style was too casual to suit the cryptic wit of Franklin P. Adams, and he had evidently lost the touch for nonsense Benchley claimed to have learned from him. His ancestry was too Anglo-Saxon for him to take advantage of Milt Gross's audience, and he was too kind to make fun of any people but his own. His own character was too sophisticated for the folksy humor of Will Rogers.

He was too old to write of flaming youth as John Held did; he was not really a part of the "Roaring Twenties." His fiction was not skillful enough to offer competition to Irvin S. Cobb's and Booth Tarkington's, and his whimsy seemed too extravagant beside Thurber's. He could not join the bitter humorists of the depression—his own income, greatly reduced now, was a healthy fourteen thousand dollars. In trying to reach an audience he seemed unsuited to, Stephen Leacock overreached himself in his humor.

His serious writing was unaffected. He published three articles in economics: "Good Times Can Come Again,"[52] "Economic Separatism in the British Empire,"[53] and "What Is Left of Adam Smith?" In the latter he warned, "This socialism, this communism, would work only in Heaven where they don't need it,

or in Hell where they already have it."[54] His publication also included a piece of literary history, "Mark Twain and Canada,"[55] and a contribution to the *Canadian Geographical Journal.*[56]

At McGill, the principalship, open since Sir Arthur Currie's death, was finally filled by Arthur Eustace Morgan, who was a better scholar than administrator. He had had no experience with a large university and he tried to run it, as Leacock said, "like a boys' school."[57] Not understanding the North American school, he started finding fault with various departments because they were not exactly like their British counterparts. The story, typical even if apocryphal, was that Morgan called Leacock into his office and said, "Professor Leacock, I am credibly informed that, of all the bad departments at this university, yours is one of the worst." Stephen Leacock looked at him quickly, leaned over the desk, and said, "What son-of-a-bitch have you been talking to?"

Stephen Leacock was too sane to worry about a grudge. He forgot his troubles with the principal and withdrew to his own department. He outlined his lectures, laid out work for his new book, planned the schedule for his department, and then played billiards at the University Club with René du Roure. He had weathered administrative storms before. Then in the summer of 1935, he received a short, terse note from A. P. S. Glassco, treasurer of McGill, which quoted part of the proceedings of the board of governors relevant to retirement, and then added:

Pursuant to the above Resolution, the Governors have instructed me to notify you that you will be retired from the University on May 31st, 1936.[58]

Hoping but not expecting the decision to be reversed, Leacock did not give up so easily. He tried not to be quarrelsome, and he tried equally hard to continue his contribution to the department he loved. He opposed the appointment of a professor whom Morgan wanted, but he wrote the dean:

My feeling is that if the Principal, with a knowledge of the facts before him wished Dr. Plaut to come, then I or anyone else ought to give way. This is what we would have done with General Currie.[59]

Principal Morgan finally got around to writing Leacock concerning his coming retirement:

Dear Leacock:

As I understood you are already aware, it has been decided by the Board of Governors that sixty-five years is to be regarded as the age of retirement of all University officers. Although it is true that the resolution of the Governors reserves to them the right in very exceptional cases to extend that period, it is the intention of the University to regard retirement at sixty-five as the normal procedure. This will be interpreted as taking effect at the end of the session during which the officer concerned attains retiring age, and for this purpose the end of the session will be taken to be the 31st of August, and not the 31st of May as

was implied in the letter sent you by Mr. Glassco in the 12th June last. . . .

In making this communication, I wish to extend to you on behalf of the Governors a very sincere expression of gratitude for the work that you have done for the University during your long tenure of office. It is my very warm hope that you will enjoy many long years of happy retirement.

Yours sincerely,
A. E. Morgan[60]

Leacock answered back with ill-concealed disappointment and distaste:

Dear Mr. Principal,

I beg to acknowledge the receipt of your letter informing me that I have been retired from the active staff of the university, and to thank you—my dear Morgan—for the personal kindliness with which you write.

S. L.[61]

When Edward Beatty, his close friend of long standing and the chancellor of McGill, wrote him with much regret but with equal firmness about the decision to retire him,

Personal
My dear Stephen,

I do not think that you need feel the least concern about the tone of a routine letter, when you remember your long years of service to the University and

the appreciation of them which you already know to be no less than world-wide. The time comes to us all to lay down our tasks, and to leave the valuing of what we here accomplished to others. There are many people in the world who will envy you the certainty with which you can expect a favourable verdict. . . .

It is to me very sad to think that I shall not much longer be able to depend on your exercise of kindly wisdom to temper the intolerance and unwisdom which I sometimes fear are creeping into the University. However, I realize that you have many years during which your influence will be increased in some way by the fact that you are no longer an active member of the staff.

For yourself, I am afraid that I have no sympathy. You have had a full life and achieved fame. Beyond that I do not see what reward any man can obtain.

I do not need to say how warmly I hope that your retirement from active work will last through many years which will be among the happiest and most useful of your life.[62]

Leacock must have seen that the struggle was about over. He still cared, however, about the department which he had worked so hard to build up, and he wrote the principal:

A. E. Morgan Esq.
Principal, McGill University

Dear Mr. Principal:
In a note of February 10, you are good enough to

say: "I should be glad if you could spare me a little time to discuss the future of the department of economics." The Chancellor also in writing to me said a short time ago: "Your influence will be increased in some way by the fact that you are no longer a member of the active staff."

On the strength of this I thought it might be of use if I set down my opinion in a brief memorandum, as follows:—

The Department of Economics has suffered greatly from the financial stringency of the past few years. It has had to forego the services of outside examiners from other universities; it has lost various scholarships which it had from McGill and from private sources for graduate students, and, most of all, it has had to suspend the publication of the monographs on Canadian problems which were a chief feature of its work.

But for all this there is no remedy but time. With the return of prosperity, all of this will come back.

I do not think it would be wise to reorganize the department so as to amalgamate it with others and destroy its distinctive character. It has to cover already a wide field. In Canada, of necessity, economics must be taught in its bearing on the Canadian environment, which is quite different from that of England. Many of us might wish that economics could be taught more as a philosophical subject and less as a practical treatment of Canadian problems.

But that is not possible here and now. The public expects from us a kind of training which will fit young men for service both with the government and with the business enterprises of Canada. In my opinion, to unite economics with other departments would rob it of the success which it has had.

I do not see that it is necessary to make any new appointment in the department. I stated to the faculty last year, before I had any idea that I was to be put out of McGill, that in the event of a vacancy among us, those who were left could easily close up the ranks and carry on. I think this still. It is possible to do this because the graduate school is much reduced in number and the other classes are capable of reorganization with a view to economy of teaching.

The saving to the university effected by such a plan is very considerable. A part of my pension is paid by the Carnegie Trust and thus only a part of it has to be paid by McGill. The immediate saving is about $3600. a year and ultimately $5,000. or a difference in capital account of $100,000.

It would seem to me that Dr. Hemmeon after his long, arduous and efficient service in the department for almost 30 years has a proper claim to promotion to the place I hold.

I am authorized by my colleagues Dr. Hemmeon and Dr. Day and Professor Culliton to say that they entirely concur in the views as to the department expressed in this letter. Mr. Forsey is ill but I have every reason to presume his acquiescence.

I have lectured at McGill since January, 1901. I have been at the head of the department for nearly 30 years. Its graduates have filled many important posts in Canada. The writings and lectures of its staff have been widely known and have influenced the public life of the country.

I thought therefore that my views might be of use in any decision to be made in regard to the future of the department.[63]

Although this letter did not wave the white flag, it certainly was conciliatory in tone and substance. Stephen Leacock, much against his will, had decided to co-operate as best he could. Two days later, however, he was required to send a copy of the letter to Dean Martin, under different circumstances.

Dean Martin
  McGill University

Dear Charlie,
  Herewith a memorandum. I sent a copy to the Chancellor. The Principal on my presenting it said that I have no right to submit it; no right to ask the opinion of junior men whose opinions were not wanted; no right to make a representation in writing by [sic] only by word of mouth to him.

His manner and language were overbearing and quite unsuited to the dignity of his position or the privilege of mine.

Will you please see that my views reach the Senate;

whether they act on them is their own proper business.[64]

After thirty-five years at McGill, Stephen Leacock had reached this state of affairs. He did not want to retire at all, certainly under such conditions, and in 1935 the failure of his humor made the dark days of retirement look even blacker to him.

XII

1936–1937

LEACOCK'S abrupt retirement was one of the few
things in his life that he never forgot and never forgave. The retirement had been a matter of policy, but
it was obvious to observers that there was something
personal in the sudden decision to enforce the retirement rule. Leacock was not the only one caught; thirteen faculty members in all were released at the same
time. Dr. Charles F. Martin, dean of the McGill medical
school and the only Canadian until recently to be
president of the American Medical Association, was retired at the same time. Principal Morgan also retired
Frank Dawson Adams, vice-principal and world-famed
geologist, who had been acting principal until Morgan's
appointment. It seemed to Leacock and his contemporaries suspiciously convenient that so many of those dismissed were men of distinction at the university, men
who, in effect, outshone the principal. Perhaps one of
the developments which hurt Leacock most was the
action of his friend, Sir Edward Beatty, knighted the

same year. Beatty, as chancellor of McGill, could have forestalled the retirements or, at least, softened the blow; but he chose to accept Morgan's recommendations and was, said Leacock, the Chief Justice who passed sentence on the "Senility Gang."[1] Certainly the precipitous and untactful action hastened the dismissal of Principal Morgan, who was, in 1937, asked by the governors to resign.

Neither Morgan's departure nor the company he, himself, shared were much consolation to Leacock. His whole life had been teaching; his writing he had considered a secondary occupation. He wrote after his retirement:

> During all my thirty-five years of college teaching I always felt that there was no profession in the world for which I would have exchanged my own. . . . The "merry month of May," says the poet. I know a merrier. Give me the murky month of February, with the snow blowing on the window pane of the classroom, the early darkness falling already and the gaslight bright in the class-room; that and a black-board, and a theorem, and a professor—the right kind, absorbed, ecstatic, and a little silly. Give me that and the month of May may keep its fronds and toadstools as it will.[2]

Stephen Leacock suspected, as did others, that his retirement had been forced by his Conservative stand on economics and politics rather than any question of his health or his ability to teach.[3] He was a Conservative

in a Liberal country and an even more Liberal province; his views were sound and honest, but they were frequently unpopular. Leacock bore no grudge except for Morgan; he showed an understanding and even some sympathy for the board of governors when he said, "I have plenty to say about the governors putting me out of the university . . . but I have all eternity to say it in. I shall shout it down to them."[4] On the other hand, it gratified Leacock when the New York *Times* proposed that some American university should arrange for Leacock "to smoke at their post-graduate students in selected groups," arguing that many colleges had maintained a resident poet, why not a "resident wit and satirist."[5]

Leacock was not one to waste his energies in a futile fight, and when his friends proposed a farewell dinner, he fell in with the idea in good spirit. It was, recalls Goforth, who was present, the biggest farewell dinner ever given in Montreal. It was a dress affair, and, in spite of its being by invitation only, the attending crowd was huge. The guest list consisted largely of students, former students, McGill staff members, the board of governors, former faculty members, and the like. Leacock was not consulted about the guest list, but Principal Morgan was conspicuously missing from a gathering honored by all the other luminaries of the school. The dinner, elaborate and friendly, was touched with a note of sadness at the departure of "old Stevie." The devoted group presented to Leacock a large charcoal portrait sketch by Richard Jack, A.R.A., and, as a fur-

ther gesture of their esteem, had bound for him in red leather the forty volumes he had written. A special bookplate designated this:

> to mark their recognition of his beneficent influence and as an affectionate tribute to his long and faithful service to the University and to mankind through his distinguished achievements in the world of letters.

When Leacock arose to acknowledge the gifts there was a general uneasiness; "the old man" had a brilliant reputation as an after-dinner speaker, but what could one say at his own academic wake? Leacock relieved them very shortly. "When I had to choose between a morocco-bound set of Shakespeare or a morocco-bound set of Stephen Leacock, I thought long. I investigated the bookshops and found that one could get Shakespeare for a quarter, but the cheapest book by Stephen Leacock cost a dollar and a quarter, so I chose Leacock." He might be retiring from teaching but he was not retiring from being a gentleman and a very funny one at that.

In honor of his retirement after a long, distinguished career, the University of Michigan granted Leacock a Litt. D. in 1936, and in the same year McGill conferred what many thought to be a much belated honor, the degree of Doctor of Laws. It was, of course, given him as soon as was ethical, it never being considered proper for an active member of a faculty to receive an honorary degree from his own school. Stephen Leacock's appearance on the stage at the convocation was greeted with nods and murmurs of approbation by the audience,

and when his name was finally called to receive the degree, the students broke into loud cheers for "Stevie." They would not be quieted until Leacock himself, with gray tufts of hair sticking out from under his mortarboard, held up his hand so that his companions, John Livingston Lowes and Ernest William Brown, could be given their degrees.[6]

It was a matter of wry irony to Leacock that his release from McGill could have resulted from his own ever-persuasive pen. His own pamphlet, *The Restoration of the Finances of McGill University,* had recommended retirement for all faculty members eligible for retirement. With this he may have signed, if not his own death warrant, as romances are fond of saying, his own resignation. Certainly his attitude and action after his retirement showed that he had not considered himself as one of those involved.

Smarting under the implication which retirement carried, Leacock turned to his writing with enthusiasm, to show that he still had something to say. Besides four articles in major magazines, ranging in subject from professional education to political science,[7] he put together a monograph, *The Gathering Financial Crisis in Canada,*[8] which had appeared originally as a series of articles in the London *Morning Post* in July of 1936.[9] In this he found fault with the government-owned Canadian National Railway, with the juggled budget presented by the Finance Minister, and with the criminally generous spending of the people's money by the

Liberal government. As usual, he mixed sound statistical argument with a telling wit: "Some [active assets] . . . are active enough . . . but others, such as the money lent to Greece in 1919 . . . seem paralyzed in their activity."[10] It was not the warning of a pessimist, however; Leacock saw Canada's salvation in her natural resources, her gold and copper and cobalt.

In his three books of the same year there was a suggestion of what the retired Leacock was to be like. *The Greatest Pages of American Humor*[11] was a well-selected anthology with Leacock's serious critical comments. Both *Funny Pieces* and *Hellements of Hickonomics in Hiccoughs of Verse Done in Our Social Planning Mill* professed to be humor, but there was an earnestness about parts of them which bespoke more than fun. In the last section of *Funny Pieces*, which he called "Personalia," he wrote seriously but good-naturedly on academic freedom and on his retirement. Surprisingly enough, the humor in *Funny Pieces* was of a higher quality than he achieved in some time. There was the exuberance of old in the first lines of "Opening Day at College": " 'What the hell are you taking Divinity for?' asked the bright-eyed co-ed."[12] With rare form, he returned to parody in his gibe at the supererudite literary critic:

SOCIETY IN ITS SIMPLEST TERMS.* *French Writer Analyses the Giddy Throng.* . . .
  *Le Contrat Social. J. J. Rousseau. Paris (Kentucky?).
   $1.40.

Monsieur Rousseau—we call him Monsieur because to us French is a second language and almost a third —writes extremely well. His *livre* lacks something of the quality of the other *livres* before, but that is only to be *expecté*. Indeed, as one says in French, *tout change,* or, as the witty Abbé Fénélon cleverly expressed it, *Toutes les choses ont une fin,* a phrase impossible to translate, as everything is in witty French. Monsieur Rousseau in his *Contrat Social* conducts us at once into a *milieu sauvage,* an expression so difficult to convey in English that we won't even try to. He finds the basis of this—the *base* so to speak—to be the principle of *liberté* (*principe de liberté*) freely accepted among men (*hommes*). To this first principle he adds that of *égalité* (or, roughly speaking, equality) and then very ingeniously connects the two of them with *fraternité.* By putting the three together he reaches the combined idea (*ideé*) of *liberté, égalité, fraternité.* After that such secondary ideas as *paternité, maternité, qualité, jollité,* etc., etc., follow themselves. In short, as with all works of real genius, the thesis once started runs of itself. . . .

We suspect that Monsieur Rousseau has drawn from a number of authorities, including certainly St. Thomas Aquinas, whom he refrains from naming. This, however, does not prevent his *livre* from having great *intérêt* and considerable *mérite.* If not exactly what one might call *une livre de poche* or *une volume de pantalon* it can at least be classed as an *essai*

de pyjamas—a thing we won't even try to put into English.

There are, of course, a number of misprints, such as "égalité" for "equality" and so forth.[13]

Other sketches, such as "History Revised" and "Interviews as They Were and Are," revealed that he was still sometimes reduced to grasping at humorous straws. *Hellements of Hickonomics*, in the same year, was for Leacock a return to verse. Leacock, having occasionally written verse, beginning with his first book, offered an evaluation of himself as a poet in *College Days:*

> Let me explain at once for those who do not know 'em,
> The kind of meters, called gas meters, which I use
> in this poem.
> Each foot begins and ends just where I end or begin
> it,
> I defy any man to scan it, though it might be possible
> to skin it.[14]

Leacock writing poetry was a little bit like the life-of-the-party wearing a lampshade for a hat. The observer generally laughed, but he was uncomfortable at the same time. Leacock used the strained rhyme which Ogden Nash used, but in Leacock's comic verse the technique was almost so obvious that it took away much of the fun. *Hellements of Hickonomics* contained the best of Leacock's attempts at humor in poetry. Thus, he was at his best in "Oh! Mr. Malthus," in which he made Malthus the figure of death, come to take pauper children whom production could not support.

That long drawn Face, the cloven Lip
The crooked Fingers all a-grip,
The sunken Face, cadaverous,
The dress, Ah, God deliver us. . . .
The Father strides with angry fist
"Out, out! you damned Economist!"
His wife restrains his threating Paw,—
    "William, it's economic Law!"
She shrieks,—"Oh, William! don't you know
The Geometric Ratio?—
William, God means it for the best
Our Darling's taken! we've Transgressed—"
    And crying, "Two times two makes four,"
She crashes swooning to the Floor.

. . . .

Such is the tale, we have it straight from
    Wordsworth's pious pen.
He happened to be out, not late, just after
    sunset when
He met a little cottage Girl, she was eight
    years old, (*she said*). . . .
    With her little Belly fully
    Satisfied, her mind got woolly;
    She was just like the rest
    Couldn't stand an acid Test,
    Took her thoughts too near the Place
    Where Digestion had its Base.
    What the child mistook for Knowledge,
    Just fresh air and lots of Porridge,—

Here is where Biology
Moves into Ontology.[15]

This was somewhat grim, but it put Malthus where
Leacock thought he belonged. It showed some kinship
to Oliver Wendell Holmes's "One-Hoss Shay," one discussing an economic concept and the other a socio-
religious one. But Leacock's verse is never the smooth
vers de société of Holmes. It was rather *vers de sociologie*
—Holmes wrote social verse; Leacock wrote scientific
verse. As a parody of Wordsworth, "Oh! Mr. Malthus"
was not brilliant, but the ease with which he worked
in the technical terms of the economic theory raised
the poem above the average, and the final couplet was
very good light verse. Much of Leacock's verse was, as
might be expected, parody of well-known poetry, but
his status as a parodist was little enhanced by it; he
was at his comic best when he burlesqued prose.

The book, however, was sound humor and sound
economics, though not very well received by liberals.
The critic for *Poetry Magazine* said, "He has some
mastery of prose, but in verse he makes so many silly
assertions and omissions that the prose *Preface* and
Appendix of this book overbalance and contradict the
poetry. Like Shaw he is unable to grasp on any tangible
resolution of capitalist contradiction. His paradoxes are
brilliant but not luminous.[16] This critic showed a remarkable lack of understanding of what Leacock was
trying to do. Stephen Leacock was not looking for
"capitalist contradiction"; he thought most of the con-

tradictions were on the other side. In "The Social Plan" he said, almost grimly:

> I know a very tiresome Man
> Who keeps on saying, "Social Plan."
> At every Dinner, every Talk
> Where Men foregather, eat or walk,
> No matter where,—this awful Man
> Brings on his goddam Social Plan.[17]

The principal aim of the book, however, was not to make fun of any political belief; it derived its humor at the expense of economics and political science themselves. It was, as he said in the preface, his farewell to economics. Perhaps retirement had brought the realization that, from his years of experience, he had something besides jokes to tell.

Leacock at leisure meant Leacock at loose ends. He was accustomed to taking his recreation when he wanted it, but he had never had it forced on him before. When it was suggested that he undertake an extended lecture tour through the western provinces, he naturally objected. It had been more than fifteen years since he had made more than three or four speeches on a single trip. Public lecturing was hard work, and he did not like it. He was good at it, but it always made him nervous. Always he was unable to eat before speaking, and the relief afterward was so great that he was at his best with his own small group immediately after a lecture.[18] He told his son that he never got over the fear which comes with speaking in public but that he had found a

way to combat it. He always picked out of the audience
a face that he liked, and he directed his whole lecture
to that face until he was over those first few bad moments which he invariably had. Besides his dislike of
public speaking, there was another reason why Leacock
hesitated to make a regular lecture tour in Canada; he
had never before taken money from a Canadian audience. While he had been charging high prices for his
humorous talents in the United States, he had been
motivated by a kind of patriotism, donating these same
talents to Canadian Rotarians, McGill Alumni Clubs,
Montreal Housewives Leagues, and any other organizations which he felt were both worthy and Canadian.[19]
There was, of course, no reason why he should not
charge for lectures in Canada; so, with the assistance
of Wallace Goforth, he made plans for the trip, partly
because he could not think of anything else to do and
partly because it had the earmarks of turning into a
triumphal tour for the retired man.

Having arranged with McGill, where his son was now
a freshman, for Stevie to accompany him, Leacock left
Montreal November 25 to see, for the first time, that
part of Canada to which all five of his brothers had
been drawn at one time or another.[20] Accompanied
by black luggage marked with bright stars for easy
identification at stops, Leacock moved through what
was easily the most exhausting and, at the same time,
the most rewarding experience of his life.[21] He went
from one enthusiastic, affectionate audience to another.
During the tour, which took him to Vancouver Island

and back in less than two months, he made more than thirty major addresses, in addition to which he frequently spoke to smaller groups when he had time. In Edmonton, for example, he spoke five times, three times in one day.[22] From Winnipeg he wrote:

> It is just like a come-to-Jesus parade. I talked at the Fort Gary Hotel [to the Women's Canadian Club] and a little while before the meeting they said, "This is the record for seats except for the Queen of Rumania," and a little later, "This beats the Queen of Rumania," and later, "The Queen is nowhere."[23]

The trip was broken by a meeting with his brother Edward at Calgary the middle of December.[24] He spent Christmas in Vancouver and his birthday in Victoria. From here he wrote proudly, ". . . never was anything like it, they said. I put a lot of work into each speech and never a note."[25] This was the end of the trek, however, and Leacock was tired. He told his niece, who was handling his correspondence, to express his regrets but to refuse all engagements "at present. Don't say *never;* I am tired but I can finish this and then I am done."[26] Exhausted but triumphant, Leacock returned to Montreal on the seventeenth of January.[27] Except for McGill alumni or other small groups he had a particular interest in, Leacock never made another real public speech.

Speaking, like many things he did, was very tiring for Leacock. He was not a frail man; on the contrary, he was robust and quite active until his death. He did

not tire easily; he tired regularly. The reason, of course, lay in the vital intensity with which Leacock turned to everything he did. He rose early; and, whether farming, fishing, speaking, writing, or entertaining, he performed the task with zest and enthusiasm. He lived every day at full speed, throwing his whole self into whatever was to be done. He did not accidentally make mountains out of molehills; he did it on purpose. The high sense of the dramatic so evident in his writing was a part of his basic personality. John Kelly, the hired man, came to Leacock's niece one day and said in a puzzled fashion, "Miss Barbara, I just don't understand Dr. Leacock. He says this whole farm depends on that pig," pointing to one small pig nuzzling up to the fence. Leacock was right, of course; attention to details made the difference between success and failure, but his dramatic emphasis had been too much for Kelly. Barbara thoughtfully recalled that living with her uncle was "a bit like living beside a volcano: there was nothing dull or routine in life."[28]

Perhaps it was this same sense of the dramatic which led Leacock to some of the peculiar economies which he practiced. He was really far from being a frugal man, but he liked to pretend that he was saving. Some of his schemes were real money savers—almost all of his manuscripts were written on the backs of examination papers he had received from students at McGill—but most of his plans were economies in form only, the sole requirement being that they seemed to be saving money or time. Leacock never counted labor into the cost of

anything. Old Brewery Bay had two furnaces in which Leacock never burned anything but wood; he had "bought a bush," and wood from the bush cost nothing. He had, of course, failed to count in the original cost of the bush, the wages of the two men who spent some time cutting, hauling, and stacking enough wood to last the winter, and the extra help who had to get up at all hours of the night to fire the furnaces; but what fun he had saying, "Oh, we grow our own wood, doesn't cost a thing." He always said he did not need an electric refrigerator. The lake froze over in the winter, and he had an icehouse. "It's no trouble to cut ice." It really was no trouble for him; he hired two men for two weeks to fill the icehouse. These might have been eccentricities, but the arrangements worked; had the house not been kept warm with wood or the icebox kept full from the icehouse, Leacock would have changed. Also, he always had an overabundance of labor that he had to keep busy somehow. He was always giving jobs to the relatives of his cook, and he had to find something for them to do.

Much of Leacock's economizing concerned his garden. He was proud of his gardening, largely a vicarious occupation for him, and he wanted the garden to be used. He discovered a soup one summer which could be made of the shells of the peas after the peas had been removed. He was not really very fond of the product, but using it made such a fine story that it was served frequently during the season. He disregarded completely the cost of raising anything he had grown.

George and Mary Leacock remember a lunch they had with Stephen. The soup was brought in, as always, in a tureen. Stephen sniffed at it suspiciously and asked what kind of soup it was. "Consommé of beef," said Barbara. "My God," shouted Leacock, "tinned soup with all those fine tomatoes in the garden." He picked up the tureen in both hands, carried it to the window, and poured it out. Then he made everyone go out into the garden and pick tomatoes to take to the kitchen. The cook must make cream of tomato soup, and they must wait for her. But no one minded; now contented, Leacock regaled them with stories while they sat at the table waiting for Tina to finish the soup.

Leacock proudly showed George his new irrigation system one year, explaining it had not "cost a cent." When George asked where he got all the pipe and fittings, Stephen airily revealed that he had torn down "that old windmill." "That old windmill," George remembered, had cost three hundred dollars the year before. Stephen Leacock never really fooled himself about his economizing. Although it was a good act and he had fun with it, he revealed, in a letter quoted by his niece Barbara, that he understood the situation:

I have a large country house—a sort of farm which I carry on as a hobby. . . . Ten years ago the deficit on my farm was about a hundred dollars; but by well-designed capital expenditure, by drainage and by greater attention to details, I have got it into the thousands.[29]

Stephen Leacock did not have to count pennies; personal economy was a game he played when it was convenient. He never let it rule his life. He burned wood in the furnace, but when he wanted a place to fish, he stocked his pond with fifteen thousand dollars' worth of trout.[30]

Leacock's effective economizing came in the way he made money, not in the way he spent it. For years he had written sketches that he could sell to magazines before he put them into a book. Now he turned his lecture tour into a series of newspaper articles for the Montreal *Daily Star* and then into a book, *My Discovery of the West*. This study of the economic situation and prospect of the western provinces was lightened by the usual Leacock humor, but it was sound observation. There was evidence of the teacher at work in his approach. Leacock admitted his own prejudices, and then explained with utmost sympathy and fairness the social or economic practices he was against. In "The Pure Theory of Social Credit," he turned a difficult technical explanation into a pleasant, easily understood essay. The book, large in scope, dealt with the political and economic histories of western Ontario, Manitoba, Saskatchewan, Alberta, and British Columbia. It bristled with statistics and legislative acts, but Leacock handled them casually and never allowed scholarship to come between him and his less academic reader. At the end of the book, in his practical fashion, Leacock offered solutions to what he had found wrong: a legislative change allowing amendment of the Constitution,

consolidation of the provincial debt into one Dominion debt, unification of the railway into all government-owned or all company-owned, and encouragement of immigration.[31] The thing Canada had to do was "be an empire."

My Discovery of the West was not the only literary result of Leacock's tour; the same year he published, with a note of defiance in the title, *Here Are My Lectures*. The publication of his lectures was in keeping with his announced retirement from the platform. Some of the lectures had drawn heavily on his earlier work; the three on "Frenzied Fiction" used excerpts from many of his parodies. Because they were drawn from his early best work, they were good, but, surprisingly, the new offerings of this volume, such as "The Two Milords" and "While You're at It: Expert Advice on Knocking Your House into Shape," were written almost at the high level of the old. In "Why I Am Leaving My Farm" there was some of the most delightful nonsense he had written. He was disheartened by finding that "the . . . manual suggested that . . . [a] snug effect can be made by covering the loggia with eucalyptus. 'Loggia' is a new word for me, though I suppose I can guess what it refers to. Personally I would just give it a coat of whitewash."[32] Later in the same sketch he was distressed at the citified turn taken by the simple old farm newspaper:

> The ceremony at which the Rev. Mr. Bray officiated, was held out of doors under a pergola, the assembled

guests being gathered in the loggia, beautified with floral decorations of bubiscus, rabies, and the flowering avunculus. Miss Primrose wore a beautiful écrin of soft tulle shot with dainty ecrus. Her father, who gave her away, wore a plain vignolette of haricot while Mrs. Primrose (mère) looked riante in a dark purple chassis de nacre.[33]

As had become his custom in recent books, some of the material, "The Advancement of Learning" and "Looking Back on Retirement," was good-natured, light discussion of subjects about which the author was obviously serious.

XIII

1937–1939

STEPHEN LEACOCK published, also in 1937, one of his most revealing titles, *Humor and Humanity*. When he sent his friend, Dr. Gerhard Lomer, a copy, he noted in sarcastic triumph, "This is the fifth book I have published since I was retired (as useless)."[1] *Humor and Humanity* and his earlier *Humor: Its Theory and Technique*, in 1935, contained his principal statements on what humor was and should be. His frequent and apt references to Bergson, Kant, Aristotle, and Eastman or even Tom Corwin and Thomas Hobbes indicated a scholarly interest in humor which had resulted in wide research. The prevailing impression in either of the two books was that Leacock knew humor, and, even more than that, respected it. Each of the critical volumes ended with a chapter on the sublimity of humor. Although both books drew on the same material and sometimes even used the same examples—the first work being the larger study—their aims were perhaps different. The

first was about the theory and technique of humor; the second was more concerned with the philosophy of humor. In his preface, Leacock stated:

The author has given to this book the title *Humor and Humanity*, rather than the obvious and simple title *Humor*, in order to emphasize his opinion that the essence of humor is human kindliness. It is this element in humor which has grown from primitive beginnings to higher forms: which lends to humor the character of a leading factor in human progress, and which is destined still further to enhance its utility to mankind.[2]

In his first sentence he defined humor as "the kindly contemplation of the incongruities of life, and the artistic expression thereof." In this statement lay his own philosophy of humor.[3]

Perhaps no author ever followed more closely his own precepts than Stephen Leacock. It is true that his friend, H. A. Innis, said, "The callous vulgarity which characterizes the humour of the medical profession is paralleled by the cynicism in the social sciences. . . . Mathematics was not the drawback to Lewis Carroll that political science was to Stephen Leacock . . . [giving] him an interest in institutions rather than persons."[4] Innis, however, was one of those social scientists who had found their studies under attack from Leacock's pen. Furthermore and more to the point, his criticism stood in opposition to every other critical comment made on Leacockian humor. Sandwell said Lea-

cock was typified by "his intense and vivid humanity."[5] The London *Times* critic was impressed by the complete absence of malice in Leacock's work.[6] Will Cuppy called him "good-natured,"[7] and the New York *Times*, "amiable."[8] Wherever Leacock chose to direct his humor, whatever the target, the humor was humane. The most easily identified characteristic of humor which Benchley could have learned from Leacock was the humorist laughing at himself; no one got hurt that way. When Leacock made fun of education, it was his own profession, and he handled it lovingly. He said of economics:

> Take enough of that mystification and muddle, combine it with the continental area of the United States, butter it up on the sides with the history of dead opinion and dress it, as the chefs say, with sliced history and green geography, and out of it you can make a doctor's degree in economics. I have one myself.[9]

The last line was obviously a kindly gesture, intended to take the sting out of the laugh for anyone who might have such a degree; there was certainly none of the cynicism which Innis thought he saw. Because Leacock was an active social scientist, it was easy for Innis to fall into the error of thinking that Leacock was a second-rate Veblen; however, Leacock was too busy following Mark Twain, and that at a safe distance. Closer to the truth than Innis was the critic who saw Leacock as

"quite free from the superciliousness of the modern satirist. He does not sneer at his butts; he rags them."[10]

For all of his belief in kindliness, Leacock thought that humor should fight back on occasion. Kindliness did not mean a calm, unquestioning acceptance; it meant simply that whatever rejection was called for would be without malice. Leacock pointed out that one of the essential points of humor was its use "as a corrective to over-sentiment."[11] The antiromanticism of American humor was a characteristic which he greatly admired.[12] His own antiromanticism was pointed out by the critic who said that Leacock's humor gave "out a satisfaction similar to that one gets watching a silk hat succumb to a snowball."[13] Puncturing the romantic bubble came easily to Leacock. Much of his parody was directed against romantic literature: the detective story, the gothic novel, melodrama. Other bits found their humor at the expense of such romantic ideas as a "back to nature" movement or spiritualism. Even the romantic profession of writing got its gibes when he wrote:

A well-known novelist of today is on record as saying, "There is only one recipe for writing that I ever heard of: take a quart or more of life-blood; mix it with a bottle of ink and a teaspoonful of human tears; and ask God to forgive the blots." It may be a recipe. But a good many writers find it easier to take a quart of whiskey and a teaspoonful of vermouth. Indeed there is no more need to use up life-blood and tears in writing than there is in the real estate business or in dry

duck farming. The Roman poet said there are tears for everything, but writing is not especially wet.[14]

The antiromanticism of his humor was a natural part of the man. As a social scientist, Leacock offered practical, pragmatic objections to idealized societies like socialism and communism; as a humorist, he offered equally sound objections to idealized professions like writing.

Coupled with Leacock's admiration of antiromanticism was his love of irreverence in humor. In Mark Twain he thought its effect "as wholesome as the sweeping of a fresh wind through a dank swamp. This . . . [was] the true 'American' humor."[15] Critics found the same sweeping fresh wind in Leacock's writing. Peter McArthur had said that the dominant note in Leacock's humor was rebellion.[16] Stephen Leacock had early shown himself to be as irreverent as the most American humorist; one of his student productions in *The Varsity* had been a formula for an obituary:

It is our painful duty to record the * * * demise of ——, graduate of this University of the year ——. For —— years previous to his death, Mr.—— occupied the position of ——, a post which he filled with the greatest ability. His probity, his unflinching honesty and indefatigable zeal, [sic] endeared him to all whose privilege it was to know him. As a public man and in the daily avocation of life Mr.—— was ever ready to fight the battle of ——. He was frequently heard to declare that ——. As a kind father, a tender

279

husband, and a loving son, his name will be cherished in the sorrowing memories of those from whom he was taken.

Most of the blanks—require no explanation. I may add a word of comment on some of the more abstruse. If the obituary is written for a baby the words "We prophesy that if it had lived, etc." are to be inserted. After "He was heard frequently to declare," the printer is supposed to insert some phrase touchingly reminiscent of the departed, such as, "that he wouldn't go home until morning." If deceased died outside the pale of the church, or had but few friends, the obituary is followed by a few lines in a jocose strain, mildly bantering his relatives on his loss.[17]

This irreverent attitude toward death was paralleled by his treatment of the classics, venerable institutions and customs, and people in high places. While he loved it, he called "God Save the King" doggerel,[18] and in one of his richest moods he recounted Mr. McCoy's audience with the Pope:

His Holiness was delightful . . . I explained to him my proposal for heating the Vatican by explosions of magnesium—in Latin, of course—I spoke Latin entirely . . . The dear old man sat and nodded his head so gently, merely saying *hic* . . . *hoc*.[19]

This had nothing of the bitter anti-Catholicism of Mark Twain, but it was irreverent in a kindly fashion. It was in the same spirit that he advised newspapermen to

learn to say "an alleged murderer" and "the alleged King of England" to avoid libel suits.[20] It was probably Leacock's irreverence which prompted Innis, somewhat pompously, to accuse Leacock of cynicism. Stephen Leacock was no cynic, but he did not like the deification of Adam Smith any more than that of Shakespeare. And he made fun of both of them.

The difference between fact and fiction, thought Leacock, was one of the principal distinctions between American and English humor. English humor depended on truth which seemed impossible; American humor depended on impossibility which seemed true.[21] As he told Cyril Clemens during a visit, English humor was based on fact while American humor was pure fancy or imagination.[22] Had he been talking about his own humor, he certainly would have placed it with the American production. One discerning critic had said "the audacity of invention" allowed the reader to watch "an alert intellect at play" in the writing of Leacock.[23] All of Leacock's humor showed evidence of fanciful origin. Almost all of his humor started with a logical beginning and built imaginatively toward an absurd, illogical conclusion. "My Financial Career" was a case in point; the trepidation with which the depositor entered the big, ornate bank was one which many men had felt. On this humble beginning he built the hilarious story of the man who became so confused that he immediately drew out all the money he had deposited by writing a check larger than he meant to. The whole canon of Leacockian humor was filled with the flash and the

glow of imagination—in character, in language, in situation, and in plot. Much of *Sunshine Sketches* was representative:

> Mr. Golgotha Gingham, the undertaker of Mariposa, [sat] on a stool. It was a part of Mr. Gingham's principles to take in an outing of this sort, a business matter, more or less—for you never know what may happen at these water parties. At any rate, he was there in a neat suit of black, not, of course, his heavier or professional suit, but a soft clinging effect as of burnt paper that combined gaiety and decorum to a nicety.[24]

The very name, Golgotha Gingham, bespoke imagination. The art of caricature, though based on fact, ultimately depends on fancy. Finally, the almost poetic quality of the comparison, "a soft clinging effect as of burnt paper," attested the creative imagination of Stephen Leacock.

In his analysis of the qualities of humor, Leacock failed to mention one which his own humor contained. Elizabeth Stern of the New York *Times* said, "While there is always the element of the fantastic in these stories, there is a certain everyday homeliness about the people and their problems which, despite their absurdities, endears them to the reader.[25] This use of the ordinary in language, in subject, and in illustrative example was frequently evident in his more serious essays: "All this you will say is exaggerated, is overcolored, is not truth. Very likely. But a half truth in argument, like

a half brick, carries better."[26] He used familiar ideas
to cut through excess verbiage or to contrast with pedan-
tic ideas which he thought fallacious:

> If [one] . . . asked [what is truth?] . . . of the econ-
> omists of today and waited for an answer, he would
> have to arrange his board for a long time in advance.[27]

This was reminiscent of Artemus Ward in whom Max
Eastman had found the same quality "of lovable honesty . . . honest provincialism in a society much over-
straining the effort to escape it."[28] Eastman was not
alone; other critics, such as Sculley Bradley, had found
"our humor . . . distinguished by homeliness."[29] Leacock's neglect of the quality of homeliness in his analysis, however, was not necessarily oversight. Although
the book did concern itself when necessary with
national differences, *Humor and Humanity* was about
all humor, regardless of origin, and Leacock had simply
identified American humor sufficiently without needing
homeliness.

With his three books in 1937, Leacock did some other
publication which was typical of his career. He wrote
two articles on Alberta's political system[30] and two on
the situation of the labor union in Canada.[31] Perhaps
a monograph which he prepared for the nickel industry
told the most about his character. *What Nickel Means
to the World* was a further discussion of the future of
Canada in terms of its mining industry, and its publication was paid for by the nickel interests. Part of the discussion was concerned with the coinage of nickel, a dis-

cussion so effective that the industry asked for and received permission to mint trial coins to Leacock's specifications.

Such publication as that for the nickel industry did little for Leacock's literary reputation, since it seemed to be a matter of writing for anyone who would put up the money. Few realized that, though Leacock had no objection to selling his art in the service of something he believed in, money alone would not move him. He had earlier written for *Collier's* a very successful little sketch called "What the Duce!" burlesquing Mussolini. The editor, thinking he had a good thing, approached Leacock about doing a similar article on the Prince of Wales. Leacock was outraged and disgusted. "Not for all the money in the United States Treasury," he snapped. Stephen Leacock's pen was not for sale; the nickel monograph had been an expansion of what he had already said—that Canada's financial future rested with her natural resources. He believed just as strongly in the expanded idea as he had in the original, and he could not have been induced to write otherwise.

The same year, Stephen Leacock received what was perhaps the highest honor he was ever to be accorded. In 1937 the Royal Society of Canada, after proper deliberation, passed a resolution:

A sane economist, an authority on Canadian history, a critic and essayist of international repute, a lecturer of magnetic personality, a teacher who has profoundly influenced many generations of students and,

above all, a writer and speaker who is the incarnation of humour, Stephen Leacock has won for himself a unique place in the Canadian scene. Adding lustre to the staff of McGill University for thirty-four years, his genius has been acknowledged with honorary degrees from Brown University, Queen's University, his alma mater of Toronto University, Bishop's College, Lennoxville, and his own university in Montreal. Author of many books on many subjects, he has illuminated with clear thinking and pungent phrase whatever theme he chose for his pen. Generous of his time and talent in helping many good Canadian causes he has contributed greatly to the growing reputation of Canadian letters.

It is therefore the privilege of the Royal Society of Canada to award the Lorne Pierce medal for the year 1937 to Stephen Leacock.[32]

Here was vindication with a vengeance. Leacock had never been very active in the society, preferring to turn his pen to more profitable and more effective writing. His recognition by the august body was not occasioned by his membership, but by his works, at which some of the group had previously looked askance.

An honor almost equal to the medal came to Leacock when he was invited by President L. S. Klick to join the staff of the University of British Columbia.[33] Vancouver, however, was a long way from Orillia and even farther from his circle of friends in Montreal. He liked the West he had seen on his recent visit, but he felt it

necessary to refuse with regret. Stephen Leacock had made his retirement a very real one, and he did not really want to go back to the classroom, as much as he loved teaching.

Leacock was more than once importuned to leave his retirement and return to public life. He was invited by Lawrence Lowell, the president of Harvard, to deliver the Lowell Institute Foundation Lectures, a series of six or eight lectures on any subject he might choose.[34] He was urged to make a good-will tour of Russia.[35] He was even invited to make an extensive lecture tour in Australia and New Zealand.[36] The offer from the Southern Hemisphere was so attractive that Stephen went so far as to investigate an itinerary, but ultimately he refused this as he had the others. He was not the kind of man to make a series of "last appearances."

When he retired from teaching, he retired at the same time from an active life in civic affairs.[37] He had been a popular and frequent speaker at service organizations; he had participated in politics; he had contributed time and talent to worthy Canadian charities. Now he had placed such things behind him. Some thought his action had been caused by bitterness at his retirement, but Stephen Leacock, while never reconciled to being called too old, was too balanced to withdraw from society on such a pretext. Instead, Leacock wanted to devote more time to serious writing, and he wanted the leisure to enjoy doing it. He was flattered by the offers from Vancouver and Australia, but he stayed in retirement.

One phase of his life which his retirement did not

affect was his wide acquaintance with interesting people. Leacock did not collect celebrities, but he did like people who were different. He kept up his connections with the important people he had known and continued to meet new ones. He knew William Lyon Phelps well enough to wire him that an old friend, Colonel Borey, would be visiting in New Haven and asked that he "treat him as one of ourselves." Afterward, he notified Colonel Borey, "Have telegraphed Billy Phelps."[38] From the first Leacock had drawn the attention of illustrious people. As early as 1917 he had received Theodore Roosevelt's letter. He was at various times a close companion of E. V. Lucas and G. K. Chesterton. Leacock's son recalls that Chic Sale visited his father in Orillia and Irvin S. Cobb was entertained in Montreal. In the latter part of his life Leacock carried on quite an extensive correspondence with Thomas B. Costain, his fellow countryman who was an editor for Doubleday.[39] On the other hand, of course, three of his favorite people were William Jones, his gardener; Bill Gentleman, janitor at McGill; and Jake Gaudaur, his fishing guide at Orillia and champion oarsman. Leacock was famous enough in his own right that he was neither attracted nor excluded by the fame of others. His own stature made an invitation from him gracious instead of forward.

Knowing almost nothing about cars, Leacock was surprised when he received notice, one day, that his truck had violated the vehicle ordinances of Ontario. He never learned to drive his car because, he said, that

would have meant having to chauffeur his guests back and forth from Old Brewery Bay to Orillia. He did not mind sending his man to drive, but he was not going to do it himself. Leacock knew only two things about cars, that they required gasoline—he asked all departing guests, "How's the gas supply?"—and that they generally went too fast.[40] One of his friends reported that Leacock liked big, fast cars,[41] but his family declare that he hated fast driving. George Leacock recalled that Stephen always cautioned the driver not to go over thirty-five miles an hour but, having given his warning, settled back and never looked at the speedometer again. When he was fined nineteen dollars in Brockville, Ontario, on May 4, 1937, for allowing his truck to be driven without flares,[42] he answered the required questionnaire gleefully: "Read—fairly well but I need spectacles. Write—Yes, quite nicely. I have written forty volumes.[43] To the court he wrote:

> I desire to say that I am fined because I permitted my driver to drive my truck without flares. I never in my life heard of flares until now; neither did my driver, and I had no notion that a truck must carry flares—nobody told me. There is no obligation on the man who sold me the truck to tell me about flares, and there ought to be, but there isn't. Now what comes next? There may be a dozen more obligations and limitations. My driver speaks French. Shall I be fined in Ontario for that? My truck is painted green. Is that legal? Or is it too Irish?[44]

The last gibe—at the Orangeman-controlled political machine in Ontario—had the subtle Leacock touch that could be devastating. He paid his fine, but he had had his fun.

Leacock reserved his sarcasm for such institutions as the court, for he never turned his scathing humor on people. It is significant that almost all his acquaintances cannot remember that Leacock ever spoke ill of anyone. Actually he had a violent temper which he was usually able to control. Barbara, his niece, recalls that he was frequently angry at people and expressed himself volubly, but it was typical of his personality that he did not impose these outbursts on those outside his home.

Barbara Ulrichson might have said too that he frequently got angry at her, but she understood him. She realized, as he did, that his affection for her was a deep one. He had never had a daughter; he had not always been very close to his son. Since 1927, Barbara had run his house, typed his letters, helped him with his books, and acted as hostess for him. It was with mixed feelings that they parted such close companionship in 1937. Barbara was getting married. Her husband, Don Nimmo, was the son of the editor of the Detroit *Saturday Night*, an old friend of Stephen's. As if she were his daughter, Leacock was glad to see her happily married, but he would miss her. With parental fondness, he planned a magnificent outdoor wedding for her at Old Brewery Bay. He put his men to work building tables to place around the lawn—"Didn't cost a thing," he told George, "built them myself." From the roof of the porch to the

edge of the terrace, he stretched an awning; and over the beautiful walk to the boathouse, he built an arbor for the ceremony itself. He covered the floor of the dining room with sawdust to make a bar of it, and mixed the drinks himself part of the time. He imported champagne, which he hated, and Scotch, which he loved. He played the gracious host, announcing, with a nice sense of fitness, that the bar would be closed twenty minutes for the wedding ritual. Such actions were a part of the man.

What followed was equally typical of Stephen Leacock. The wedding over, Leacock was satisfied. The tables, and awning, and arbor were to be taken down, but he would get to it. Weeks later, when George visited him again, the tables were still standing in the rain, now beginning to topple. The awning sagged from the porch, displaying a large hole where a dog jumped out of an upstairs window and through the fabric, in chase of a rabbit. Not until the arbor collapsed and blocked the walk was it removed. Because Leacock had not needed the things and had known where they were, he had left them.

Because of the publication of *My Discovery of the West*, Lord Tweedsmuir presented Leacock, in 1938, the Governor-General's Prize, Canada's top literary award.[45] The prize, in the nonfiction class, pointed up what had become increasingly plain, that Leacock was never a very good fiction writer and that his greatest mastery of letters lay in his ability to explain in inter-

esting, lucid language an intricate political, economic, or social problem.

Two of the articles he wrote in 1938 demonstrated the technique which had won the Governor-General's medal for him. "The World's Muddle over Gold"[46] and "What's Next in Europe?"[47] both were clear and sometimes witty discussions of economic and political situations. His other two articles were more literary. "Emigration in Literature" considered the influence of the spreading Empire on the writing that was done during the expansion, beginning with the settlement of colonial America.[48] The other was a biographical sketch of Sir Andrew Macphail, occasioned by his death. In it Leacock recalled that he had served with Sir Andrew on the advisory board of the *University Magazine,* and that on his coming to Montreal he had joined the Pen and Pencil Club, where he had known Macphail as well as Paul Lafleur, John Logan, Robert Harris, Maurice Cullen, and Jack McCrae.[49] He had looked upon Andrew Macphail with great affection and had rejoiced with him when he was knighted.

Only one book by Leacock appeared in 1938. *Model Memoirs* was, as its subtitle said, "sketches from simple to serious." It showed his usual command of parody in bits like "My Victorian Girlhood," and it showed in "All Is Not Lost" his impatience with professional politicians and political reporters:

The Lats (I think it was) had sent what was practically an ultimatum—the nearest they could write to

one—to the Slats and there was no likelihood that a high-chested people like the Slats would swallow it. As I say, I think it was the Lats and Slats, or it may have been the Checks and Shorts; at any rate, some of those high-chested people that fill the center of Europe, who used to be content before the great war to play the hand-organ and make toy clocks, and who now fill our whole fore ground. . . .

So I came home feeling pretty sick. And then, after all, it turned out that the Slats hadn't "picked up" the affront—by lucky chance—and, of course, if you don't pick up an European affront right away, it goes bad.[50]

This was the kind of foolishness that early Leacock fans had learned to expect from him, though they had missed it recently. They were glad to see it come back.

In *Model Memoirs*, Leacock used a trick which he frequently employed in his writing, that of putting real people into his sketches, sometimes even using the real names. *Sunshine Sketches*, of course, had been filled with identifiable people. In "The Dissolution of Our Dinner Club" in the current volume, two characters named Woodenbean and Des Rois appeared. These were obviously Dean Woodhead, classical scholar at McGill, and Leacock's friend, Captain René du Roure. Du Roure appeared often simply as "Capt. R.," as he did in "Golf Season" in *The Iron Man and the Tin Woman*. Melpomenous Jones in *Literary Lapses* had taken his name from a very real Septimus Jones, and

Bill Jingleman, the janitor in "Opening Day" of *Funny Pieces,* was certainly Bill Gentleman of McGill's maintenance staff. In the "Epilogue" to a later book he spoke of fishing with Charlie Janes, the father of his student of the middle twenties, Henry Janes.[51] Still later he told of his intention to buy Christmas presents for Charlie, for George and Mary, and for an old professor who took his classes for him years before.[52] Charlie and George were his brothers; Mary was George's wife and Professor Needler actually had taken his classes while he attended his examinations at Toronto. The gardener in *Arcadian Adventures,* who would not let his employer touch any of the flowers, walk on the lawn, or stand on the paths, sounded very much like Bill Jones of Orillia.[53] May Shaw remembers driving into town with Trix Leacock for fresh vegetables because "our Mr. Jones" would not allow picking from the Leacock garden he tended. However, none of the people who found themselves in Leacock's stories objected, because Leacock treated them so gently.

Bill Jones, Leacock's gardener from 1918, had evidently learned to cope with the fantastic schemes which Leacock proposed and put into practice.[54] Leacock always took his gardening very seriously at first, determined to prove that he could raise turkeys or melons as well as anyone. When, however, he had grown a twenty-four-pound Montreal melon or had produced enough fine birds to send one to each of his family for Christmas, he lost interest in the project and either stopped it completely or just let it run down.

Leacock was serious in 1939 when he wrote a seed company, complaining of eight hundred asparagus roots which had not even come up. Eight hundred was, of course, far too many for Leacock to handle, but he liked to do everything on a grand scale. The company answered that such orders could not be guaranteed; local conditions must be unfavorable or perhaps there was "something wrong with the method of planting."[55] This phrase Leacock underlined in red, and, with the same pencil, he scrawled at the top of the page, "This is an insulting letter—Stephen Leacock." In their next letter, the seed firm again disclaimed all responsibility but then added in a somewhat confused tone that eight hundred asparagus roots were being sent to replace the earlier ones.[56] By the time they got there, Leacock was probably interested in something else.

Stephen Leacock, a man who could not tie his tie so that it would stay and who always needed a haircut, kept very accurate and precise records on his farm. All the neatness he possessed was concentrated in his orderly mind. He wrote his niece:

I find that from May 1st to May 15th we served 333 meals, and they cost 17 cents for outside supplies, but as many things represent "stocking up" (having just come up from Montreal) and as inside supplies increase greatly with broilers and vegetables, I hope to get down close to 10 cents. . . . The fowls, eating by the measured pound of food of which I know the cost, are running at about a little over $15 a month; but

the hens lay not far from 50 cents a day (20 cents a day cash and the rest we eat), so that the hens are very nearly feeding the 225 broilers.[57]

This Leacock called "putting the college to it," a phrase he used very frequently.[58] When he raised the several varieties of peas which he had imported from England, he had the children count the number of shelled peas one could expect from a box of unshelled peas, and he noted carefully which variety produced the most uniform peas and which the greatest number.[59] He fastened up a bulletin board on the barn where he posted precise orders for the day: "Pick the peas. Put them in baskets. Take them to the market." The board had, too, a system of bells for calling various workmen—two rings for one, three for another. The only trouble with this was that the men could never remember what their signals were; and therein lay the secret of the whole system. Duties would have been onerous indeed, had Leacock insisted on results from all of his elaborate plans. But Leacock, himself, paid little attention to his statistics or records once he had compiled them. He just liked to keep records.

The number and variety of journals, ledgers, and notebooks remaining among his effects attested to his love of getting things down in writing. One such notebook, bearing the inscription "23 Grad Hall," contained lectures dated from October 2, 1900, to November 9, 1900. Another which he had named "Books Read and Books Looked Over" had carefully noted entries in 1938

and 1939, some time after his retirement from McGill. Still another listed the daily expenses from February, 1938, to August, 1939, and one called "Petty Cash" had even been indexed. The titles, themselves, indicated the methodical quality of the man's mind:

Orillia Garden and Orchard Book 1933
Day by Day 1937
Lumber 1937—& 1938—
Livestock and Poultry Feed Book [indexed]
Orillia Day Book
Orillia New Day Book Beginning August 1st 1940
House Garden and Fish Book Vol. 2 1943[60]

The first of this list contained a typical entry. On one page was an intricate drawing of plans for rebuilding a cottage, even including markings where drains were to be dug before construction started. Sometime later, Leacock turned back and carefully noted in the margin, "Cancelled in favor of a lodge." Bookkeeping was a game for Stephen Leacock, one he played as enthusiastically as he did billiards, but he seemed never to impose it on others.

The most detailed of his records were compiled after his retirement, when he spent more time at Old Brewery Bay, coming from Montreal as soon as the weather permitted. Even when he had been teaching, Leacock had wanted to get back to his fishing as soon as possible; after he retired, he hurried every spring to the trout stream he leased from John Drinkwater. He was on his way to his fish stream one day when he picked up a

young boy hitchhiking. Asked where he was going, the boy replied that he was going out to Drinkwater's to fish. "Some old guy has the place leased, but nobody ever catches you." When Leacock asked if he might go along, the boy agreed and then guided the man straight to his own stream, where they fished all afternoon. The boy never knew he had been with the "old guy" who leased the place, but Leacock told John Drinkwater that he wanted better protection on his lease. With the stream for trout and the lake for bass, Leacock was a busy and a happy fisherman.

Having bought his first boat when he was seventeen, Leacock was never again without a seaworthy craft of some kind. He named his last boat *Selwyn* after the school his son had attended, but he never learned, says his brother George, to run the motor himself. He kept a man to drive the boat just as he kept one to drive the car. When George asked him if one man could not do both, Stephen replied, "No. What if I want to go fishing and have the car pick me up on the other side of the lake? See, George, see that's where most people don't have it!" Leacock never really realized that it was the money, not the idea, that most people did not have. If he could not run the motor, he must have, at least, learned to steer, for on July 9, 1939, he helped save the life of Percy Bartleman whose canoe had turned over. Leacock and John and Tina Kelly put out from shore when they saw the boy's situation. Kelly was driving the boat, but when they had to return to land because Tina was ill, Leacock took over the wheel. On the next run,

Leacock, showing the same skill he had as a young man with a sailing craft, cut close enough to Bartleman for Kelly to throw him a rope.[61] Such an action by so famous a person naturally made good headlines, even gaining the front page of the New York *Times*. Leacock soon tired of the talk of heroism and stated to one reporter:

> Why the first thing you know they'll make a lifeboat station out of me. . . . You may quote me as saying that in the future I will rescue no one, not even women.[62]

Still, for a man sixty-nine years old, it had been quite a feat, one which reassured him that his retirement had not proven him useless.

XIV

1939-1941

LEACOCK had moved into the Windsor Hotel around the first of the year, and he had found himself comfortable there. On his return to Montreal in the fall of 1939, Leacock decided to give up permanently his Cote des Neiges house, though he retained title to the property until his death. John and Tina, instead of going with him to Montreal as they usually did, remained behind to take care of Old Brewery Bay. Leacock drew up an elaborate contract as to their duties and salary under the new plan, even providing for his will to supercede the contract in the event of his death.[1] Having already wired his publisher of his change of address, he moved into his new quarters in the Windsor Hotel.[2]

Leacock's serious periodical publication for the year was nationalistic in tone. "Charles Dickens and Canada" was a piece of literary scholarship which grew out of his earlier biography of the English humorist.[3] "Canada and the Monarchy" was another of his empire

299

studies, concerning the loose-knit but strong ties with the mother country.[4] Leacock turned critic in his other article of the year: in "Writers of Quebec," a review of Ian Forbes's *Spirit of French Canada,* Leacock revealed a wide knowledge of the literature of his country, French as well as English.[5]

When Great Britain entered the war in September of 1939, Canada immediately followed suit. Stephen Leacock, the imperialist, was particularly affected by the action. The next month he published *All Right, Mr. Roosevelt* (*Canada and the United States*). This forty-page pamphlet was a gentle, kindly statement which was at the same time an appeal and a challenge. Canada would accept any help the United States felt it could offer, even man power:

> If any of the McGruders of Mississippi,—they were Highlanders, weren't they originally?—want to come over and join the Royal Highlanders of Toronto, we've a tartan and a sporran and a jorum (one forgets these Highland terms) for each of them. Let them all come. Perhaps they can bring the Virginia Robinsons and Randolphs with them, or "round heads" from Connecticut still stamped with the image of the Ironsides: or the Lowells or the Cabots from Boston,—but no, I forgot, they don't talk to anybody—or to nobody that they'd meet in Europe.[6]

But Leacock made it clear that his real purpose was to impress both countries that their long-standing international friendship was the greatest contribution that

either could make to a troubled world. As in the first World War, Leacock began early to apply his own particular talents to the war efforts of his country.

The same year, he wrote *Too Much College*, a book for which he had made elaborate preparations. Stephen Leacock had taught in college for thirty-five years, and he did not like what he saw happening to education. *Too Much College* was basically a serious accusation of colleges, hitting at their philosophies, their curriculums, and their methods. "Education Eating Up Life" was an argument that young people had to go to school too long. At one time, said Leacock, men were out of school and into debt by the time they were thirty:

> Now it is all changed. Children in school at six years old cut up paper dolls and make patterns. They are still in high school till eighteen, learning civics and social statistics—studies for old men. They enter college at about nineteen or twenty, take prerequisites and post-requisites in various faculties for nearly ten years, then become demonstrators, invigilators, researchers, or cling to a graduate scholarship like a man on a raft.[7]

He had all the major schools of Canada and the United States send him catalogues. He studied them carefully and then wrote such telling essays as when he attacked teaching methods in "Mathematics Versus Puzzles" and "Parlez-Vous Français?" and when he attacked what was being taught in colleges in "Teaching the Unteach-

able." In "Psychology the Black Art of the College," he wrote:

> John F— in school made life miserable for his teacher and also for the other children. He threw erasers across the room. He threw snowballs through the window. He dumped the waste paper all over the floor. He erased all the things the teacher had on the board. . . .
>
> In the days when I taught school, half a century ago, I think I could have solved the John F—— problem to ten places of decimals with three feet of bamboo.[8]

Colleges were training people to do, not to know. He felt that one learned to teach by teaching, learned business by losing money, learned journalism by writing, and learned marriage by nursing the baby. He said "College is meant to train the mind, not the thumb,"[9] and he saw no reason for giving academic credit for the mere acquisition of skills. It was in his return to writing of education that he again spoke of his retirement:

> Listen; it's like this. Have you ever been out for a late autumn walk in the closing part of the afternoon, and suddenly looked up to realize that the leaves have practically all gone? You hadn't realized it. And you notice that the sun has set already, the day gone before you knew it—and with that a cold wind blows across the landscape. That's retirement.[10]

Here was some resignation, but not all the bitterness was gone yet. Most of the contents of *Too Much College* was

in the recent Leacock vein, serious subjects presented in a jocular manner. The form he used was the essay and he used it with telling effect, in a book which required fifteen printings.

Too Much College had been as thriftily put together as some of his earlier books. There had been twenty-eight short anecdotes syndicated and released by Miller Services, Ltd., between November 12, 1938, and May 13, 1939.[11] Leacock took twenty-two of these, under the heading "Little Stories for Good Luck," to fill the last portion of his book. The short stories indicated something of Leacock's reputation as a raconteur. As host at his own table and as guest at others, he had always enjoyed celebrity as an anecdotist. "In America," he said, ". . . we suffer from the story-telling habit."[12] The technique was not a new one for him; he had filled *Here Are My Lectures* with what he called "Interleaf Stories," the same kind of short, personal anecdotes. The anecdotal structure—the introduction of the narrator into the story—was one Leacock used often in even his longer sketches; he liked to tell his own stories. And he correctly viewed it as part of his kinship with American humor. The very last part of the book, the "Epilogue" on bass fishing, Leacock said he put in for himself as "It ought to be the privilege of an author to reserve some part of his book for his own.[13] It must have been personal intervention, too, which placed the drawing of the frontispiece in the hands of Peggy Shaw, the now grown former playmate of Stephen, Jr.

Laugh Parade, in 1940, was a kind of anniversary

volume for Leacock: it had been ten years since his other anthology, *Laugh with Leacock*. In 1930 it had seemed that Stephen Leacock had written the last of his humor. By 1935, he had written three more books of humor, though he still seemed unable to recapture the touch of nonsense he exhibited in his early writing. His increased production in serious and critical work indicated that he saw the end himself. With his retirement, however, Leacock found either new life or new leisure, and he certainly found a new style. The content of his work became more important, and the humor, while it became quieter, regained the sure touch of old. He turned from nonsense to common sense. After 1936 when he published *Funny Pieces*, Leacock employed his humor more often as a vehicle for serious thought. Though he spoke with a great deal of charm and a disarming, good-natured humor, when he talked of academic freedom, or modern drama, or the changes in language, he meant what he said. As the humor became a bit more incidental, it grew sharper, so that the new sketches, though different in style from the old, were almost the equal in quality of *Literary Lapses* and *Sunshine Sketches*. His continuing sales, though not so large as at first, had been steady, and his publisher thought it reasonable to bring out *Laugh Parade*, which justified its existence by requiring a second printing within two months.

The only other book to bear his name in 1940 was *Our British Empire*. This was in the same vein as his earlier popular treatments of political science. Both its purpose and its wit were foretold by the preface:

I write this book in the hope that it may be of service in the present hour. It is a presentation of the British Empire, not for the pageant of its history but for its worth to the world. The Empire is united not by force but by goodwill. It means co-operation, not compulsion. In it we live as free men.

The link of our common history, the bond of our common language, the identity of our outlook hold us closely associated with the United States. With France, the long record of bygone wars that once divided us is now but a common glory. In the hour that is, we share that comradeship in arms which faces a common danger with a united endeavor. Through these associations we may see a vision of a world of peace.

In dealing with the mass of statistical material that goes with the making of such a volume as the present, it is unavoidable that errors and misprints will find their way in. For these I apologize beforehand. For instance, in Chapter III, I stated that the number of hogs in the world is 200,000,000. I now believe this wrong. There seem to be more than that. Reviewers whose one idea of reviewing is to mop up misprints will add more hogs.[14]

Occasioned by the war, *Our British Empire* defended the system of government under which the Empire operated as the very system which the whole world would have to come to eventually—one of good will and mutual benefit. An interesting note was Leacock's insistence that

"to a certain degree modern Britain . . . [was] the child of America."[15] It was the discovery of America which started the growth of the British Empire, and, having made a mistake in handling the first colonies, England never made the same error again. *Our British Empire* was the production of a loyal British citizen who thought imperialism as beneficial in 1940 as he had thought it in 1907.

At the age of seventy, shortly after an operation on his throat, Leacock, in response to a question put by a newspaperman, said of death, "I have a suspicion it is inevitable, but give me my stick, I'll face it."[16] This statement expressed the quiet determination with which the man had lived his life, but Leacock's love of the dramatic and his skill in choosing an apt and telling phrase made it doubtful that the statement was very significant. Many viewed him as an agnostic, and, indeed, his attendance at services and his attention to church duties had been slight since his youth. On one of the rare occasions when he attended services at the Anglican church in Orillia, Leacock found himself without any money when the offering plate was passed. He calmly tore the flyleaf out of the prayerbook and scrawled "I O U $2.50." When, however, he treated religion in his humor, the fun was directed at individuals or practices, and not at beliefs. Such humor was always very gentle, and the only church he presumed to laugh at was his own. He spoke of Sir Arthur Currie as walking "close to the shadowed curtain of the In-

finite." And Wallace Goforth said that, though Leacock never mentioned religion, an abiding faith was a very real and obvious part of the man. Perhaps it was because of his advancing age, but in Leacock's last few years his writing took on more concern with things of the spirit—whether human or divine. "The fault with economics," he said, "was the assumption that what *can only be done by the Spirit* could be done by material interest."[17] His clearest, least affected statement, because it was in the framework of humor in which he spoke best, was in a small allegory he wrote shortly before his death. Science, Philosophy, and Theology meet at the funeral of Dead Certainty:

> The interment is over, and the three turn away together.
>
> "Incomprehensible," murmurs Theology reverently.
>
> "What was that word?" asks Science.
>
> "Incomprehensible; I often use it in my litanies."
>
> "Ah, yes," murmurs Science, with an almost equal reverence, "incomprehensible!"
>
> "The comprehensibility of comprehension," begins Philosophy, staring straight in front of him.
>
> "Poor fellow," says Theology, "He's wandering again; better lead him home."
>
> "I haven't the least idea where he lives," says Science.
>
> "Just below me," says Theology. "We're both above you."[18]

Certainly the thought of death must have been as distressing to Leacock as to anyone else, but perhaps he meant it when he said, "I'll face it."

Boston University wanted to confer on Leacock an honorary Doctor of Humanities in 1939. With the honor came an invitation to speak at the "Sunset Supper"— a gathering of alumni.[19] He was not up to it, however, and had to reply:

> I cannot tell you how greatly I appreciate the honour which you suggest on behalf of Boston University. Unfortunately an illness and a serious operation of last year has rendered my health extremely uncertain and prevents me from undertaking so long a journey or incurring the strain involved on such an honorable & agreeable occasion.
>
> I need hardly say with what regret I find myself compelled to forego the conspicuous distinction proposed.[20]

Leacock made a better recovery from his difficulty than he had anticipated, but at times he was quite concerned about his condition.

About this time Leacock received a request to sit for a portrait. The artist, Fredrick B. Taylor, was somewhat surprised when the elderly man consented. But Taylor had been a student at McGill, and his studio was close to the Windsor Hotel where Leacock was living. After he had started sitting every weekday from twelve to one, Leacock explained that he hoped someone would

want his portrait; surely McGill would want one, and he hoped the University Club would want to remember him. Active even as he grew older, Leacock was a difficult subject, partly because he could not sit still and partly because he made the artist laugh so hard. The work went so slowly that Taylor was reluctant to display how little he had accomplished, but at the third sitting he asked Leacock if he would like to see how it was coming. "Do you want me to see what you've done?" asked Leacock; when Taylor confessed he would rather wait, Leacock said, "You will only see one of my unfinished manuscripts over my dead body so why should I see your unfinished painting!"[21] With supreme understanding, he never showed the slightest interest in the canvas until it was ready.

Taylor found it a difficult portrait to finish. He continued to dabble at it, unsatisfied with the result but dealing with a completed picture. After watching him closely, Leacock remarked, "You know I've always believed that it takes two to paint a portrait, the painter and someone to knock him in the head when it's finished."[22] Taylor readily agreed, and Leacock got his first look at his likeness. It was not a splendid picture; it was too vivid in color and too devoid of character. The hands, done in a photographic manner, served as the focus instead of the face. Leacock grasped the arms of his chair, turned red, and then in a gasp of laughter chose the kindest words he could have said, "My God, Taylor, that's exactly how I feel!"[23] As he

intended, the artist took it as a compliment, and Leacock escaped.

In 1941, besides writing two articles,[24] Leacock had one of the most interesting publishing experiences of his life. Samuel Bronfman of the House of Seagram determined to publish a history of Canada. This would be the distillery's contribution to culture; it was certainly not a promotional venture. The Gazette Printing Company in Montreal was given the job and an advisor was brought in from New York. The New Yorker, casting around for an editor or author, approached the superintendent of the printing company, Furness. Furness suggested Stephen Leacock as a distinguished Canadian who might accept the task, and, after some discussion, they wired him. They were a little nonplused by his prompt answering telegram: "Come along and bring your fishing poles." When they arrived at Old Brewery Bay late in the afternoon, Leacock met them in one of his typical fishing outfits—baggy slacks, once white; a nondescript sweater; a hat, now totally shapeless; and scuffed, comfortable soft shoes. Giving them no opportunity to talk business, he hurried them into the boat and onto the lake. Humoring Leacock, they fished until well after dark and brought to shore finally one small bass. Their host took them back to the house where, during a late dinner, they tried to explain to him what they wanted. Leacock breezily told stories and made his usual interesting conversation; then he abruptly stood up. "Well, I'll see you fellows in the morning. You can sit here all night if you want to, but

I'm going to bed." He left them, telling them that if he were not around when they got up, his man would give them breakfast.

The efficient American was incensed; calling Leacock a "has-been," he was determined to return to Montreal at once. Furness persuaded him to stay, though he himself was not quite sure why. The next morning, Leacock was nowhere in sight, and they each received for breakfast half of the fish they had caught the night before. Since Leacock had still not appeared, they decided to wait in the boathouse to bid him good-by. From his study above the boathouse, Leacock came down the stairs heavily, bearing a sheaf of notes in his hand. "Gentlemen, I was up about five this morning, and I have the whole thing drafted out. I know what you want, and here is what I suggest." And he presented to them a detailed outline of the history of Canada. Furness and his companion were astounded, but before they left they signed a ten-thousand-dollar contract with Leacock to do the book in the next four months.[25] After thirty-one years, Stephen Leacock returned to the Gazette Printing Company, printers of his first book.

Canada, the Foundations of Its Future was one of the finest examples of the bookmakers' art; Seagram had plenty of money, and nine of the outstanding artists of Canada were commissioned to do thirty-one full-page illustrations, plus small decorative sketches through the book. The subtitle implied what Leacock said in his foreword:

Here are great cities that within living memory were solitary prairie, crowded harbours where but half a century ago the sea rolled in unheard, unheeded. This very novelty is an inspiration. This very lack of history is the foundation of history itself. We can begin at the beginning.[26]

This was Stephen Leacock's seventh volume of history, and he was to write two more. His first one in 1907, on the growth of responsible government in Canada, had grown out of his knowledge of political science, but his approach was the study of big personalities—Baldwin, Lafontaine, and Hincks. The next three, all in 1914— *Adventures of the Far North, The Dawn of Canadian History,* and *The Mariner of St. Malo*—were even closer to Leacock's idea of real history. To Stephen Leacock, history had the immediacy of human endeavor. He might have agreed with Carlyle that "History is the essence of innumerable biographies." He wrote history well because Jacques Cartier and Abraham Lincoln and Baron Lahontan were, to him, real people; furthermore, they were the kind of people he admired most, those who pushed out and accomplished something. His own friendship with contemporary explorers stemmed from the same admiration. Intimate with Amundsen and Shackleton, he inspired Vilhjalmur Stefansson to write *Unsolved Mysteries of the Arctic,* for which he wrote the introduction.[27] There was less of hero worship in these friendships than might be imagined; he thought of these men as having experienced history rather than

having made it. Leacock felt, as strongly as anyone else, that history was something lived by people. It was important to him that he had touched history. In *Canada*, he said, "It is strange this, and peculiar to our country, the aspect of a town grown from infancy to old age within a human lifetime.[28] When he sent a friend the book, he wrote, "Read the pages on Toronto in the Confederation period. It's real history, being my own recollection of 1876–78."[29] Just as when he wrote humor, Leacock could not forget humanity: it was people who made and were history.

XV

1942-1944

C*anada* was the first history Leacock had written in seven years, but its influence was evidently great. As if burdened by a sense of history, Leacock published, the next year, 1942, two books and two articles in this rediscovered field. He considered *Montreal, Seaport and City* the best book of his career, telling his brother that he had finally achieved a mature serious style just when he felt he might be past writing good humor. This is a book which Leacock had had no notion of writing, as much as he loved Montreal. The first suggestion of such a project came to him in a letter from Thomas B. Costain, whom he had known first back in the 1920's as the editor of *MacLean's Magazine*. Costain had moved on to the *Saturday Evening Post*, where he had again had some correspondence with Leacock. Now, as an editor of Doubleday, Costain wrote:

Dear Mr. Leacock:
I have a suggestion up my sleeve that I have been saving in the hope that we could get together. How-

ever, time is passing along so I think perhaps I should let you know now what it is all about.

You may have noticed that we are publishing a series of books on famous American ports. Already we have treated Gloucester, San Diego, Seattle and Baltimore and several others are now in the works. We now want to take it beyond the bounds of the United States and naturally our first thought is of Quebec, the most colorful of all ports on the American continent.

Would you be interested in doing the book on Quebec for us? In view of the research work you did for your recent history, I imagine that you could approach the task without feeling that it would prove too onerous. In fact, I feel pretty sure you would find it a pleasant assignment, the story of Quebec being so full of color and drama. Does the idea appeal to you?[1]

Leacock had earlier published three books with Doubleday—*Charles Dickens, The Greatest Pages of Dickens,* and *The Greatest Pages of American Humor*—and he was intrigued by the idea. He suggested, however, that Montreal would make a better subject for a number of reasons—one practical one being that the local sales in Montreal would be greater than in Quebec. The book ought to be, he said,

> a happy blend of history and geography, romance and commerce, with plenty of present day interest both for U.S. and Canada.[2]

This must have been a surprising answer for Costain and the other Doubleday editors, but Costain was quick to reply:

I am delighted that you will do the port book and think you are entirely right about the choice. Montreal is the better from other standpoints besides the matter of local sales. It will be the terminus if or when the St. Lawrence Waterway plan goes through, which will make it an outstanding world port; and the story of Montreal has been tied up with the United States at every stage, particularly in the efforts made to capture the city during the two wars.

Therefore we bow to your superior judgement in the matter and want you to do the port of Montreal for us.[3]

Leacock had come to view Montreal with great affection in the more than twoscore years he had lived there, and he felt it had played an important part in history. He gloried in telling that story.

Leacock felt so strongly that history had a lesson for the world that he relinquished royalties on the first five hundred copies of *Our Heritage of Liberty* to enable the publisher to print the book, which promised little sale.[4] In it he reviewed the history, the struggles, and the accomplishments of democracy. Out of his knowledge of the past, he predicted the future in "New Program for Canada,"[5] and "Was Hochelaga a Myth" was an evaluation of Jacques Cartier's account of the fabulous Indian city he found on the site later to be

Montreal.[6] It was a year of important serious publication for Stephen Leacock, but he did not neglect his humor.

His other book of the year, *My Remarkable Uncle, and Other Sketches*, was distinguished by its title sketch, "My Remarkable Uncle," certainly some of the finest writing Leacock had ever done. The subject of the character sketch was his father's younger brother, E. P. Leacock. The accuracy with which he drew the old fraud did not lessen the sympathy which the reader felt for him. E. P. might have been a twin to Beriah Sellers of Mark Twain's *Gilded Age:*

> His activities were wide. He was president of a bank (that never opened), head of a brewery (for brewing the Red River) and, above all, secretary-treasurer of the Winnipeg, Hudson Bay and Arctic Ocean Railway that had a charter authorizing it to build a road to the Arctic Ocean, when it got ready. They had no track, but they printed stationery and passes, and in return E. P. received passes all over North America.[7]

E. P. was not really a charlatan; "all his grand schemes were as open as the sunlight—and as empty."[8] He simply told stories and then found himself believing them. He was a man with vision in a boom time of dreams, and he saw what he wanted to see—actually saw it.

Perhaps one reason Leacock's treatment of the character was so sympathetic lay in Leacock's own personality. He had something of the same quality himself. Once when Francis Hackett was visiting him, Leacock

showed him the garden still covered with last year's weeds, saying, "There are the peas, and there are the melons." Hackett, marveling, said to Barbara, "He really sees them, doesn't he?" Mary Leacock recalls that Stephen hugely enjoyed standing by the front door as they arrived, ushering them in with great ceremony. He would turn to one of the little country girls he had finally trained to stand still and say grandly, "Take Mrs. Leacock's luggage to the west bedroom." The bedroom was on the west side of the house, but it was hardly worth the buildup he gave it. The beds were equipped with hard, thin mattresses, and the lights might or might not be working at the moment. As far as Stephen Leacock was concerned, if a thing worked at all it was enough. Once when his truck broke down, George offered Stephen one of his to use until it could be fixed. Stephen wrote back that the two hired men had "put in a new clutch and ground hell out of everything else"; it still leaked something from underneath, but the motor ran and Stephen was satisfied. E. P. Leacock was not really a remarkable uncle; he was a proper uncle for such a man as Stephen Leacock.

My Remarkable Uncle was further marked by the inclusion of the only serious short story Leacock ever published. It was not serious in the sense of art, but its purpose was the story and its form was fiction; it was not a narrative vehicle for fun. "The Transit of Venus" told the story of a college professor whose bumbling courtship of one of his students almost failed and then succeeded. It was not a superb story, but it was

typical of Leacock to try serious fiction at least once.

The book contained, however, mostly pieces of writing which might best be classified as familiar essays. The essay, a form Leacock depended on more and more in his last literary period, had appeared in his work as early as 1913. *Behind the Beyond* of that year contained, as one of its best offerings, "Homer and Humbug":

> Let me take another example from the so-called Catalogue of Ships that fills up nearly an entire book of Homer. This famous passage names the ships, one by one, and names the chiefs who sailed on them, and names the particular town or hill or valley that they come from. It has been much admired. It has that same majesty of style that has been brought to an even loftier pitch in the New York Business Directory and the City Telephone Book. . . .
>
> This is what I should like to do. I'd like to take a large stone and write on it in very plain writing,—
>
> "The classics are only primitive literature. They belong in the same class as primitive machinery and primitive music and primitive medicine,"—and then throw it through the window of a University and hide behind a fence to see the professors buzz!![9]

But he made fullest use of the essay in his late work. In *My Remarkable Uncle*, his discussion of the British soldier and of the passing of the kitchen and of adult education and of the gentleman—"Gentlemen embezzle

but don't steal"—were high examples of a medium Leacock had employed from the first.

Leacock's essays differed from the sketches in their intent. They really had something to say; they were not intended for fun only. They managed, nevertheless, to be a pleasant mixture of sense and nonsense. In "Three Score and Ten," a very true comment on age became fun in his hands:

> You begin as "little man" and then "little boy," because a little man is littler than a little boy; then "sonny" and then "my boy" and after a while that "young man" and presently the interlocutor is younger than yourself and says, "Say, Mister." I can still recall the thrill of pride when a Pullman porter first called me "doctor" and when another one raised me to "judge," and the terrible shock it was when a taxi man swung open his door and said, "Step right in, dad. . . ." Presently I shall be introduced as "this venerable old gentleman" and the axe will fall when they raise me to the degree of "grand old man." That means on our continent any one with snow-white hair who has kept out of jail till eighty. That's the last and the worst they can do to you.[10]

This was the same technique he had used in "Oxford as I See It," and he showed no lessening of powers now. In even their strictest form, Leacock's essays were never formal; they were warm and personal essays, containing his own opinions or observations. It was a seri-

ous comment written in a pleasant style when he wrote
"Good-bye Motor Car!":

> The only amusement for a youth came to be going
> out in a car with a girl, or going out in a car to look
> for a girl, or going out with a girl to look for a car.
> Since you can't drive all the time, they had to invent
> the pop and hot dog stand, and since you can't stand
> and eat all evening, they had to build a dance hall
> beside the pop stand.
>
> You can't dance forever, so that had to expand into
> a sort of Inn, called the Old Saw Mill, or the Old
> Forge, or the old anything at all that a new thing
> isn't.
>
> With that, money, money, money every minute
> . . . money for gasoline, money for pop, money for
> ice cream, more money for gas, money for the right to
> dance, money for the right not to dance. . . .
>
> Thus staggered the world along, bankrupt with its
> own pleasure . . . the rich bankrupted by the rich-
> ness of their golf club . . . the young bankrupted on
> soft drinks; the old bankrupted on hard ones.[11]

Though he was having fun, Leacock meant what he
said. In his new serious role, he found the humorous
essay the form best suited for what he wanted to say
and what he wanted to do. Leacock no longer tried to
be hysterically funny; in 1943, he wanted to teach as
well as amuse.

It was evidently during this busy year that Leacock

started thinking seriously about an autobiography. He wrote his publisher realistically:

> I should not wish to publish this till the war is over as I think it would attract more attention in a quieter world.[12]

That he would write a good autobiography was evidenced by the remarkable memory he displayed in a chance meeting with Dan McArthur the same year. Dan was the son of Peter McArthur, the editor of *Truth* when Leacock first began to publish. As a kind of parlor trick, Leacock went through a copy of *Literary Lapses* with the young McArthur, identifying which of the sketches had appeared in *Truth* and indicating by dates the issues in which they were printed.[13]

The next year, 1943, was one of Leacock's busiest writing periods.[14] Already at work on two books to be published later, he wrote, besides four articles concerning Canada, a series of short sketches and stories in support of the War Loan. He resurrected Mariposa as the little town trying to make its quota in the Loan drive, and, though the writing was good, the town was not the Mariposa of *Sunshine Sketches*. Leacock, however, knew the little town could not live again, and he did not even try to use the same characters. He included the eight sketches in his new book of humor, *Happy Stories*, in spite of the hint of hasty composition which such public relations writing was sure to show. Besides "Mariposa Moves On," the name he gave the eight little Victory Loan sketches, there were several other good pieces.

There was quite a representation of Leacock's old humor, as in "Mr. McCoy Sails for Fiji":

It goes without saying that the McCoys were out in the "Forty Five," every man of them, out and back. My friend is very proud of a dirk of the Young Pretender that they have at McCoy Castle; they have his dirk, and his gold watch and chain, and his gold pencil, and his cuff links. The Young Pretender, it seems, while hiding in Scotland spent a night at McCoy Castle.[15]

A burlesque, "The Life of Lea and Perrins," was very good, as was "Pawn to King's Four," a gibe at the leisurely pace of a chess club. Perhaps the best of the lot was "Boom Times," a fictionalized account of further adventures of his "remarkable uncle." The fact that some of the pieces were not so effective was likely to recall to the reader that it had been some time since Stephen Leacock had written a bad book. Certainly this one was still far above the level of most of the humor he wrote between 1925 and 1935. The uneven quality of *Happy Stories* was probably the result of Leacock's not having worked hard enough on the book. It undoubtedly would have been better if he had not been more interested in another book he was working on at the same time.

He wrote his friend, Dr. Lomer:

This book How to Write is like a favorite child to me because I wrote it purely to suit myself with no

eye on editors or sales or the public. If that means that it fails then it is a favorite all the more, as the feeble child always is to the fond parent.

So what more fitting book to present to the unbiassed mind of a Librarian.

With best regards,
Stephen Leacock[16]

How to Write demonstrated again what his humor had shown for a long time, that he knew precisely what he was doing when he wrote. In spite of the wit with which he presented his advice, his introduction was sound. If he chose to write chapters on "The Laws of Grammar and Free Speech," "How not to Write Poetry," and "How not to Write More Poetry," he was able to make the beginning writer understand the actual labor of composition. South Africa ordered fifteen hundred copies of *How to Write* when it was adopted as a reference text.[17] The book was further honored by a decision to publish it in Braille.[18] His chapters on the writing of humor were largely taken from *Humor: Its Theory and Technique,* but if he had been right the first time, there was little he could say that was different. The outstanding feature of the book was its pragmatic approach:

How do you get started?

The best practical advice that can be given on this subject is, don't *start*. That is, don't start anywhere in particular. Begin at the end: begin in the middle, but *begin.* If you like you can fool yourself by pretending

that the start you make isn't really the beginning and that you are going to write it all over again. Pretend that what you write is just a note, a fragment, a nothing. Only get started.[19]

With the easy, familiar air he always used in his humor, Leacock lent confidence to the prospective writer. There was a conspiratorial air about the book, as if a guild member were giving away secrets which could not fail. At any rate, *How to Write* was a good critical analysis of the practical art of writing.

It was in 1943 that Stephen Leacock gave his old friend, Joe McDougall, a special lesson in how to write. McDougall received a rather mysterious telephone call, asking him somewhat guardedly if he could consent to come for an interview with regard to writing a book to order. Bewildered but interested, he arranged the meeting and during it discovered that the book was to be in support of private enterprise against socialism. As the prospective employer reeled off the requirements of the book, McDougall grew more convinced that they had called the wrong man. When he finally stopped the man to inquire why he, who did not even understand the questions, had been chosen, the interviewer hesitantly admitted that McDougall had not been his choice. He had approached Professor Leacock, but, unfortunately, he was already at work on a similar volume. Leacock, however, had said that there was only one person in Canada ideally suited for the assignment; that was Joe McDougall. Not wanting to contradict his

friend, McDougall agreed to think it over and rushed back to his office.

Calling Leacock immediately, he found that he had, indeed, been recommended. "Stephen," he said, "you know me very well by now and if there is one thing you know about me better than any other thing it is that I know nothing whatsoever about the subject of economics." Leacock quickly replied, "Joe, you haven't a thing to worry about. I've just had somebody mail you a letter which covers the whole thing. All you need to do is refer to the sections of the books I have mentioned and anybody can put the thing together satisfactorily from this outline." He went on to warn McDougall not to read more than he had indicated—pages 178–91, for example—for "the rest is balderdash and will only confuse you." The next morning McDougall received a typical Leacock manuscript which it took him an hour to decipher, he recalls, but the whole book was there; all it would take was some industrious hack work. McDougall hardly knew what to do; he did not really want to do the book, but he did not want to hurt Leacock either. The problem solved itself when those who proposed the work revealed how little they were willing to pay. McDougall knew his friend would approve his refusing the task on financial grounds.[20]

Stephen Leacock was spending more and more time at his Orillia home. Since he had given up his home in Montreal, Old Brewery Bay remained the only place where he could live and entertain as he wished. The establishment did not run smoothly, but it ran. Leacock

liked to give huge parties, but he never seemed to have enough silver or dishes to serve them properly. The maids were always rushing the soup spoons out to the kitchen to wash them in time for dessert. It was just such a mixture of the elaborate and the makeshift which marked Leacock's social life. He was very fond of intricate meals, from hor d'oeuvres on through, but the hor d'oeuvres, themselves, were likely to be sardines still in the tin and cucumbers served with a knife so the guest could cut his own. He was not a heavy eater himself, but he knew good food, and he served good food. He did not, however, really care how it was served. He invited George and some others to go fishing one time after lunch. As lunch was delayed they considered taking the meal with them but decided to eat before they left. As they entered the dining room, Leacock, who hated to miss a moment of fishing, was still upset. "This won't do," he said, "we have to get on. We can take it with us." Distributing the party around the table-cloth, he had them pick the whole works up and carry it to the lake. There they laid it in the bottom of the boat, meat pies, salad, cherry tarts, and all. Leacock threw back his head and laughed with a real sense of accomplishment. "That's why," said Mary, "he never had a matching cup and saucer."

It was to Orillia that Henry Janes came in 1943 to offer Leacock a writing assignment. Janes, now a public relations man, had been Leacock's student in the twenties. Pan American Airways was preparing a series of public service advertisements on the world after the

war, and they wanted Leacock to do one of them. They offered a thousand dollars for a thousand words, but Leacock told Janes that he was so busy he did not think he could get to it. He would try, however, to deliver something in the next two weeks. The next morning Leacock arose at his usual early hour and when Janes came to breakfast handed him the finished manuscript.[21] He explained that he had proceeded to write the article because he simply could not get started on the writing he had planned to do. "Henry, it just won't go," he complained. "I can't make it go." As it began to rain, they called off their planned fishing trip, but Leacock suggested they go down to look at the lake anyway. By the time they had reached the shore, his writer's mind was evidently working again. Standing in the light rain, totally unaware of it, Leacock recalled the sea battle between the *Chesapeake* and the *Shannon*. Using his cane as a pointer and the squally lake as a map, he lectured for forty-five minutes on the famous sea fight, quoting tonnage, crew, captains, and armament from memory.

The book that started again at the lake was *Canada and the Sea*, his only literary production of 1944 except one article.[22] The history was concerned with many of the things Leacock liked best, the sea and sailing, exploration and military engagements. This kind of history came rather easily to Leacock; it was as much a labor of love as his humor was. It was a suitable book to be the only one published the year of his death.

Early in 1944 Leacock was incapacitated by failing health. He wrote Gladstone Murray in late January:

> . . . getting better & hope soon to be out of the woods —as an aftermath of flu something went wrong with my swallowing—I believe (and please God), it is clearing up now. . . .[23]

As the plea in the last line indicated, Leacock was concerned about his condition, and well he might be. His earlier operation on his throat had been for what was thought to be cancer. The difficulty in swallowing should have frightened him terribly. Perhaps it did; he was not one to impose his troubles on others unless they were very close to him. His next letter, however, revealed that his optimism was wearing thin:

> At the present I am a very sick man. With good fortune I may pass a present corner and go on for a good time yet, even years. But at the present I find it very hard.[24]

As the disease progressed, Stephen Leacock of the hearty laugh and the flexible voice, had trouble making himself heard. It was obvious that cancer, the malady he had fought so hard after his wife's death, had now struck him again.

But the innate courage of the man stood him in good stead. He went on with his work as well as he could. He had already made arrangements for Barbara to publish a posthumous volume made up of whatever

works he might leave uncollected.[25] He went through his manuscripts and one time soberly labeled one stack:

Sorted
All Ready
None Needed for—
Barbara's Book[26]

This was February 22. Unable to speak easily, in increasing pain, Leacock, still in bed, worked steadily with his pen until the middle of March. On March 16 he was operated on for cancer of the throat.[27] Though not of superior physique, Leacock had always had good health, and that, with all the determination of his strong will, began to pull him back toward recovery.[28] However, Leacock at seventy-four was past his prime; he could not hold out long enough. He suffered a relapse and on March 28, 1944, X-rays were taken to determine if anything could be done for him. He labored even for the shallow breaths he was drawing, but his eyes twinkled as he smiled up at the radiologist and said huskily, "Did I behave pretty well? Was I a good boy?"[29] Two hours later Stephen Leacock was dead.

XVI

STEPHEN LEACOCK, seldom ostentatious in life, wanted neither display nor disturbance at death. In accordance with his wishes, his body was cremated and the ashes were taken to St. George's Church at Sibbald's Point. There, the scene of many long, happy summer days in his childhood, the wind blew sharply up the steep bank from his beloved Lake Simcoe, whirling more snow to the already-covered ground. The bad weather and the distance from Toronto and Montreal worked together to give Stephen Leacock the quiet service he wanted. With six members of his family as pallbearers, including his brothers, George and Charles, the ceremony was simple, but it was conducted by the highest religious official of the dominion, the Most Reverend Derwyn Owen, Primate of all Canada. Archbishop Owen, a long-time friend of Stephen's, had come fifty miles from Toronto through the snow to assist the local rector in the last rites of Canada's most famous author. Owen had also come to help in the funeral services of one

of the distinguished Sibbald family. Upper Canada College honored one of its most outstanding head boys in sending its principal. On March 31, under a bare umbrella elm where his mother, Jim, and Dick had preceded him, the ashes of Leacock were interred.[1] The next day, All Fools' Day, 1944, newspapers all over the world carried the news of the burial of the humorist.

Though his death brought to an end a career which could only be called successful, Stephen Leacock had not followed a uniform course in his writing. However, after his retirement in 1935, Leacock concentrated on his literary career, increasing his production to an average of almost two books a year. Though the tone of it changed, his humor regained its superior quality. Only occasionally writing nonsense, he left that medium to younger men, like Max Shulman or Will Cuppy, and he turned his attention and talents to the informal essay. In his later years, among his contemporaries, he resembled most E. B. White, Corey Ford, Wolcott Gibbs, and a host of columnists who tempered their comments with laughter. From the new perspective of retirement, Stephen Leacock had viewed the world in a more kindly fashion than ever before, and his good-natured gibes ceased only with his death in 1944.

But not even death really stilled Leacock; there were four books yet to come. One of them was certainly to be expected. *The Leacock Roundabout* was an anthology selected from the whole Leacock canon, the sort of book which usually comes at the death of a popular author.[2] It could not really be called the voice of Lea-

cock; it was an echo. *Last Leaves* was a different matter; though it had not been put together by the author, it was all new. Leacock's niece, Barbara, collected the last of Leacock's periodical publications, as her uncle himself would have done. The resulting volume contained some of his finest writing. Because they were dated by their concern with the war, a large number of the selections, unfortunately, could not last as his earliest work had, but the style in which they were written was the same mature, clear style Leacock had found in *Canada* and *Montreal*. In such sketches as "Rebuilding the Cities" and "The School Is the Lever," the theme was one which he had found much earlier—that society had a responsibility to its least fortunate members—and he stated it with as much enthusiasm and courage as he had when he first discovered it.[3] Even the nonsense of the last volume was good, better than it had been recently. Leacock had been so pleased with "Living with Murder" that he had written George, "it encourages me to go on writing." He might have said the same thing of "A Lecture on Walking" or his light-hearted spoofing of postwar planning, "This Business of Prophecy."

One essay stood out as typical of the style he had been steadily developing since his retirement, a style made possible by the mind which took all knowledge as its province. In "Common Sense and the Universe" he undertook to explain the contemporary position of science. He explained it beautifully and, in doing it, presaged the case study method of teaching science on

a popular level that James B. Conant and Lincoln Barnett were to employ later. In the late nineteenth century, said Leacock, science had explained the whole universe.

Once started, the nebulous worlds condensed into suns, the suns threw off planets, the planets cooled, life resulted and presently became conscious, conscious life got higher up and higher up till you had apes, then Bishop Wilberforce, and then Professor Huxley.[4]

Then came the discovery of radioactivity and Rutherford's work with the atom. The concept of the atom as a small but solid particle had to change:

Let us try to show what Rutherford did to the atom. Imagine to yourself an Irishman whirling a shillelagh around his head with the rapidity and dexterity known only in Tipperary or Donegal. If you come anywhere near, you'll get hit with the shillelagh. Now make it go faster; faster still; get it going so fast that you can't tell which is Irishman and which is shillelagh. The whole combination has turned into a green blur. If you shoot a bullet at it, it will probably go through, as there is mostly nothing there. Yet if you go up against it, it won't hit you now, because the shillelagh is going so fast that you will seem to come against a solid surface. Now make the Irishman smaller and the shillelagh longer. In fact, you don't need the Irishman at all; just his force; but Irish

determination, so to speak. Just keep that, the *disturbance*. And you don't need the shillelagh either, just the *field of force* that it sweeps. There! Now put in two Irishmen and two shillelaghs and reduce them to one . . . body. . . . What you have now is a hydrogen atom.[5]

Then came Einstein's theory of relativity in time and space. It was in his explanation of the necessity of relation between dimensions that Leacock shone at his brightest:

You can see it better still if you imagine the universe swept absolutely empty: nothing in it, not even *you*. Now put a *point* in it, just one point. Where is it? Why obviously it's nowhere. If you say it's right there, where do you mean by there? In which direction is there? In *that* direction? Oh! Hold on, you're sticking yourself in to make a direction. It's in *no* direction; there aren't any directions. Now put in another point. Which is which? You can't tell. They *both* are. One is on the right, you say, and one on the left. You keep out of that space! There's no right and no left.[6]

Here was none of the condescension which usually accompanies popular explanations of intricate subjects; rather here was all the charm of the boy explaining a new game to his companions, never realizing for a moment that he is superior to everyone on the playground. The clarity of his explanations resulted from the homely quality of his illustrations, as when he explained the

dimension of time: "It just means that information about an occurrence is not complete unless we know both where it happened and when it happened. It is no use to tell me that Diogenes is dead if I didn't know that he was alive." The introduction of the quantum theory and the statistical method into physics he correctly interpreted, calling it the funeral of Dead Certainty. It was just such a mixture of common sense and special knowledge, leavened with humor, that Leacock had been working toward; in his last books he achieved the combination beautifully.

The book that was occupying Leacock's time when he recommended Joe McDougall for a similar task was *While There Is Time; the Case Against Social Catastrophe.* In it he sounded anew his alarm against socialism. To the trained observer like Leacock, it was obvious that the war was going to speed up social reform. Since 1920 he had talked social responsibility of one man for another. What he feared was that man, the individual, would shift that responsibility to the state until man had neither responsibilities nor rights. Unlike his earlier works on the subject, *While There Is Time* made its appeal directly to Canadians and its application specifically to Canada.

The last book to come from Leacock's pen was not completed. *The Boy I Left Behind Me* was the beginning of the autobiography he had discussed with his publisher as early as 1942. Leacock had intended to call it "My Memories and What I Think," but such a comprehensive title hardly fitted the small, slim volume which

he had time to complete.[7] Much of *The Boy* was written during Leacock's last illness. First the inactivity and finally the pain made the writing difficult for the author, and there was in this production a shortness of temper which he had never displayed anywhere else in his writing. Probably as reliable as the word of most men on themselves, *The Boy* spoke too harshly of the poverty he suffered in his childhood. Though in some years the Leacocks were in less comfortable circumstances than in others, poverty was never theirs. There is also the possibility that Leacock's sense of the dramatic overcame his sense of history. Leacock's demonstrated skill as an historian, however, makes such reasoning improbable. Part of the answer undoubtedly lay in his treatment of his father. He said, in one of his prim, Victorian moments, "[It was] a shadowed, tragic family life into which I need not enter. I always feel that it is out of place in a autobiography to go into such details."[8] Wanting to get the feel of his troubled youth into the book, he was stopped by his sense of decency from blaming his father. Instead, he laid the blame on an impersonal quality, that of finances. Whatever the reason, the autobiography, for all of its valuable color and insight, was unreliable in some places.

One particular charm of *The Boy I Left Behind Me* was its use of digressions in an almost eighteenth-century fashion. At the slightest opportunity, Leacock would stop the narrative of his life to give a short history of education, a description of the battle between the *Chesapeake* and the *Shannon*, a criticism of the methods

of teaching French in Ontario, or a discussion of the English public school. Even the fragment of the intended book which Leacock left indicated that it truly was not going to be just an autobiography; it was also going to be "What I Think."

The settlement of Stephen Leacock's estate revealed that it was not an astonishingly large one—he had spent a great deal of money—but it was a comfortable amount. After small bequests to his brothers, the servants, his niece, and Mrs. Shaw had been settled, there remained in a trust fund for his son an inheritance exceeding a hundred thousand dollars. The will itself showed the thoughtfulness of its maker. Drawn up in late 1942, it made bequests of three hundred dollars each to Bill Jones and Tina Kelly, but only a month before his death, Leacock added a codicil which increased the amounts to five hundred dollars. To his brother Charles, with whom he shared his lakeside home at various times, he left his boats and fishing tackle. To May Shaw, a neighbor almost since he began to write, he left five hundred books from his library—the books to be chosen by her. To his devoted, dependable niece, Barbara Nimmo, he left the copyright of all unpublished material he might leave. And to McGill, where his friend Dr. Lomer was building a Leacock collection, he left all his manuscripts which were immediately "findable." Such special bequests, frequently in addition to money, indicated much of the kindly, loyal character of Stephen Leacock.[9]

The settlement of the estate revealed other things which would have pleased Leacock, also. He was no

longer earning the almost fantastic royalties which the
twenties had brought, but his books had brought him
more than eleven thousand dollars from Dodd, Mead
and Company in the three years preceding his death,
and the two months after his death saw his writing still
selling, adding a thousand dollars more to the estate
in that time.[10] As a practical economist, Leacock was
vindicated by the status of his holdings in stocks and
bonds. His fifty thousand dollars' worth of securities
was so widely scattered that no single investment was
worth more than five thousand, and many were as small
as fifty dollars. Yet of the many issues which he held,
only one small mining stock was selling below par. Since
most of his investments were in oil, paper, or mining, it
was easy to see that Stephen Leacock had followed
his own teaching; Canada's future lay in its natural
resources.[11]

Awarded seven honorary doctorates, honored three
times with significant medals for literary excellence,
Leacock might have felt himself amply rewarded for
his work; few men receive so much. But more honors
followed after his death. On July 4, 1944, a little more
than three months after his death, a Liberty ship, the
SS *Stephen Leacock* was launched. A letter explained:
"Liberty ships were named for eminent Americans—
patriots, writers, artists, statesmen, etc., or other deceased persons who had contributed to the history
and culture of America. Mr. Leacock's name was selected by the Ship Naming Committee as that of a person in this category."[12] George Leacock, who furnished

the library of the ship with a set of his brother's books, was told that Stephen Leacock was the only noncitizen thus honored.

The honor which he probably would have appreciated most came from Orillia. He had immortalized it as "Mariposa," and the people wanted to repay him. On June 21, 1944, the Leacock Memorial Committee was formed,[13] the action of the committee taking two forms. Emanuel Hahn, leading medalist of Canada, was commissioned to design a Leacock Memorial Medal for Humour to be awarded annually for the best book of humor written by a Canadian; Leacock would have liked even the nationalistic touch. The group also decided to honor Leacock with a Memorial Collection of his works and material about him, the collection to be housed in the Public Library. Elizabeth Wynn Wood, noted sculptor and native Orillian, was asked to do a portrait bust of the famous author. Through the untiring efforts of the Mariposians themselves, both projects were completed. The first medal was presented in 1946, and the bust was unveiled by the Premier of Ontario, Leslie Frost, September 14, 1951.[14] The annual dinner for the presentation of the medal is the kind of occasion Stephen Leacock would approve of: they remember him, but they remember him with laughter.

In 1957 the town of Orillia itself moved to help keep alive the memory of one called "Canada's greatest writer." Leacock's favorite spot on earth, The Old Brewery Bay, was purchased by the town and established as the Stephen Leacock Memorial Home. Mr.

Louis M. Ruby generously bought Leacock's library and personal papers and presented them to the home. Cataloguing the some twenty thousand items began, and in 1958 the Home was first open to the public. The town intended, through the display of its collection, "to retain the charm and vitality and personality of the man."[15]

Such honors were not just gestures to an undeserving figure; Leacock's career had been long, distinguished, and varied. At his death he had written a remarkable total of sixty-one books in more than half a dozen fields. Besides his thirty-five volumes of humor, his bibliography could list in the social sciences alone six titles in political science, two in economics, and nine in history. One volume in the field of professional education bore his name. In a more literary vein, he wrote five books of criticism and three of biography, including his own autobiography. Of the twenty-seven serious books which came from his pen, at least a dozen would have to be classified as professional or scholarly publications.

The production of well over half a hundred successful books was in itself enough to assure the distinction accorded Leacock, but there was more. The remarkable man had written, besides the humor which appeared in periodicals, eighty-eight articles on widely divergent subjects. The number of articles testified to Leacock's industry; the distribution testified to his qualifications as a philomath, one who loved all learning. Naturally, the largest body of publication was in his own professional area—thirty-eight articles in political science and

twenty-one in economics—but surprisingly the remainder of the work was divided among many fields. Education drew his attention six times, as did history. He wrote two biographical sketches. He published twelve pieces of literary criticism, and to the literature of geography he contributed three articles. Even more surprising, in most of these categories he published articles which an academic scholar might have listed in his professional bibliography. Of course, a professor at a university as large as McGill was expected to produce some scholarly works for his department, and twelve of his titles in political science and eight in economics would be classified by the academic world as scholarship. It was unusual, though, to find a man capable of doing acceptable research and criticism in many other departments. Leacock published learned articles in history—two; in education—two; in geography—three; and in literature—seven. These thirty-four articles, of which at least two dozen appeared in major journals, indicated a career marked by learning as well as wit.

A separate area of scholarship to which Stephen Leacock also contributed was that of reference works. He had, early in his life, written for eleven divisions of the Encyclopaedia Britannica. The Encyclopedia Americana listed him as the author of six articles in that work. Five of them—"Clergy Reserves," "Imperial Federation," "Local Government," "The Ashburton Treaty," and "Washington Treaty"—were divisions of the larger entry on Canada.[16] The sixth was on "Riel's Rebellion" of 1885, in which his brother Dick had fought.[17] He

was credited in Compton's Encyclopedia with being a contributor in biography, though it identified no specific entry,[18] and he wrote sketches of humorists Charles Farrar Browne, Robert Henry Newell, and Edgar Wilson Nye for the Dictionary of American Biography.[19]

Leacock's works, in spite of their scattered subject matter, had a consistency which was unusual. If one note was dominant in his whole bibliography, it was humanism. This philosophy was one that Stephen Leacock was admirably suited to speak for in all of its meanings. Beginning with a good classical background at Upper Canada College, his education continued its way through the humanities in history, literature, and modern languages. A gracious host, Leacock liked companionship; he liked an audience; people were as necessary to him as was thought.

As an historian, Stephen Leacock was interested in the people of history. Like Carlyle, he believed that history was the story of important figures. His first contribution to history in 1907, concerning the coming of responsible government to Canada, was significantly named *Baldwin, Lafontaine, Hincks;* the human agency, not the system which it brought, was important to Leacock. From then on, the history that came from Leacock's desk was about those who made history—Mackenzie, Sir John Franklin, Cartier, Lincoln, Baron de Lahontan. Leacock, however, enjoyed the human failings of his heroes; in *Canada,* speaking of Prince Rupert, the godfather of the Northwest Territory, he digressed to comment, "In one and the same letter we find him

spelling 'dog' two different ways."[20] Dates themselves meant little to Leacock; they were merely useful in that they told when a man did something. Battles were not movements of "troops"; they were the actions of people, with Wolfe here and Montcalm there. Even when writing of a city, Leacock did not change his style. A reviewer said, "Stephen Leacock has written with skill, humane understanding, and unfailing good humor. . . . Montreal has been fortunate in its historian. To read this book is to have a new understanding of the quality of the city."[21] Leacock tried to bring to everything he wrote, including history, this "humane understanding"; he almost always succeeded.

In his studies in political science and economics, Leacock followed the same pattern as in his histories. People were important. Figures, by themselves, were not. His concern with the human side of the social sciences did not, however, keep him from being a competent scholar. One critic said that his proposals in *The Unsolved Riddle of Social Justice* were "fifteen years ahead of time,"[22] in their discussion of social legislation. Leacock was an ardent advocate of private enterprise who feared socialism greatly. But his concern for the people who needed social justice made him see that private enterprise was not likely to serve the need; the government would have to extend its protection. This same solicitude for humanity colored Leacock's whole approach to his professional field: he never read Adam Smith without the knowledge that the economic man did not really exist; he never studied Malthus without

remembering that people were not ciphers. A depression was not just an interesting economic problem to him; it meant someone was going without food. Totalitarianism was not merely a political structure to him; it meant someone was going without freedom. His own Empire was a brotherhood more than a form of government. Both economics and political science were, for Stephen Leacock, tools to serve mankind. When they became intellectual playthings for learned minds, he grew disgusted with them.

Having decided early that all good humor must be without harm, Stephen Leacock spent almost half a century turning theory into practice. For all of his success as an historian, a critic, an economist, an *homme d'esprit*, his position with posterity, of course, depends upon his humor. There was evident in all his humorous writing a kindness and lack of malice which was rare. As Leacock wrote it, even satire, usually a biting art, was far from destructive. Professor Pacey, who made a bit too much of Leacock's similarity to the neoclassical writers, was right when he said, "His values are eighteenth century ones: common sense, benevolence, moderation, good taste. His method of presenting the values, however, is the genial one of Addison rather than the savage one of Swift."[23] But even this criticism did not go far enough; there was never in Leacock the condescension which sometimes appears in Addison. Further, in Leacockian humor the reader's sympathy lay with the butt of the joke. Leacock laughed at the little man who was baffled by his own society; this was

the basic incongruity from which his humor came: the system and the citizen of the system, unsuited for each other. The explanation was simple; the system, because it was a system, was partly mechanical, and the man, because he was human, was nonmechanical. Leacock liked the humanness of man, even if the very thing that made him wonderful sometimes made him ineffective.

It was fortunate that Leacock liked the contrary, human side of man, for he was filled with it himself. The most striking qualities of the personality of Stephen Leacock were his human inconsistency and his kindness in recognizing the trait in others. He had little use for the fool, but he did not like the all-wise either. As for him, he had no idea what a clutch was for, though he understood time as a dimension. In his parodies he attacked sentimental fiction, but in other works he played on nostalgia himself. In so far as the human is what *is* and not an ideal which ought to be, Leacock fitted the pattern well. It was a human sentiment which made Leacock want to give his niece a big outdoor wedding. And then, quite humanly satisfied with a job well done, he let the awning, arbor, and tables stand until the weather brought them down.

It is unlikely that Leacock saw the inconsistencies in his life. He recognized no incongruity between his untied bow tie and the dozens of handkerchiefs he might use in one day, or between the tennis court he gradually allowed to become a lawn and his carefully preserved lectures. For an enthusiastic billiards player, he put up

with a table which was in bad repair most of the time he played on it. Leacock's answer, and the real answer to the whole paradox, would have been that he could still play on it; utility was Stephen Leacock's criteria for much in life. Even when his humor slipped, it never slipped so far that it stopped selling. When his repaired truck still leaked, he was not bothered; it carried the produce to Orillia anyway.

Another characteristic of Stephen Leacock might be called magnanimity. Quick to anger, he was quick to forgive—although he was human enough to prefer to make amends without an apology. In a long, active, vociferous life, the only two people he never forgave—his father and Principal Morgan—had hurt him very deeply. The same bigness governed his writing. One tribute said that "he had both courage and humor, but he never confused the two."[24] He never laughed at pain and he was never amused by injustice. And when he turned his attention to cancer or politics, it was a full-scale fight. In a gentler vein, his courtesy to women amounted almost to chivalry. Whatever he did, he did in an expansive way. His friend, Joe McDougall, said, "If you had any kind of a discussion with him you came away feeling that what he had said was extraordinarily worth repeating."[25] Stephen Leacock always gave the effect of being a personage.

By his own admission in his criticism, Leacock was an American humorist, by heritage. A Canadian critic placed him "in the tradition of Thomas Haliburton and Mark Twain and Artemus Ward."[26] By the admission

of Robert Benchley, Leacock gave as freely of the tradition as he got. The exuberance, the style, the technique —indeed, the whole of Stephen Leacock's contribution to laughter—placed him well within the pale of the world's most admired humor.

An international figure, Leacock was mourned by the world. Even at an advanced age, his death was untimely. The New York *Times* said, "We wish he could have stayed longer, but he had and gave the rest of us a good time."[27] Many papers paid him the high tribute of an editorial at his death, but Leacock, represented on at least one list of one hundred best books,[28] would have liked best the fitting words of the *Christian Science Monitor:*

On the train this morning we saw a man chuckling— chuckling as he might not have done if Stephen Leacock had not just passed on. [His] . . . passing . . . caused the newspapers to reprint some of his . . . remarks. . . . It is all that a man can ask that his fellows should be unable to remember him without a smile, that laughter should be the ultimate expression of their love.[29]

Notes

N. B. *All notes appearing at the back of the book are documentary in nature. Unless otherwise noted, all correspondence and other personal papers are quoted from the files in the Stephen Leacock Memorial Home, The Old Brewery Bay, Orillia, Ontario.*

CHAPTER I

1. Register of Baptisms, Parish of Swanmore, p. 72.
2. "Diary: Agnes Leacock," p. 4. This is a small typewritten ms. prepared by Agnes Leacock because "my children often ask me to tell them about their English relations and my own early life." A copy of the diary is in the Stephen Leacock Memorial Home.
3. *Ibid.*, pp. 1–7.
4. *Ibid.*, pp. 11–13.
5. *Ibid.*, p. 12.
6. *The Boy I Left Behind Me*, New York, 1946, p. 19; hereinafter cited as *Boy I Left*.
7. "Diary," p. 11.
8. *Boy I Left*, p. 15.
9. "National Head Dr. Cuddy Opens Sons of Canada Here," *News-Chronicle* (Port Arthur), August 8, 1944.
10. *Boy I Left*, pp. 21–27.
11. *Ibid.*, p. 43.
12. *Ibid.*, pp. 21–27.
13. Letter from Stephen Leacock to W. P. Leacock, [1875].
14. Letter from Stephen Leacock to W. P. Leacock, [January, 1876].

15. *Boy I Left,* p. 23.
16. *Ibid.,* pp. 50–51.
17. *Ibid.,* pp. 51–53.
18. *Ibid.,* p. 59.
19. *Ibid.,* pp. 60–73.
20. *Ibid.,* p. 78.
21. *Ibid.,* 65–71.
22. *Ibid.,* pp. 83–84.
23. *Ibid.,* pp. 74–78.
24. *Ibid.,* pp. 76–78.
25. "What I Read as a Child," *The Library and Its Contents,* ed., Harriet P. Sawyer, Classics of American Librarianship, 1925, pp. 143–44.
26. *Boy I Left,* pp. 81–82.
27. The date is from the bulletin of the Church of St. George-the-Martyr, Sibbald's Point, Ontario; the remainder is documented below.
28. *Boy I Left,* pp. 92–93.
29. Barney Milford, "There's Still a Lot of Leacock in Orillia," *Maclean's,* LXVIII (February 13, 1955), p. 81.
30. *Boy I Left,* pp. 93–94.
31. *Ibid.,* pp. 87–88.
32. *Ibid.,* pp. 96–99.
33. "My Remarkable Uncle," *My Remarkable Uncle, and Other Sketches,* New York, 1942, p. 5.
34. *Boy I Left,* p. 99.

CHAPTER II

1. *The Roll of Pupils of Upper Canada College; January, 1830, to June, 1916,* Kingston, Ontario, 1917, p. 365.
2. *Boy I Left,* pp. 130–32.
3. *Roll of Pupils,* p. 365.
4. *Boy I Left,* pp. 113–16.
5. *Ibid.,* pp. 107–12.
6. *Ibid.,* p. 99.
7. Date from the memorial stone in the cemetery at Sibbald Memorial Church.

Notes

8. *Boy I Left*, p. 134.
9. "Memories and Miseries as a Schoolmaster," *College Days*, New York, 1923, pp. 15–16.
10. Charles W. Gordon, *Postscript to Adventure*, New York, 1938, p. 44.
11. Stephen Leacock to W. P. Leacock, June 28, 1884.
12. *Boy I Left*, p. 135.
13. Award certificate pasted inside the front cover of this book (Patterson's Shilling Library, Edinburgh, 1883) in library at the Stephen Leacock Memorial.
14. *Boy I Left*, p. 100.
15. Masthead of *College Times*, VI (1886–87).
16. "U. C. C. Literary and Debating Society," *College Times*, VI (January 2, 1886 [sic.]), p. 27. The date should be 1887, the masthead not having been changed for this first edition of the new year.
17. *College Times*, VI (April 17, 1887), pp. 75–76.
18. *Boy I Left*, p. 100.
19. *The Surviving Trustee of the Will of T. M. Leacock deceased In Account With the Children of W. P. Leacock deceased*, in the files at the Stephen Leacock Memorial.
20. "Junior Matriculation, July 1887," *University of Toronto: Class and Prize Lists, 1888*, Toronto, 1888.
21. Draft of a letter from Stephen Leacock to the editor of *Cap and Gown*, magazine of Wycliff College.
22. *University of Toronto: Class and Prize Lists, 1888*, Toronto, 1888, pp. 19–24.
23. *Boy I Left*, p. 156.
24. *Ibid.*, pp. 157–58.
25. "Boarding House Geometry," *Literary Lapses*, New York, 1910, p. 26.
26. *Boy I Left*, pp. 159–60.
27. *Ibid.*, pp. 165–67.
28. *Ibid.*, pp. 172–74.
29. *Ibid.*, p. 176.
30. *Ibid.*, pp. 180–84.
31. "Soda Biscuits Here and a Whole Roast Ox There," *Star Weekly* (Toronto), June 10, 1922.

32. *University of Toronto, Register of Graduates, &c. Examination Papers, for 1890*, Toronto, 1890, p. 111.
33. *University of Toronto: Class and Prize Lists, 1890*, Toronto, 1890, p. 27.
34. "The Meds' Banquet," *Varsity*, X (December 9, 1890), p. 115.
35. "'Midst the Mortarboards," *Varsity*, X (March 17, 1891), p. 240.
36. "'Midst the Mortarboards," *Varsity*, X (December 16, 1890), p. 132.
37. "A Lost Work [By the Sanctum Philosopher]," *Varsity*, X (November 18, 1890), p. 77. Brackets are in the original.
38. "Editorial Comments," *Varsity*, X (December 2, 1890), p. 99.
39. *University of Toronto: Class and Prize Lists, 1891*, Toronto, 1891, p. 32.
40. H. A. Innis, "Stephen Butler Leacock," *Canadian Journal of Economics*, X (May, 1944), pp. 216–17.
41. Bruce Murphy, "Stephen Leacock—the Greatest Living Humorist," *Ontario Library Review*, XII (February, 1928), p. 68.

CHAPTER III

1. *Roll of Pupils*, p. 56.
2. Douglas S. Robertson [D.S.R.], "In the Spotlight," *Telegram* (Toronto), April 1, 1944.
3. *Boy I Left*, pp. 169–70.
4. Pelham Edgar, "Stephen Leacock," *Queen's Quarterly*, LIII ([May], 1946), pp. 175–77.
5. *Ibid.*, pp. 173–81.
6. Robert B. Pattison, "Stephen Leacock at Play," unpublished ms., in the Leacock Memorial Collection at the Orillia Public Library, Orillia, Ontario, pp. 2–5.
7. Edgar, "Stephen Leacock," p. 173.
8. Pattison, "Leacock at Play," pp. 1–4.
9. Edgar, "Stephen Leacock," pp. 176–77.
10. Pattison, "Leacock at Play," p. 4.
11. Edgar, "Stephen Leacock," pp. 174–75.

12. "Leacock, as Master, Made Boys Kiss Each Other Each Minute for Forty Five Minutes," *Star Weekly,* December 18, 1926.
13. Certificate No. 13050, Bureau of Records and Statistics, City of New York.
14. Stanley Kunitz, *Authors, Today and Yesterday,* New York, 1933, p. 398.
15. Record of Work, Stephen Butler Leacock, University of Chicago.

CHAPTER IV

1. R. L. T. [Charles Vinning], "Mr. Leacock," *Globe* (Toronto), December 13, 1930.
2. *Ibid.*
3. "The Flight of College Time," *McGill Fortnightly Review,* I (November 21, 1925), 3.
4. Innis, "Stephen Leacock," p. 219.
5. All figures concerning income unless otherwise documented come from Leacock's own records preserved at the Stephen Leacock Memorial Home. These include duplicate income tax forms after the tax law was passed in 1917.
6. John Philip Collins, "Stephen Leacock, Ph.D.: Savant and Humorist," *Living Age,* CCXCI (December 30, 1916), 800.
7. *Proceedings of the Canadian Club, Toronto, for the year 1905–06,* III (1905–06), 114–18.
8. Innis, "Stephen Leacock," p. 219.
9. *Ibid.*
10. *Royal Colonial Institute: Report of Proceedings,* XXXVIII (1906–07), London, 1907, 336.
11. J. P. Day, "Professor Leacock at McGill," *Canadian Journal of Economics,* X (May, 1944), 227–28.
12. Orillia, N. S., Book 2, Registry Office, Simcoe County, Ontario, p. 346.
13. Trent G. Frayne, "The Erudite Jester of McGill," *Maclean's Magazine,* LXVI (January 1, 1953), 38.
14. "The Limitations of Federal Government," *American Political Science Association Proceedings,* V (1908), 37–52.

15. *American Political Science Association Proceedings*, VI (1909), 5–6.
16. B. K. Sandwell, "Stephen Leacock, Worst-Dressed Writer, Made Fun Respectable," *Saturday Night* (Toronto), LIX (April 8, 1944), 17.
17. Holograph note by Leacock, dated Dec. 12, 1934, on the flyleaf of the copy of *Literary Lapses* in the Friedman collection, Redpath Library, McGill.
18. Draft of letter from Leacock to Mr. Larkin, April 4, 1910.
19. Draft of letter from Leacock to Mr. Tanguay, February 3, 1910.
20. Helen Palk, *The Book of Canadian Achievement*, Toronto, c. 1951, p. 130.
21. Holograph note by Leacock in the Friedman copy of *Literary Lapses*, Redpath Library, McGill.
22. *Sunshine Sketches*, p. 74.
23. First published in 1910, *Literary Lapses* was reprinted by John Lane, The Bodley Head, in 1911, 1912 (3 times), 1914, 1915, 1916, 1917 (2 times), 1919, 1920, 1922, 1924, 1926, 1927, 1930 (2 times), 1931, 1937, 1941, 1948, and 1950.

CHAPTER V

1. Frayne, "Erudite Jester," p. 39.
2. *Roll of Pupils*, p. 56.
3. Barney Milford, "There's Still a Lot of Leacock in Orillia," *Maclean's Magazine*, LXVIII (February 13, 1955), 82.
4. Gladstone Murray, "Stephen Leacock and His Humor," *Gazette* (Montreal), September 20, 1951.
5. Fredrick B. Taylor, "I Painted Stephen Leacock," *McGill News*, XXXI (Summer, 1950), 49.
6. *Literary Lapses*, p. 207.
7. *Ibid.*, pp. 26–27.
8. Robert Benchley, *My Ten Years in a Quandary*, New York: Harper & Bros., 1936, p. 115.
9. Collins, "Stephen Leacock, Ph.D.," p. 802.
10. B. K. Sandwell, "Here Stephen Leacock Lives and Writes," *Saturday Night* (Toronto), LVIII (October 10, 1942), 4.

Notes

11. Letter from Leacock to Mr. Irwin, February 5, 1943, in the Leacock Memorial Collection at Orillia Public Library, Orillia, Ontario.
12. Barbara Nimmo, "Preface—'Stephen Leacock,'" *Last Leaves*, p. xiv.
13. Edgar, "Stephen Leacock," pp. 182–83.
14. Sandwell, "Stephen Leacock, Worst-Dressed Writer," p. 17.
15. William Arthur Deacon, "Leacock Loved the Little Town Which He Christened Mariposa," *Globe and Mail* (Toronto), April 1, 1944.
16. *Sunshine Sketches*, p. xi.
17. Milford, "There's Still a Lot of Leacock," p. 80.
18. Letter from Leacock to George Rappley Bunting, Oakville, Ontario, dated September 29, 1943, in the possession of Mr. Bunting.
19. Sandwell, "Stephen Leacock, Worst-Dressed Writer," p. 17.
20. A. R. M. Lower, "The Mariposa Belle," *Queen's Quarterly*, LVIII (Summer, 1951), 220–26.
21. *Here Are My Lectures*, New York, 1937, p. vii.
22. Letter from Julia B. Morley to Leacock, July 11, 1913.
23. Letter from Nina Marcus Cohen to Leacock, [July, 1913].
24. *Behind the Beyond*, New York, 1913, p. 73.
25. Letter from E. V. Lucas to Leacock, December 5, 1913. The ellipsis is Lucas's.
26. Letter from E. V. Lucas to Leacock, February 4, 1914.
27. Letter from Paul Wilstach to Leacock, December 13, 1913.
28. Letter from Fredrick Eckstein to Leacock, January 22, 1914.
29. Letter from Frank Crowninshield to Leacock, September 26, 1914.
30. *University Magazine*, XII (December, 1913), 540–49.
31. *National Review*, LXI ([July, 1913]), 986–98. This issue was incorrectly dated May, 1912.
32. "Nominates Prof. Mavor," *Telegram* (Toronto), December 2, 1913.
33. Desmond Pacey, "Leacock as a Satirist," *Queen's Quarterly*, LVIII (Summer, 1951), 211.
34. *Arcadian Adventures*, p. 267.
35. *Literary Lapses*, p. 28.

Notes

36. *New Republic,* IX (December 2, 1916), 120–22.
37. *Wet Wit and Dry Humor,* New York, 1931, pp. 188–89.

CHAPTER VI

1. William Caldwell, "Impressions of Ontario; a Visit to a Canadian Author," *Canadian Magazine,* LIX (May, 1922), 58.
2. Letter from Faith Baldwin to Leacock, December 28, 1913.
3. Letter from F. Scott Fitzgerald to Leacock, [1916].
4. Letter from Kenneth Roberts to Leacock, January 16, 1917. By courtesy of Anna M. Roberts and the Canal National Bank of Portland, Maine, Executors of the Estate of Kenneth Roberts.
5. Letter from Leacock to Agnes Leacock, 5:30 P.M., August 19, 1915.
6. Diary, p. 7.
7. *Maclean's Magazine,* XXIX (August, 1916), 7–8, 77–99; (October, 1916), 12–13.
8. *Star* (Toronto), September 23, 1916.
9. *Further Foolishness,* New York, 1916, pp. 234–36.
10. This letter is in the possession of Stephen L. Leacock.
11. *Frenzied Fiction,* pp. 10–14.
12. "Social Unrest after the War," August 31, 1919, IV, 1; "The Road of Freedom," September 7, 1919, IV, 7; "Man's Work and His Wage," September 14, 1919, IV, 7; "Work and Wages and the Peril of the Industrial Balance of Power," September 21, 1919, III, 4; "Social Control for Equal Opportunity," October 2, 1919, IX, 2; and "Socialism in Operation: a Prison," October 5, 1919, X, 10.
13. In the author's collection by the kindness of Mrs. Benchley.
14. *Ibid.*
15. *Ibid.*
16. *Ibid.*
17. Nathaniel Benchley, *Robert Benchley,* New York, 1956.
18. "Preface," *Of All Things,* by Robert Benchley, London, 1922.
19. Autographed volume in library at the Stephen Leacock Memorial Home.
20. Letter from Benchley to Frank C. Dodd, April 21, 1930, in the files of Dodd, Mead and Company. For more extensive

treatment see, Ralph L. Curry, "Leacock and Benchley; an Acknowledged Literary Debt," *American Book Collector,* VII (March, 1957), 11–15.

21. Edgar, "Stephen Leacock," p. 183.
22. N. B. Zimmerman, "Stephen Leacock, Toastmaster of Mirth," *Tribune* (Winnipeg), March 30, 1944.
23. Telegram from Benchley to Leacock, February 11, 1935.
24. Letter from Leacock to Jefferson Jones, November 22, 1920; in the files of Dodd, Mead and Company.
25. Letter from Jefferson Jones to Leacock, November 24, 1920; in the files of Dodd, Mead and Company.
26. *Winsome Winnie,* New York, 1920, p. 13.
27. *Ibid.,* p. 38.
28. Letter from Maud B. Davis to Leacock, December 25, 1916.
29. Letter from Charles A. Littlefield to Leacock, December 24, 1920.
30. Letter from Ella McLean to Leacock, December 24, 1920.
31. *The Unsolved Riddle of Social Justice,* New York, 1920, pp. 127–28.
32. *Boy I Left,* p. 161.
33. Letter from Sir Arthur W. Currie to Leacock, July 20, 1931. The signature has been clipped out to be framed with the memorial bit Leacock wrote at Sir Arthur's death. The framed clipping and signature stood on the mantel of his study.
34. Frayne, "Erudite Jester," p. 19.
35. "Medal Will Act as Stimulus to Other Writers," *Packet and Times* (Orillia), June 19, 1947.
36. "Professor Leacock is Opposed to Prohibition as a Matter of Principle," *World* (Toronto), April 4, 1921.
37. "Stephen Leacock in England," *Star* (Toronto), October 13, 1921.
38. Letter from Yves Guyot to Leacock, March 27, 1920.
39. "Ontario Courts Chided by Stephen Leacock," New York *Times,* May 6, 1937.
40. Nimmo, "Preface," p. viii.
41. Frayne, "Erudite Jester," p. 38.
42. *Globe* (Toronto), September 19, 1921.
43. "A Master of Satire," *The Times,* September 27, 1921, p. 12.

Notes

CHAPTER VII

1. "Leacock Lurking in the Limelight," *Star* (Toronto), September 29, 1921.
2. "Mr. Stephen Leacock's Lectures," *The Times*, October 14, 1921, p. 8.
3. *My Discovery of England*, New York, 1922, pp. v–viii.
4. "Mr. Stephen Leacock's Lectures," p. 8.
5. Stephen Leacock, "Barrie and O. Henry," *Mark Twain Quarterly*, II (Fall, 1937), 3.
6. *Boy I Left*, p. 15.
7. Letter from Leacock to E. V. Lucas, November 18, 1923, in Leacock Room, Redpath Library, McGill.
8. "Leacock's Can-Opener," *Star Weekly* (Toronto), February 25, 1922.
9. "Mr. Stephen Leacock on London," *The Times*, December 10, 1921, p. 12.
10. "Mr. Stephen Leacock's Tour Ended," *The Times*, December 24, 1921, p. 8.
11. Letter from Leacock to Mr. Christy, December 30, 1921, in the Leacock Memorial Collection at Orillia Public Library, Orillia, Ontario.

Leacock had made fifty addresses:

October	4	Thirsk, York
	17	London
	18	Eastbourne
	19	London
	19	Southend-on-sea
	20	London
	21	London
	25	Shrewsbury
	26	Wokingham, Berks
	31	Litchfield
November	1	Folkestone, Kent.
	2	Ipswich, Suffolk
	3	Carshalton, Surrey
	7	Cardiff, Wales
	9	Bristol
	10	Wolverhampton

12 Malvern
14 Birmingham
15 Harrogate, Yorks.
16 Manchester
17 Moseley, Birmingham
18 Bristol
21 Glasgow, Scotland
22 Edinburgh, Scotland
23 Aberdeen
November 23 Aberdeen
24 Falkirk, Scotland
25 Greenock, Scotland
26 Bridge-of-Allan, Stirlingshire
28 Glasgow, Scotland
29 Glasgow, Scotland
30 Leeds
December 2 Rotherham, Yorks.
3 Barrow-in-Furness
5 Tunbridge Wells
5 Eltham
6 Hampstead
7 Brighton, Sussex
7 Westbourne Park
8 London
10 Goodhurst, Kent.
13 Ossett, Yorks.
14 Dewsbury, Yorks.
15 Dumfries, Scotland
16 Dundee, Scotland
17 Tunbridge Wells
18 Newcastle-on-Tyne
19 Blundellsands, Lancs.
20 Northwich, Cheshire
21 Kingston-on-Thames
23 Bournemouth, Hants.

12. Nimmo, "Preface," p. viii.
13. *LeColon* (Roberval, Quebec), June 15, 1944.

14. *My Discovery of England,* p. 12.
15. *Ibid.,* p. 14.
16. *Ibid.,* pp. 36–40.
17. *College Days,* p. 81.
18. *Ibid.,* p. 150.
19. *Over the Footlights,* p. 48.
20. *Ibid.,* p. 159.
21. The exact figure was $39,011.73.
22. Frayne, "Erudite Jester," p. 19.
23. Convocation Program, April 28, 1923.
24. Letter from Max Elsner of the Metropolitan Newspaper Service to Leacock, January 24, 1924.
25. *The Garden of Folly,* New York, 1924, pp. ix–x.
26. *The Theory and Technique of Humor* on technique and *Humor and Humanity* on philosophy.
27. Letter from Dodd, Mead to Leacock, April 18, 1923, in the files of Dodd, Mead and Company, New York; the three letters which follow immediately have the same location.
28. Letter from Dodd, Mead to Leacock, April 1, 1925.
29. Letter from Dodd, Mead to Leacock, January 10, 1925; and telegram from Leacock to Dodd, Mead, January 19, 1925.
30. "Mrs. Leacock Ill Now in England," *Star* (Toronto), November 28, 1925.
31. Telegram from Sir Arthur Currie to Leacock, December 7, 1925.
32. *Last Leaves,* p. 4.

CHAPTER VIII

1. *Winnowed Wisdom,* New York, 1926, p. 211.
2. *Ibid.,* p. 153.
3. *Ibid.,* pp. vi–vii.
4. *Review of Reviews,* LXXIV (October, 1926), 370.
5. *The Institute Bulletin,* IV (March, 1926), 2–8.
6. Henry Janes, Public Relations Service Limited, Toronto.
7. T. H. Harris, *Herald,* Montreal.
8. Frayne, "Erudite Jester," p. 39.
9. Day, "Professor Leacock at McGill," p. 227.

10. "Memorandum to the Income Tax Department on My Income Tax," by Stephen Leacock, dated April 19, 1937; a typed carbon of this remains in the files at the Stephen Leacock Memorial Home.
11. *Sunshine Sketches*, p. xi.
12. "Professor Stephen Leacock Died," *News-Letter* (Orillia, Ontario), March 29, 1944.
13. Letter from Leacock to Dodd, Mead, September 15, 1927, in the files of Dodd, Mead and Company, New York.
14. Letter from Dr. Oscar Schloss to Dr. Alton Goldbloom, April 26, 1926, in the Leacock Room, Redpath Library, McGill.
15. Letter from Leacock to Goldbloom, May 4, 1926, in the Leacock Room, Redpath Library, McGill.
16. Letter from Leacock to Goldbloom, [n.d.], in the Leacock Room, Redpath Library, McGill.
17. *Telegram* (Toronto), May 2, 1927.
18. *The Times*, July 1, 1927, p. 21.
19. "Leacock Denounces Quacks," New York *Times*, September 25, 1926.
20. Telegram from John C. A. Gerhster to Leacock, January 24, 1928.
21. Statement from the Montreal *Star* Company, Ltd., to Leacock, January 24, 1928.

CHAPTER IX

1. *Short Circuits*, New York, 1928, p. 301.
2. "The Future of American Humor," St. Louis *Post-Dispatch*, Supplement, American Section, December 9, 1928, pp. 4–5.
3. The printed nomination sent other members remains in the files at the Stephen Leacock Memorial Home.
4. *Royal Society of Canada: Proceedings and Transactions*, XXII (May, 1928), Series 3, section 2, pp. 213–32.
5. Written across the bottom of a letter from McDougall to Leacock, February 16, 1928, in the possession of J. E. McDougall, Montreal.
6. These dated blueprints remain in the Leacock effects at the Stephen Leacock Memorial Home.

Notes

7. Letter from R. F. Curry to Leacock, December 7, 1928.

8. Frayne, "Erudite Jester," p. 39.

9. Program, dated August 17, 1929.

10. Program, dated December 31, 1929.

11. A Canadian Soldier, "An Impudent Sketch," *Bodleian*, printed in Thomas L. Masson, *Our American Humorists*, New York, 1922, pp. 226–27.

12. Letter from Leacock to Gerhard R. Lomer, [n.d.], but marked "Received Jan. 13, 1930," in the Leacock Room, Redpath Library, McGill.

13. "For the Last Time He Says That'll Be All for Today," *Newsweek*, VII (May 16, 1936), 44.

14. A Canadian Soldier, "An Impudent Sketch," p. 229.

15. "Canada Mourns Rum Loss," Philadelphia *Record*, April 29, 1929, and "Leacock Advises Canada to Throw off U. S. Dominance," Montreal *Gazette*, November 6, 1929.

16. Many copies of these hastily scrawled notes remain at the Stephen Leacock Memorial Home.

17. This habit is evident from the numerous letters thanking Leacock for such gifts.

18. *The Iron Man and the Tin Woman*, New York, 1929, p. 129.

19. *Ibid.*, p. 8.

20. Letter from Frank Dodd to Leacock, August 28, 1929.

21. Letter from Frank Dodd to Leacock, September 6, 1929.

22. Carbon of telegram from Leacock to Frank Dodd, February 18, [1930].

23. Carbon of letter from Leacock to Frank Dodd, February 28, [1930].

24. "On Empire Trade," *The Times*, April 12, 1930, p. 11.

25. "Imperial Economics," *Times Literary Supplement*, 1930, p. 723.

26. "Dr. Leacock's Book Widely Distributed," *Globe* (Toronto), October 17, 1930.

27. "The Fall of the Pound Sterling," Montreal *Daily Star*, October 10, 1931, pp. 1, 21, and "Beating Back to Prosperity," *Mail and Empire* (Toronto), November 28, 1931, p. 3.

28. *Wet Wit and Dry Humor*, New York, 1931, pp. 74–75.

29. *Ibid.*, pp. 80–92.

Notes

1. *Saturday Review*, London. This comment and the following one were printed on the back of *Stephen Leacock's Plan.*
2. *British Empire Review*, London.
3. Innis, "Stephen Leacock," pp. 216–26.
4. Collins, "Stephen Leacock, Ph.D.," p. 800.
5. In the files at the Stephen Leacock Memorial Home.
6. "Some Anecdotes of McGill," *McGill News*, XXIV (1945), 103–10.
7. Letters from the Bank of Montreal to Leacock, January 7 and March 7, 1938, report purchase and sale of the stock in East Malartic Mines.
8. Burton S. Keirstead and Fredrick M. Watkins, "Political Science in Canada," *Contemporary Political Science: a Survey of Methods, Research, and Teaching*, UNESCO. 1950, p. 172.
9. Memorandum, October 20, 1932; the deletions are the author's.
10. *Papers and Proceedings of the Canadian Political Science Association*, III (1931), 260.
11. *Ibid.*, IV (1932), 1, 259.
12. *Ibid.*, V (1933), 247.
13. *Ibid.*, VI (1934), 5–16.
14. Holograph note by Leacock, [n.d.], in the Friedman copy in the Redpath Library, McGill.
15. *Mark Twain*, New York, 1935, p. 3.
16. *Ibid.*, p. 59.
17. *Ibid.*, p. 147.
18. "Baron Lahontan, Explorer," *Canadian Geographical Journal*, IV (May, 1932), 281–92.
19. *Canadian Institute Mining and Metallurgy Bulletin*, August, 1932, pp. 430–36.
20. *Stephen Leacock's Plan*, p. 6.
21. *Papers and Proceedings of the Canadian Political Science Association*, V (1933), p. 21.
22. "Leacock, the Humorist, Pens Serious Note Resigns from Royal Society for Economy," *Mail* (Toronto), May 27, 1932.

23. Edgar, "Stephen Leacock," p. 179.

24. *Royal Society of Canada: Proceedings and Transactions,* XVII (May, 1923), Series 3, p. xxxi.

25. "Stephen Leacock," *Bookman,* LXXVI (February, 1933), 151.

26. "General Currie: An Appreciation by Stephen Leacock," *Herald* (Montreal), December 6, 1933.

CHAPTER XI

1. *Charles Dickens,* Garden City, New York, 1934, p. 65.

2. *Ibid.,* p. 98.

3. Letter from William Dike Reed to Leacock, January 13, 1934.

4. Draft notes for letter from Leacock to Frank Dodd, January 29, 1934.

5. Quoted in Innis, "Stephen Leacock," p. 224.

6. The copy containing this inscription, dated March 11, 1934, is in the Leacock Room, Redpath Library, McGill.

7. *Papers and Proceedings of the Canadian Political Science Association,* VI (1934), 5–6.

8. New York *Times Magazine,* August 19, 1934, pp. 6–7.

9. "Is Canada Breaking Up?" New York *Herald Tribune,* December 16, 1934, pp. 12–13, 20; and "The Last Five Years in Canada: How the Country Reacted in a Period of Depression," *The World Today,* New York, 1934, pp. 22–25.

10. *Yale Review,* XXIV (September, 1934), 118–29.

11. New York *Times Magazine,* April 22, 1934, pp. 8–9.

12. Letter from R. B. Bennett to Leacock, July 2, 1932.

13. Letter from J. Earl Lawson to C. C. Ballantyne, February 13, 1935.

14. Letter from J. Earl Lawson to Leacock, April 1, 1935; Mr. Bennett's personal gratitude was expressed in a letter to Leacock, April 18, 1935.

15. Letter from R. B. Bennett to Leacock, July 12, 1935.

16. J. E. McDougall, "Memories of Stephen Leacock," a typed manuscript which Mr. McDougall kindly prepared at the author's request, in the author's collection. Unless otherwise documented, the information on radio is from this source.

17. Letter from Leacock to J. E. McDougall, April 14, 1934, in Mr. McDougall's possession.
18. Nimmo, "Preface," p. xii–xiii.
19. Letter from Gladstone Murray to Leacock, June 5, 1937.
20. Nimmo, "Preface," p. xiii.
21. "Mrs. Agnes Leacock Dies at Orillia," *Globe* (Toronto), January 30, 1934.
22. Letter from Leacock to Cyril Clemens, July 28, 1930, in Mr. Clemens's possession.
23. "Leacock Says Humor Badly Needed Today," *Columbia Missourian*, January 16, 1935.
24. *Humor: Its Theory and Technique*, New York, 1935, p. 28.
25. *Ibid.*, p. 35.
26. *Ibid.*, p. 100.
27. *Ibid.*, pp. 28–30.
28. "The Last of Leacock," *Times Literary Supplement*, XLVII (January 10, 1948), p. 19.
29. "Stephen Leacock, Humorist," *Living Age*, CCCXI (November 5, 1921), p. 353.
30. *Nonsense Novels*, New York, c. 1938, p. 76.
31. *Humor and Humanity*, p. 157; *Humor: Its Theory and Technique*, p. 120.
32. *Short Circuits*, p. 77.
33. *Here Are My Lectures*, New York, 1937, p. 72.
34. Quoted in *Humor: Its Theory and Technique*, p. 29.
35. *Humor and Humanity*, p. 87.
36. "American Humor," *Nineteenth Century*, LXXVI (August, 1914), p. 450.
37. *Here Are My Lectures*, p. 3.
38. *Literary Lapses*, p. 207.
39. Mildred Clara Struble, "Stephen Leacock, Jester," an unpublished thesis submitted for the degree of Master of Arts, University of Washington, 1920, p. 13.
40. *Humor and Humanity*, p. 158.
41. *My Remarkable Uncle*, New York, 1942, p. 176.
42. *Humor and Humanity*, p. 192.
43. *Ibid.*, p. 157.
44. "Here . . . Leacock . . . Writes," p. 4.

45. G. G. Sedgewick, "Stephen Leacock as a Man of Letters," *University of Toronto Quarterly*, XV (October, 1945), p. 25.
46. *Sunshine Sketches*, pp. 65–66.
47. "Our Living Language: A Defense," New York *Times Magazine*, February 26, 1939, p. 9.
48. New York, 1922, p. 212.
49. *Humor and Humanity*, pp. 192–93.
50. *Model Memoirs*, New York, 1938, p. 312.
51. "How to Keep Education from Eating Up Life," New York *Times Magazine*, October 30, 1938, p. 3.
52. *Current History*, XLII (June, 1935), 233–39.
53. *Quarterly Review*, CCLXV (July, 1935), 1–11.
54. *Canadian Journal of Economics and Political Science*, I (February, 1935), 41–51.
55. *Queen's Quarterly*, LXII (Spring, 1935), 68–81.
56. "The Lake Simcoe Country," XI (September, 1935), 109–16.
57. Taylor, "I Painted Stephen Leacock," p. 49.
58. Letter from A. P. S. Glassco to Leacock, June 12, 1935.
59. Letter from Leacock to Dean Woodhead, June 29, 1935.
60. Letter from A. E. Morgan to Leacock, November 13, 1935.
61. Copy of letter from Leacock to A. E. Morgan, November 21, [1935].
62. Letter from Edward Beatty to Leacock, December 14, 1935.
63. Copy of letter from Leacock to A. E. Morgan, February 13, 1935.
64. Copy of letter from Leacock to Charles Martin, February 15, 1936.

CHAPTER XII

1. *Funny Pieces*, New York, 1936, p. 260.
2. *Ibid.*, pp. 251–53.
3. "Stephen Leacock and His Connection with Orillia," *Packet and Times* (Orillia, Ontario), March 30, 1944.
4. "Leacock Retired by McGill," New York *Times*, December 19, 1935.

Notes

5. "Leacock at Leisure," New York *Times*, December 21, 1935.
6. "McGill Confers Honors," New York *Times*, May 28, 1936.
7. "Academic Freedom," *Maclean's*, XLIX (February 1, 1936), 38–39; "Canada Won't Go Yankee," *American Mercury*, XXXIX (September, 1936), "Edward VIII and Canada," *Review of Reviews*, XCIII (March, 1936), 29–30; and "Social and Other Credit in Alberta," *Fortnightly Review*, CXLVI (November, 1936), 525–35.
8. Toronto, 1936.
9. *Ibid.*, p. [ii].
10. *Ibid.*, p. 2.
11. Garden City, New York, 1936.
12. *Funny Pieces*, p. 33.
13. *Ibid.*, pp. 67–68.
14. *College Days*, p. 82.
15. *Hellements of Hickonomics*, New York, 1936, pp. 41–43.
16. John Wheelwright, "The Poet as a Funny Man," *Poetry*, L (July, 1937), 211.
17. *Hellements of Hickonomics*, p. 3.
18. Nimmo, "Preface," pp. vii–viii.
19. *Ibid.*, p. xi.
20. "My Trip," a journal which remains at the Stephen Leacock Memorial Home.
21. Nimmo, "Preface," p. xi.
22. "My Trip," December 16.
23. Nimmo, "Preface," p. xi.
24. "My Trip," December 17.
25. Nimmo, "Preface," p. xi.
26. *Ibid.*
27. "My Trip," January 17.
28. Nimmo, "Preface," vii.
29. *Ibid.*, p. xvi.
30. Frayne, "Erudite Jester," p. 39.
31. *My Discovery of the West*, New York, 1937, pp. 255–59.
32. *Here Are My Lectures*, pp. 208–9.
33. *Ibid.*, p. 211.

Notes

CHAPTER XIII

1. Letter from Leacock to Gerhard Lomer, November 19, 1937, in the Leacock Room, Redpath Library, McGill.
2. *Humor and Humanity*, New York, c. 1938, p. [v].
3. *Ibid.*, p. 1.
4. Innis, "Stephen Leacock," pp. 221–23.
5. Sandwell, "Stephen Leacock, Worst-Dressed Writer," p. 17.
6. "Mr. Leacock's Uncle," *Times Literary Supplement*, XLI (July 25, 1942), 370.
7. Will Cuppy, ed., *World's Great Mystery Stories*, Cleveland, 1943, p. 12.
8. "Stephen Leacock," New York *Times*, March 30, 1944.
9. "Lost in the Jungle of Economics," New York *Times Magazine*, August 20, 1939, p. 18.
10. "The Dry Pickwick," *Times Literary Supplement*, XXXI (March 17, 1932), 200.
11. *Humor and Humanity*, p. 60.
12. *Ibid.*, p. 218.
13. Nancy Ladd, "Stephen Leacock's Best," New York *Times Book Review*, December 15, 1946, p. 24.
14. *How to Write*, New York, 1943, p. 6.
15. *Humor: Its Theory and Technique*, pp. 104–5.
16. Peter McArthur, *Stephen Leacock*, Toronto, 1923, p. 134.
17. "Sanctum Philosopher," *Varsity*, X (October 24, 1890), p. 20.
18. *Humor and Humanity*, p. 178.
19. *Happy Stories*, New York, 1943, p. 9. Ellipses are Leacock's.
20. *Too Much College*, New York, 1939, p. 147.
21. *Humor and Humanity*, pp. 199–200; *Humor: Its Theory and Technique*, pp. 203–4.
22. Cyril Clemens, "An Evening with Stephen Leacock," *Catholic World*, CLIX (June, 1944), 240.
23. "Lewis Carroll of Canada," *Current Literature*, LIII (November, 1912), 585.
24. *Sunshine Sketches*, p. 75.
25. Elizabeth R. Stern, New York *Times Book Review*, January 24, 1944, p. 21.

26. "Is Education Eating Up Life?" New York *Times Magazine,* October 23, 1938, p. 1.

27. "Lost in the Jungle of Economics," p. 16.

28. Max Eastman, *Sense of Humor,* New York, 1922, pp. 84–85.

29. Sculley Bradley, "Our Native Humor," *North American Review,* CCXLII (Winter, 1937), 362.

30. "Alberta's Fairy Story," *Commentator,* I (June, 1937), 67–72; and "Social Credit," *Review of Reviews,* XCV (January, 1937), 65–66.

31. "Labor and Law in Canada: an Interpretation of the Oshawa Strike," *Standard* (Montreal), May 1, 1937, p. 1; and "Labor Should Organize But Do It the Right Way," *Telegram* (Toronto), May 1, 1937.

32. "The Lorne Pierce Medal," *Royal Society of Canada, Proceedings and Transactions,* XXXI (1937), 40.

33. "Vancouver Wants Leacock," *Star* (Toronto), December 11, 1937.

34. Letter from A. Lawrence Lowell to Leacock, March 9, 1937.

35. Letter from Louis Kon to Leacock, March 11, 1937.

36. Letter from W. T. Conder to Leacock, November 19, 1936.

37. "Local Aspects of the World," *Packet and Times* (Orillia, Ontario), March 30, 1944.

38. Consecutive telegrams in *"Canadian National* All Telegrams after Sept. 10 37. Continued Mat 1938." This book of carbon copies remains in the files of the Stephen Leacock Memorial Home.

39. Letters from all these figures remain in the files at the Stephen Leacock Memorial Home.

40. Nimmo, "Preface," p. xvii.

41. William Caldwell, "Impressions of Ontario; a Visit to a Canadian Author," *Canadian Magazine,* LIX (May, 1922), 58.

42. "Leacock is Woeful at Ontario Justice," *Star* (Toronto), May 5, 1937.

43. "Ontario Courts Chided by Stephen Leacock," New York *Times,* May 6, 1937.

44. "Humble Prayer to the Magistrate at Brockville," May 3, 1937.

45. "Stephen Leacock, Humorist is dead," Philadelphia *Inquirer*, March 29, 1944.
46. *Nation's Business*, XXVI (January, 1938), 18–20, 103.
47. *Barron's, the National Financial Weekly*," XVIII (November 7, 1938), 3.
48. *Quarterly Review*, CCLXX (April, 1938), 204–20.
49. "Andrew Macphail," *Queen's Quarterly*, XLV (November, 1938), 447–49.
50. *Model Memoirs*, New York, 1938, p. 309.
51. *Too Much College*, p. 246.
52. *My Remarkable Uncle*, pp. 190–91.
53. Pp. 178–79.
54. Herbert L. MacDonald, "Leacock Memorial," *Standard* (Montreal), October 8, 1949.
55. Letter from William Rennie Seeds, Ltd., to Leacock, June 1, 1939.
56. Letter from William Rennie Seeds, Ltd., to Leacock, June 7, 1939.
57. Quoted in Nimmo, "Preface," p. xvii. It is an interesting note on the entertaining habits of Leacock that this fifteen-day period averaged more than twenty-two meals a day or an average of seven people a day.
58. *Ibid.*
59. Letter from George Leacock to the author, October 6, 1954, in the author's possession.
60. All of these volumes remain in the library at the Stephen Leacock Memorial Home.
61. "Leacock Braves Storm," New York *Times*, July 10, 1939.
62. "Leacock Fed Up on 'This Hero Business,'" *Star* (Toronto), July 13, 1939.

CHAPTER XIV

1. "Agreement with John and Tina Kelly," September 1, 1939.
2. Telegram from Leacock to Dodd, Mead, February 12, 1939, in the files of Dodd, Mead and Company, New York.
3. *Queen's Quarterly*, XLVI (February, 1939), 28–37.
4. *Atlantic Monthly*, CLXIII (June, 1939), 735–43.

5. *Saturday Review,* XX (June, 1939), 10.
6. *All Right, Mr. Roosevelt,* Toronto, 1939, p. 5.
7. *Too Much College,* p. 4.
8. *Ibid.,* pp. 130–31.
9. *Ibid.,* p. 142.
10. *Ibid.,* p. 175.
11. Letter from Miller Services, Ltd., to Leacock, March 9, 1939.
12. "Stories and Story-tellers," *Outlook,* CXXX (February 1, 1922), 183.
13. *Too Much College,* p. [239].
14. *The British Empire,* New York, 1940, p. v. The American edition was entitled *The* rather than *Our* British Empire.
15. *Ibid.,* p. 2.
16. Frayne, "Erudite Jester," p. 19.
17. *Last Leaves,* New York, 1945, p. 106. The italics are Leacock's.
18. *Ibid.,* pp. 50–51.
19. Letter from Daniel L. Marsh to Leacock, April 14, 1939.
20. Letter from Leacock to Daniel L. Marsh, April 19, 1939.
21. Taylor, "I Painted Stephen Leacock," pp. 48–49.
22. *Ibid.,* p. 50.
23. *Ibid.* This portrait now hangs in the Leacock Room of the Redpath Library, McGill.
24. "The Question Nobody Answers," *Canadian Banker,* XLVIII (July, 1941), 459–65; and "The Whole Duty of a Citizen," *Canadian Spokesman,* I (January, 1941), 1–4.
25. Address of Henry R. Mainer at the Leacock Memorial Dinner, June 29, 1953, at Orillia. A tape recording of the speech is in the Leacock Memorial Collection in the Orillia Public Library.
26. *Canada, the Foundations of Its Future,* Montreal, 1941, p. xxviii.
27. New York, 1939, pp. v–viii.
28. P. 156.
29. Quoted in F. D. L. Smith, "As Stephen Leacock Saw Toronto 70 Years Ago," *Globe and Mail* (Toronto), April 6, 1944.

Notes

CHAPTER XV

1. Letter from Thomas B. Costain to Leacock, December 8, 1941.
2. Quoted in letter from Thomas B. Costain to Leacock, December 16, 1941.
3. *Ibid.*
4. Letter from Leacock to Dodd, Mead, July 6, 1942, in the files of Dodd, Mead, New York.
5. *Saturday Night*, LVIII (November 28, 1942), 14.
6. *Standard* (Montreal), February 28, 1942, magazine section, p. 10.
7. *My Remarkable Uncle*, p. 6.
8. *Ibid.*, p. 9.
9. *Behind the Beyond*, pp. 193–95.
10. *My Remarkable Uncle*, p. 300.
11. *Last Leaves*, pp. 30–31.
12. Written on a contract with Dodd, Mead concerning the proposed autobiography, dated August 21, 1942, in the files of Dodd, Mead, New York.
13. Frayne, "Erudite Jester," p. 38.
14. "Britain and America," *Thought, Fordham University Quarterly*, XVIII (June, 1943), 204–7; "Plea for Geographical Science," *Queen's Quarterly*, L (February, 1943), 1–13; "Tale of Two Cities," *Maclean's*, LVI (March 1, 1943), 7–8, 40–42; and "What's Ahead for Canada?" *Maclean's*, LVI (May 1, 1943), 12, 22, 24. This last article also appeared in expanded form in the *Financial Post* in weekly installments from December 4, 1943 to February 5, 1944.
15. *Happy Stories*, New York, 1943, p. 5.
16. Letter from Leacock to Lomer, January 11, 1943, in the Leacock Room, Redpath Library, McGill.
17. Lomer, *Stephen Leacock*, p. 33.
18. Embossed in 3 Volumes, American Printing House for the Blind, Louisville, Ky., 1943.
19. *How to Write*, New York, 1943, p. 27.
20. McDougall, "Memories of Stephen Leacock."

21. This advertisement appeared in many magazines and then was published by Pan American Airways in a volume; "To Every Child We Must Give the Chance to Live, to Learn, to Love," A *Forum of the Future: 1942 through 1943*, c. 1944, n.p.

22. "Canada Can Support 100,000,000 People," *Rotarian*, LVX (October, 1944), 16–18.

23. Letter from Leacock to Gladstone Murray, [January], in the possession of Gladstone Murray, Toronto.

24. Letter from Leacock to Gladstone Murray, February 4, 1944, in the possession of Gladstone Murray, Toronto.

25. Letter from Frank Dodd to Leacock, August 15, 1941.

26. Memorandum by Leacock, February 22, 1944.

27. Frayne, "Erudite Jester," p. 19.

28. "Stephen Leacock, Humorist, Is Dead," New York *Times*, March 29, 1944.

29. Percy Ghent, "In the Spotlight," *Telegram* (Toronto), April 11, 1944.

CHAPTER XVI

1. Ken MacTaggart, "Stephen Leacock Buried on Blustery March Day," *Telegram* (Toronto), April 1, 1944.

2. *The Leacock Roundabout*, New York, 1946.

3. *Last Leaves*, pp. 83–87, 103–5.

4. *Ibid.*, p. 40.

5. *Ibid.*, pp. 41–42.

6. *Ibid.*, p. 43.

7. *The Boy I Left*, p. [3].

8. *Ibid.*, p. 100.

9. Copies of the will, the codicil, and the schedule of settlement are in the files of Paul Copeland, Q. C., Orillia, Ontario.

10. Interdepartmental Memo, May 26, 1944, in the files of Dodd, Mead and Company, New York.

11. From schedules in the files of Paul Copeland, Q. C., Orillia, Ontario.

12. Letter from C. S. Manning, Jr., to the author, January 18, 1954 [sic—the date should be 1955], in the author's collection.
13. "Memorial to Stephen Leacock," *Ontario Library Review*, XXVIII (November, 1944), 405.
14. Program of the Leacock Memorial Dinner, September 14, 1951.
15. Ralph L. Curry, "Stephen Leacock Memorial Home," publicity brochure available at the Home.
16. "Partial List of Contributors to Vol. V," *Encyclopedia Americana*, New York, 1945, n.p.
17. "Partial List of Contributors to Vol. XXIII," *Ibid.*, n.p.
18. *Compton's Pictured Encyclopedia*, 1941, I, x.
19. *Dictionary of American Biography*, New York, 1937, Index vol., p. 209.
20. *Canada*, p. 75.
21. Henry Beston, "Canada's Greatest Port," *Books*, November 29, 1942, p. 3.
22. Wheelwright, "The Poet as a Funny Man," p. 211.
23. D. Pacey, "Leacock as a Satirist," *Queen's Quarterly*, LVIII (Summer, 1951), 212.
24. "Stephen Leacock," New York *Herald Tribune*, March 29, 1944.
25. Letter from McDougall to the author, July 13, 1954, in the author's possession.
26. A. L. Phelps, *Canadian Writers*, Toronto, c. 1951, p. 70.
27. "Stephen Leacock," New York *Times*, March 30, 1944.
28. *Have You Read 100 Great Books?*, New York, c. 1950, p. 73.
29. "Perfect Tribute," *Christian Science Monitor*, March 30, 1944.

INDEX

A33

STEPHEN LEACOCK

Humorist and Humanist